£3·75 net

D0297928

An Annotated Bibliography of Jane Austen Studies
1952-1972

Barry Roth   Joel Weinsheimer

Ohio University

Published for the Bibliographical Society of
the University of Virginia

The University Press of Virginia
Charlottesville

THE UNIVERSITY PRESS OF VIRGINIA
Copyright © 1973 by the Rector and Visitors
of the University of Virginia

First published 1973

ISBN: 0-8139-0544-3
Library of Congress Catalog Card Number: 73-86212
Printed in the United States of America

"LET THIS EXPIATE!"

"What becomes of the old giants?" said
Short, turning to him again after a
little reflection.

"They're usually kept in carawans to
wait upon the dwarfs," said Mr Vuffin.

Preface

The past twenty years have witnessed the most concentrated, continuous, and enlightening literary criticism of Jane Austen to date. This body of knowledge is of such bulk and value that a scholarly tool locating and summarizing research is needed to determine the present state of Austen studies. And, beyond clarifying what has been done, such a tool is a necessity if future criticism is to proceed in the most informed manner possible. Consequently, to fulfill this dual function, the present bibliography includes all Austen studies first published from 1952 to 1972 (and those from 1973 as they came to hand) and significant material which, though initially appearing before 1952, was judged valuable enough to be reprinted during the last two decades. Specifically, within these qualifications, and allowing for human fallibility, we list and annotate every book, essay, article, and doctoral dissertation on Austen, the critical matter appended to every edition of her works in English and to selected translations, as well as significant mentions. By presenting this range of both original and reprinted material, we offer the reader a comprehensive guide to Austen scholarship.

Every aspect of the work is determined by consideration of the needs such a bibliography will supply. For clarity and ease of reference the bibliography is divided into three sections. The first covers books, essays, and articles devoted to Austen, including all reviews of the book-length studies. The second section presents doctoral dissertations wholly or in part on Austen. Section three lists significant mentions, which are included regardless of length when they offer an unusual, perceptive, or otherwise striking idea. Within the divisions entries are arranged chronologically and, within each year, alphabetically by critic's name. Book reviews are presented alphabetically by journal for each year.

All entries have annotations, which provide a clear and concise statement of the critic's thesis. We let the author speak for himself, quoting, when feasible, the thesis sentence, and, in general, we aim at objectivity and avoid evaluation. As a rule, the maximum length of annotation for an average essay-length study or dissertation is approximately seventy-five words. Though we enter all discrete Jane Austen items, we do not duplicate annotations. Thus, an article later incorporated in a book is annotated only if its thesis would otherwise be omitted.

We abbreviate periodical titles according to the listing in the first volume of the 1970 MLA International Bibliography,* the latest available to us during composition, and furnish readily recognizable abbreviations for those absent from the MLA list. For books published simultaneously in the United States and abroad, only the American publisher is supplied; otherwise, of course, the earliest publisher is given. For reprinted material, brackets indicate the date of original publication and the edition when it differs from that in the entry proper. We locate, in the original entry, all reprinted forms of an essay, with the exception of the essay's appearance in a collection exclusively devoted to Jane Austen. For this information the reader is referred to the Index of Authors. We cross-reference continuing critical disputes and bring together under one entry all extended correspondence within a journal. Three indexes are appended to the bibliography--authors, titles and subjects.

The bibliography excludes editions and translations without critical matter, abridgements, standard reference works (such as encyclopedias), master's theses, materials in other than printed media, and study-note series for high school and college students.

We would like to thank the many people who have assisted in the preparation of the bibliography. Especially helpful has been the patient and industrious research of Ann Telfair Johnson, Interlibrary Loan Librarian at Ohio University, and of her assistants, Miriam Markley and Anne Gusmano, all of whom have contributed so much. And, in general, we have found most encouraging the efforts of the entire staff of Ohio University's library. Likewise, we appreciate the attention of our colleagues in the English Department, especially Frank B. Fieler and R. Vance Ramsey, for their consistently intelligent advice.

*There is one exception to this rule: Modern Philology is not abbreviated according to MLA usage, to prevent confusion with Mansfield Park (MP).

To the Ohio University Research Committee we are also
indebted for its liberal support.

Our special thanks are owing to Mrs. Alberta H.
Burke for her generous and unique cooperation in our
project, and to both Mr. and Mrs. Burke for their most
gracious hospitality. Others to whom we are grateful
for items we might otherwise not have obtained are John
Horden, Harrison T. Meserole, Sir Hugh Smiley, Carl T.
Berkhout, Keiko Izubuchi, J. C. C. Mays, Joseph A.
Kestner, III, Anne Mallinson, Duane Schneider, Jim
Trupin, Werner Senn, Joseph G. Fucilla, and Philip
Waldron.

Those who have contributed long hours to the work
of translation also deserve our gratitude. They are
Gita Yuckman, Zenon Kuk, Bartolomeo Martello, Dean
McWilliams, Svetozar Pejovich, Anny West, Grafton
Conliffe, Ernest Johansson, and Barry Thomas.

A debt, finally, is owing to our families, who have
endured much: our wives--Roberta Roth and Joyce Wein-
sheimer--and our children--Alexis and Miranda Roth and
Aaron Weinsheimer.

Contents

Key Abbreviations

JA	Jane Austen
S and S	Sense and Sensibility
P and P	Pride and Prejudice
MP	Mansfield Park
E	Emma
NA	Northanger Abbey
P	Persuasion

Other Jane Austen titles are given in full.

I. Books, Essays, and Articles

1 Austen, Caroline. _My Aunt Jane Austen: A Memoir._
      Alton, Hampshire: Jane Austen Society, 1952.

      Rev. in _TLS_, 20 June 1952, p. 406.

      "It is not much that I have to tell--for I mean
   to relate only what I saw and what I _thought_ my-
   self--I was just twelve years old when she died."

2 Becker, May Lamberton. _Presenting Miss Jane Austen._
      New York: Dodd, Mead, 1952.

      Rev. (with other works) in _NCF_, 7 (1952), 149-
   50; in _TLS_, 4 July 1952, p. 434; by Léonie Villard
   in _EA_, 7 (1954), 233.

      (Imaginatively rendered biography.)

3 Chapman, R. W., coll. and ed. _Jane Austen's Letters
      to Her Sister Cassandra and Others._ 2nd ed.
      London: Oxford Univ. Press, 1952.

      Rev. in _TLS_, 26 Sept. 1953, p. 630; by Léonie
   Villard in _EA_, 7 (1954), 119-22.

      "Introduction," pp. xxxix-xlv. The enchantment
   of JA's letters "will be admitted by those only in
   whose own experience little things--like nicknames,
   or family jokes, or the arrangement of the furni-
   ture--are inseparable from the deeper joys, and even
   from the deeper sorrows of life." "Even if Jane
   Austen had no other claim to be remembered, her letters would be memorable," for they yield a picture
   of "the upper middle class of that time which is
   surely without a rival."

4 Kennedy, Margaret. "'How Ought a Novelist . . . ?'"
      Fortnightly, 172 (1952), 337-44.

      "It is this leisurely neglect of important

characters, until it is time for them to come forward and say something, which confers such aston-
ishing authority upon Miss Austen's statements
about them." JA reflects the single law governing
artists: "what you can do you may do."

5 Mudrick, Marvin. Jane Austen: Irony as Defense and
       Discovery. Princeton: Princeton Univ. Press,
       1952. Mudrick's chapter on MP appears also in
       The Nineteenth-Century Novel: Critical Essays
       and Documents, ed. Arnold Kettle (London:
       Heinemann Educational Books, 1972), pp. 83-
       107. See also 99, 200, 281, 311, 737.

       Rev. by Léonie Villard in EA, 5 (1952), 255-56;
   by DeLancey Ferguson in New York Herald Tribune Book
   Review, 8 June 1952, p. 13; by Edd Winfield Parks in
   NCF, 7 (1952), 132-37; in Spectator, 5 Dec. 1952, p.
   793; in TLS, 19 Sept. 1952, p. 610; in VQR, 28
   (1952), lxvii-lxviii; by Royal A. Gettmann in JEGP,
   52 (1953), 269-71; in Listener, 8 Jan. 1953, p. 73;
   by Earl R. Wasserman in MLN, 68 (1953), 258-62; by
   Stuart M. Tave in PQ, 32 (1953), 256-57; by Frank
   Bradbrook in CambridgeJ, 7 (1954), 572-74; by
   Winifred Husbands in RES, 5 (1954), 305-08; by
   Harold F. Folland in WHR, 8 (1954), 360-61.

       Juvenilia: JA adopts irony (consisting "in the
   discrimination between impulse and pretension, between being and seeming") as her characteristic defense against commitment and feeling. Whether at-
   tacking literary or social conventions, in the juvenilia she herself never becomes morally or emotionally engaged. The juvenilia are essentially parodic, yet pieces like "Catharine or the Bower" foreshadow the novels in the attempt to create a self-
   sustaining world.

       NA: In NA, JA tries simultaneously to parody
   the Radcliffean form of the Gothic novel and create
   her own domestic novel. She juxtaposes Gothic types
   and bourgeois anti-types, showing the actual world
   to contain evil on a smaller scale. But because she
   is always "the willfully ironic and detached spectator," JA sacrifices the characters' consistency to
   their satiric function. She ends by rejecting the
   world of romance as well as the characters who
   helped disprove it.

       S and S: S and S shows JA's movement away from
   parody toward a mature consideration of personality.
   JA here adds social convention to irony as a defense
   against personal commitment. She judges as good the

insipid and limited characters, who accept society's forms. Because she sees all feeling, and not just false feeling, as bad, JA betrays Marianne, who is "an unacknowledged depth of her author's spirit" and the true "life and center of the novel."

P and P: JA now consistently uses irony that is internal, one not deflected by any need for self-justification. Through this irony P and P discloses the free individual. Like her creator, Elizabeth Bennet is an ironic observer, discriminating between simple and complex personalities, the former type being unaware and powerless, the latter possessing self-awareness, which allows for choice. The heroine becomes increasingly conscious of the social pressures able to abridge the individual's freedom.

Lady Susan and The Watsons: "Her first completed masterpiece," Lady Susan is JA at her most typical: her irony is "neither warm nor simple," but "hard," "analytic," "detached." The heroine is a tragic victim forced to waste her passionate, intelligent nature in the narrow and hollow social world. In contrast to this steady ironic vision is JA's simplistic vindication of genteel morality in The Watsons. Here, in a way reminiscent of S and S, her stiff moralism subverts artistic vision.

MP: MP is JA's grand "apostasy from irony." Seeking to justify the ethical basis of her own world, she fails artistically; she sacrifices every character to her severely moral thesis. Custom is defended against personality, "obedience against expression, system against energy." All issues are faced without compromise, and the end is "a norm of orthodox nonentity."

E: E differs from the other novels in JA's absolute assured mastery of her technique, "without intrusion of derivativeness or fatigue or morality." The book appears light but is dense, shaped by interlocking and internal ironic reverberations. The chief irony involves an individual's superficial attractiveness, which signals a separation of wit from feeling. The heroine, probably unregenerate at the end, manipulates people in order to avoid human commitment.

P: The book's new impulse is personal feeling. The exasperation JA now feels for knaves and fools is as sure a sign of authorial commitment as the warmly sensitive treatment accorded the good

characters. The novel's conflict is between the
vestiges of feudalism and the new middle class, and
its focal concern the individual's emotional opposition to society's encroachments. Irony is "controlled and uncompulsive," and casuistry "examined in
the light of personality."

Sanditon: Its use of surroundings, the Romantic
poets, and sex is new for JA, as is the awareness of
the inherent ambiguity "of all her materials,"
social and personal. Her irony finally develops
into a "free, exploring, undefensive agent of perception." In P feeling had been liberated, and in
Sanditon JA "was undertaking with fresh impulse
another liberation," "the liberation of irony."

Appendix on "Mrs. Leavis's Jane Austen": Though
occasionally illuminating, Mrs. Leavis' propositions
about JA the person and artist (see 396) are generally invalidated because they ignore the basic fact
that JA alternates "between an ironic and a conventional view of her materials."

6 Neill, S. Diana. "Fiction during the Regency," in A
     Short History of the English Novel. 1st Amer.
     ed. New York: Macmillan, 1952 [London: Jar-
     rolds, 1951], pp. 123-29.

"Behind the comedy of sex there are glimpses of
resentment at the limitations of an economic world.
. . . Death takes no toll of her characters and the
worst of all sins is vulgarity."

7 Parks, Edd Winfield. "Exegesis in Austen's Novels,"
     SAQ, 51 (1952), 103-19.

JA's "use of exegesis in each book seems to
rest finally on the concept of the heroine. When,
like Catherine Morland, the heroine is too immature
or, like Fanny Price, too weak to assume the full
burden of central intelligence, Miss Austen is
frequently the exegete as well as the novelist;
when a fully rounded character is mystically
created . . . less explanation is needed, and less
is given."

8 Parks, Edd Winfield. "Jane Austen's Lure of the
     Next Chapter." NCF, 7 (1952), 56-60.

As illustrated in P and P, JA's "most effective
device for enticing us on into the story" is the
summary of character, which arouses "curiosity by
making us feel that only a part of the evidence is
in," and that additional evidence may modify our
opinion. "Episodes may end, but her people continue
to grow, and it is this growth which she entices us
to follow avidly."

9   Praz, Mario. "Jane Austen," in La casa della fama:
    Saggi di letteratura e d'arte. Milan and
    Naples: Ricciardi, 1952, pp. 311-27. This
    essay appeared originally as the preface to
    Praz's translation of E, 1951.

Limited yet profound, JA presents, in E as in
her other novels, "conversation pieces," studies of
men in society where the rhythm of life is calm and
slow, and manners are urbane. The most typical
eighteenth-century English novelist, she cultivates,
like other classicists, reason, elegance, and comfort, and focuses always on characters.

10 Pritchett, V. S. "Introduction" to Pride and Prej-
    udice. London: Collins, 1952, pp. 9-14.

Her characters "are ruthless and what adds to
their ruthlessness is the harmony of the design
they live in, a design which by pointedly, brilliantly, breathlessly keeping to the surface of
life, holds the realities we all know in terrifying
silence beneath it." Cool and hard, stressing good
sense, social irony, and "gaiety of intellect," she
is "the only artist in the English novel . . . the
last voice of a happier age."

11 Rugg, Winnifred King. "Of Jane's Good Company."
    Christian Science Monitor, 22 Aug. 1952, p. 10.

JA's "comedy is a little sly, a little prim,
more often than not a little sharp, and entrancing
in its felicity of expression. To me it is the dash
of lemon juice to make the sauce supreme."

12 Schorer, Mark. "Fiction and the 'Analogical Ma-
    trix,'" in Critiques and Essays on Modern Fic-
    tion, 1920-1951: Representing the Achievement
    of Modern American and British Critics. Sel.
    John W. Aldridge. New York: Ronald Press,

1952, pp. 83-98. This essay appeared originally, with the title "Fiction and the 'Matrix
of Analogy,'" in KR, 11 (1949), 539-60; it
appears also, with the title "Fiction and the
'Analogical Matrix,'" in The World We Imagine:
Selected Essays by Mark Schorer (New York:
Farrar, Straus and Giroux, 1968), pp. 24-45,
and in Essays in Stylistic Analysis, ed. Howard
S. Babb (New York: Harcourt, Brace, Jovanovich,
1972), pp. 339-52.

"Persuasion is a novel of courtship and marriage with a patina of sentimental scruple and moral
punctilio and a stylistic base derived from commerce
and property, the counting house and the inherited
estate. . . . The basis of the comedy lies in the
difference between the two orders of value which the
metaphors, like the characters, are all the while
busily equating."

13 Suddaby, Elizabeth. "A Sentence in Pride and Prej-
      udice." Corr. in TLS, 11 Apr. 1952, p. 251.

The construction "has anger" occurs also in
Clarissa and means "incurred anger."

14 Tucker, A. E. H. "Religion in Jane Austen's Nov-
      els." Theology, 55 (1952), 260-65.

Although JA believed that "the religion of her
time was not interesting or absorbing enough to
write about," she still does make use of it: she
indicts the clergy by her silence about their sacer-
dotal function. Mr. Collins' piety is summed up in
his sycophancy, and Edmund Bertram attends a ball
within forty-eight hours of his ordination.

15 Usborne, Margaret. "Jane Austen--The Lefroys."
      Spectator, 29 Feb. 1952, pp. 257-58.

"I believe that, between 1796 and 1798, an
entreaty to Jane Austen to be serious would have
produced assurances of some attachment to Tom
Lefroy." The Lefroys, who in JA's time were a
"literary" family, did not retain that reputation
later in the nineteenth century.

1953

16 Chapman, R. W. Jane Austen: A Critical Bibliogra-
        phy. Oxford: Clarendon Press, 1953. The sec-
        ond edition, 1955, corrects a few errors from
        the first and enlarges the addenda.

            Rev. in TLS, 6 Nov. 1953, p. 716 [and see corr.,
        R. W. Chapman, 13 Nov., p. 725]; by Andrew H. Wright
        in PQ, 33 (1954), 100; by Winifred Husbands in RES,
        6 (1955), 331-32.

            "Addressed to Austenians in general rather than
        to the fastidious collector," this selective and
        critical bibliography is chiefly concerned with bi-
        ography and criticism, and includes "all the edi-
        tions of the novels before 1890," later reprints
        with "introductions of interest," translations, edi-
        tions of the minor works and letters, and a few
        autobiographical scraps.

17 Clark, E. V. "Some Aspects of Jane Austen." Con-
        temporaryR, 183 (1953), 236-40.

            The apparent contradiction between JA's atti-
        tude toward children in the letters and that in the
        books can be resolved by acknowledging that the bad
        behavior of children in the novels is attributed to
        and in part defines the moral deficiencies of their
        parents and does not reflect the author's dislike of
        children.

18 Cohen, Louise D. "Insight, the Essence of Jane
        Austen's Artistry." NCF, 8 (1953), 213-24.

            A comparison of the rejected and the final ver-
        sions of P's conclusion demonstrates that "Jane
        Austen's art depended upon her confidence in her own
        insight." The contrived situations and uneconomic
        phrasing of the early draft are replaced with events
        and diction that derive from JA's full realization
        of the emotions of her characters and the probable
        situations into which these emotions would impel
        them.

19 Fryxell, Donald L. "A Note on Jane Austen's Meth-
        od." N&Q, 198 (1953), 299-300.

            The episode of Harriet's "Most precious

treasures" in E may have been modeled on a similar
incident in which Fanny Knight, JA's niece, became
excited over a "dirty Shaving Rag."

20 Greene, D. J. "Jane Austen and the Peerage." PMLA,
      68 (1953), 1017-31.

      When JA "creates families with any pretensions
to gentle birth, she almost always endows them with
names belonging to actual British families." Possibly she expected "her readers to find in the arro-
gant possessors of the great Whig names of Fitzwil-
liam and D'Arcy a satire" on Whiggism. JA's double
commitment to both aristocracy and democracy does
not indicate a lack of feeling, but rather a tendency to feel both sides of the question too acutely.

21 King, Noel J. "Jane Austen in France." NCF, 8
      (1953), 1-26.

      JA was probably unaware of the French transla-
tions of her works. Raison et Sensibilité, trans-
lated by Isabelle de Montolieu, did enjoy some
popularity--though probably because of its transla-
tor's reputation. Because Mme. de Montolieu viewed
JA's "restraint with stern disapproval," the result
of her labor was a sentimentalized "imitation" of S
and S. Mme. de Montolieu's La Nouvelle Emma and La
Famille Elliot are more orthodox translations, the
second of which does more justice to JA's art.

22 MacInnes, Helen, Mark Van Doren, and Lyman Bryson.
      "Jane Austen: Emma," in The Invitation to
      Learning Reader on Popular Classics. No. 9.
      Ed. George D. Crothers. New York: Muschel,
      1953, pp. 53-60.

      The blows Emma gets "from trying to interfere
with people's lives and making a fool of herself
would not have meant anything if the chorus, the
Greek chorus, hadn't been there in the position of
Mr. Knightley to point out" her errors. JA, "a
virtually perfect artist" and "a very wise woman
. . . with the highest standards for human conduct," gives her standards to her heroine.

23 Needham, F. R. D. "'. . . And the Boulanger.'"
      Corr. in TLS, 11 Dec. 1953, p. 801. See also

corr. in TLS, Margaret Dean-Smith, 18 Dec.
1953, p. 817; Lucy Galton and R. W. Chapman, 25
Dec., p. 833; Violet Alford, 1 Jan. 1954, p. 9;
Margaret Dean-Smith, 8 Jan., p. 25; Arnold
Palmer, 15 Jan., p. 41.

(On the dance mentioned in P and P.)

24   Paul, David.   "'Syringa, Iv'ry Pure.'"   TC, 153
     (1953), 302-08.

"Much as she loved Cassandra, the letters are
curiously un-intimate. Jane never puts herself into
her letters." The letters' value consists in the
fact that "one can just trace here and there hints
of the beginnings of the process by which the common
object or experience assumes its special meaning
within a created unity."

25   Rubinstein, Annette T.   "Jane Austen," in The Great
     Tradition in English Literature: From Shake-
     speare to Shaw.   New York: Citadel Press, 1953,
     pp. 328-74.

JA is unsparingly realistic and unsentimental.
"One finds an especial piquancy in the rapid and
skillful social dissection carried on while the
lady's air of courteous attention to the story dis-
claims all knowledge of her right hand as well as
her left. And of course the need for such a pose is
in itself Miss Austen's sharpest comment on woman's
position in the best of polite society."

26   Shand, John.   "The House Where Jane Lived," in The
     Bedside Guardian: 2.   Sel. Ivor Brown.   London:
     Collins, 1953, pp. 34-37.

(A description of the origin and development of
the Jane Austen Society.)

27   Shibata, Akinori.   "Some Criticisms on Jane Austen's
     Emma."   The Humanities (Journal of the Yokohama
     National University), Sect. II, No. 2 (1953),
     pp. 28-33.

Since Emma realizes "she has been in the
wrong," the novel appears to conform to the rules of
French comedy. But JA's "good-humoured sympathy for

her characters does not square with the imperson-
ally critical spirit of French Comedy." Her incor-
rigible minor characters are in the spirit of
Shakespearean comedy.

28   Stern, G. B. "Introduction" to Emma. London: Col-
       lins, 1953, pp. 11-18.

With wit, irony, and intricate craftsmanship,
JA presents in E a heroine who commits faults from
the best of motives and "a glorious company of bores
always ready to rescue us from boredom!" "We are
left with an impression of figures painted with the
bloom, the genial suavity of a Renoir landscape, who
'fleet the time carelessly as they did in the Golden
World.'"

29   Stern, G. B. "Introduction" to Mansfield Park.
       London: Collins, 1953, pp. 11-20.

"It would be enlightening to discover" what it
is that makes us so "contentedly spell-bound" while
reading MP. There is no reasonable response to all
the urgent questions we ask, "and only Jane Austen's
genius has supplied its own unreasonable answer."

30   Stern, G. B. "A New Jane Austen," in A Name to Con-
       jure with. London: Collins, 1953, pp. 156-66.

"To be a Janeite is really a form of posses-
sion, with a profound contentment in being thus
possessed."

31   Van Ghent, Dorothy. "On Pride and Prejudice," in
       The English Novel: Form and Function. New
       York: Rinehart, 1953, pp. 99-111.

The limitations of time, setting, and situation in P and P define the form and meaning of the
book. By their language JA's characters show themselves as variously perceptive, foolish, or calcu-
lating. She focuses on the incongruities of civilized society--incongruities between utilitarian
and nonutilitarian values, between economic compul-
sion and love. But the protagonists' "emotional
intelligence" ultimately reconciles "the common
culture and the individual development."

32 Ward, A. C. "Introduction" to <u>Sense</u> <u>and</u> <u>Sensibili-</u>
      <u>ty</u>. London: Collins, 1953, pp. 11-16.

      Though flawed, her first published book gives
   us "just the counterpoise of·<u>sense</u> and <u>sensibility</u>
   that sustains the equilibrium of all Jane Austen's
   novels and infuses them with [their] unique sanity."
   As a narrator she is generally objective and, in her
   overall outlook, she is sceptical, unsentimental,
   and often "savagely satirical."

33 Wright, Andrew H. <u>Jane</u> <u>Austen's</u> <u>Novels</u>: <u>A</u> <u>Study</u> <u>in</u>
      <u>Structure</u>. New York: Oxford Univ. Press, 1953.
      Wright's appended bibliography is updated in
      the second edition (London: Chatto and Windus,
      1961) and again in the first reprint of the
      second edition (London: Chatto and Windus,
      1964).

      Rev. in <u>Adelphi</u>, 30 (1953), 90; by Emma Gurney
   Salter in <u>ContemporaryR</u>, 184 (1953), 380-81; by
   David Daiches in <u>Manchester</u> <u>Guardian</u> <u>Weekly</u>, 8 Oct.
   1953, p. 10; by V. S. Pritchett in <u>New</u> <u>Statesman</u>, 19
   Sept. 1953, pp. 318-19; in <u>Spectator</u>, 13 Nov. 1953,
   p. 550; in <u>TLS</u>, 16 Oct. 1953, p. 663; by F. W.
   Bradbrook in <u>CambridgeJ</u>, 7 (1954), 502-03; (with
   other works) by <u>Frederick</u> T. Wood in <u>ES</u>, 35 (1954),
   277; by Léonie Villard in <u>EA</u>, 7 (1954), 333-34; in
   <u>Listener</u>, 11 Feb. 1954, p. 271; by May Lamberton
   Becker in <u>New</u> <u>York</u> <u>Herald</u> <u>Tribune</u> <u>Book</u> <u>Review</u>, 31
   Jan. 1954, p. 13; by Edd Winfield Parks in <u>NCF</u>, 9
   (1954), 72-75; by James V. Logan in <u>PQ</u>, 33 (1954),
   104-05; by Dorothy Van Ghent in <u>MLN</u>, 70 (1955), 214-
   16; by Edith C. Batho in <u>MLR</u>, 51 (1956), 460; (with
   another work) by Ray Mathew in <u>LondonMag</u>, NS 3 (Apr.
   1963), 81-82.

      Materials and Themes: What raises JA above the
   objections of her detractors is her ironic vision,
   which consists in the juxtaposition of two mutually
   incompatible views of life. Hers is an "interested
   objectivity," "detached but not indifferent, with-
   drawn but not removed." Viewed in this way, JA's
   novels consistently evidence a clash of contradic-
   tory ideals, between which the author judges and
   chooses, but never with absolute certainty.

      Narrative Management: JA utilizes six distinct
   points of view: seemingly neutral "objective report-
   age"; indirect comment that by a word or phrase
   indicates a view neither of the author nor

characters; direct comment, in which JA enters the
narrative in propria persona; common-sense maxims,
usually ironic; dramatized dialogue; and, finally,
disclosures of others' thoughts or feelings to a
degree impossible in life. JA's "very omniscience
argues that a single point of view would not comprehend the intent of the novels fully."

S and S: The lesson of the novel is that
neither Elinor nor Marianne, neither the mode of
sense nor sensibility, is adequate; "each contra-
dicts the other--and there is no happy medium."
Edward Ferrars is too broadly outlined to be convincing, and Willoughby's final penitence is inappropriate.

NA: NA goes beyond the parody of Gothic sentimentalism to explore the limitations of good sense
itself. Catherine learns that good sense cannot
deal with or explain her expulsion from the Abbey.
John Thorpe is the least interesting of JA's vil-
lains, and Henry Tilney is the only one of her
heroes who threatens the formal primacy of the
heroine.

P and P: The "ironic theme of the book might
be said to center in the dangers of intellectual
complexity." The hero and heroine, precisely because of their deep percipience, are subject to
failures of perception. Further, the novel shows
that "intimacy blurs perception: intelligence fails
if there is insufficient distance between mind and
object." "Against clarity, in Pride and Prejudice,
involvement is set: both are desirable, but each,
ironically, works against the other."

MP: MP proves that JA is not always ironic.
Fanny is a simple didactic figure, who, nevertheless, has a "compelling sweetness which takes us
over such bumps as her objections to producing a
play at Mansfield Park." Although Henry Crawford
is a much more interesting character than Edmund
Bertram, he is nevertheless morally defective.
Crawford's elopement with Maria and his subsequent
"fall" are consonant with his development throughout the novel.

E: Emma's detachment is just as important as
her vanity in her misinterpretation of experience.
And these faults are not merely a foil to Mr.
Knightley's merits--his kindness, openness, and

willingness to be involved. Moreover, her cleverness, charm, subtlety, and receptivity are as thoroughly beloved by JA as his virtues. E has no villain: Frank Churchill commits no gross crime other
than selfishness, the want of consideration for
others.

    P: Here JA exposes more clearly than in the
other novels the conflict between the values of
prudence and those of love. Anne relies on both,
and the resulting contradiction causes her nearly a
decade of misery. Wentworth's real rival is not
William Walter Elliot but over-conventionality.

    Styles: JA's irony derives its sharpness and
point from the Johnsonian tradition. Examples in
her canon of understatement, litotes, antiphrasis,
and syntactic anti-climax indicate the variety of
ironic devices she employs. JA avoids metaphorical
language, assigning it only to characters we are
meant to dislike. JA's style is ultimately original and this as much as anything else is responsible
for her front rank among the English novelists.

1954

34 Allen, Walter. "The Nineteenth Century: The First
        Generation," in The English Novel: A Short
        Critical History. New York: Dutton, 1954, pp.
        113-26.

    JA was a "pure" novelist, ordering her works in
such a way that their design itself constitutes a
criticism of life. She is, with Johnson, "the most
forthright moralist in English." "Her novels represent a feminization of Fielding's" and extend his
dramatization of action in dialogue. What finally
makes JA a great novelist is her undeviating scru-
tiny of behavior.

35 Bowen, Elizabeth. "What Jane Austen Means to Me."
        Everybody's, 15 May 1954, pp. 19 and 39.

    JA "made manifest to me the wisdom (that is,
for a novelist) of confining one's art in the bounds
of a world one knows. In my day, that is more difficult than it was in hers." "One knows more worlds
than she did, but no single one so well."

36   Bradbrook, Frank W.   "Jane Austen and Choderlos de
       Laclos."   N&Q, NS 1, (1954), 75.

       In E and MP, JA may have been influenced by
     Laclos' Les Liaisons Dangereuses.

37   Bradbrook, Frank W.   "The Letters of Jane Austen."
       CambridgeJ, 7 (1954), 259-76.

       JA's letters are less limited in scope and tone
     than her novels and thus give a broader and clearer
     idea of her England. The letters often describe
     incidents later transmitted to the novels, and, like
     the fiction, her correspondence leaves the impres-
     sion of "courage rather than timidity." The criti-
     cism of art and life in JA's letters is comparable
     to that recorded by Stendhal upon his first visit to
     England in 1817.

38   Carpenter, T. Edward.   The Story of Jane Austen's
       Chawton Home. Alton, Hants: Jane Austen Memo-
       rial Trust [1954].

       (This booklet provides physical description of
     JA's Chawton home.)

39   Chapman, R. W.   "Jane Austen's Titles."   NCF, 9
       (1954), 238.

       "Jane Austen's subject-titles set a fashion."
     After "1813 titles made up of pairs of abstracts
     became frequent."

40   Chapman, R. W., ed.   Minor Works: Now First Col-
       lected and Edited from the Manuscripts, Vol.
       VI in The Works of Jane Austen: With Illustra-
       tions from Contemporary Sources. 6 vols.
       London: Oxford Univ. Press, 1954. There were
       revisions to this edition in 1963, and further
       revisions by B. C. Southam in 1969.

       Rev. in Listener, 23 Sept. 1954, p. 495; in NY,
     25 Sept. 1954, p. 143; by F. Wölcken in Archiv, 191
     (1955), 97-98; by Winifred Husbands in MLR, 50
     (1955), 569-70; in TLS, 20 May 1955, p. 263; by J.
     M. S. Tompkins in RES, 7 (1956), 88-90.

       (This, the standard edition, includes the

juvenilia, Lady Susan, The Watsons, Sanditon, and
other short pieces.)

41   Chapman, R. W. "A Reply to Mr. Duffy on Persua-
       sion." NCF, 9 (1954), 154.

     Duffy (see 44) is mistaken in placing Sir
Walter Elliot in the aristocracy; nor was the aristocracy in any danger of dissolution or displacement
by an imaginary "energetic naval class." Further,
P's description of Charmouth is not more "romantic"
than similar passages in JA's other novels.

42   Douglas, Felicity. "Real Life Stories, No. 34, Jane
       Austen." Girl (London), 20 Oct. 1954, pp. 8-9.

     (Biographical.)

43   Duffy, Joseph M., Jr. "Emma: The Awakening from
       Innocence." ELH, 21 (1954), 39-53.

     E dramatizes "the awakening of a normal, intel-
ligent young woman to the possibilities of physical
love and the direction, often chaotic, taken by her
curiosity in an effort at discovery of that love."
In her manipulation of Harriet, Emma tries to experience love vicariously, and in her flirtation with
Frank she attempts to will love. Her belief that
Harriet loves Mr. Knightley, however, reveals to
Emma the reality of emotional and physical love.

44   Duffy, Joseph M., Jr. "Structure and Idea in Jane
       Austen's Persuasion." NCF, 8 (1954), 272-89.
       See also 41.

     P's complexity appears in the novel's three
governing forces: time, society, and the individual. Time is manifested in the "pervasive symbols
of decay" and in the characters' responses to time's
ravages. Socially conceived, P mirrors the displacement of the moribund aristocracy by a vital
naval class. On the personal level, P dramatizes
"the opposition between proportion and profound
carelessness as principles of action."

45   Duncan-Jones, E. E. "Jane Austen and Crabbe." RES,
       5 (1954), 174.

The name "Fanny Price" may have been borrowed from Crabbe's The Parish Register, Part II.

46   Firth, Canon J. D'E.   "Jane Austen's Last Home."
       Good Housekeeping (London), 66 (Aug. 1954), 28-
       30.

     (Illustrations and description of the Win-
chester house where JA died.)

47   Gorer, Geoffrey.   "A Passage in Mansfield Park."
       Corr. in TLS, 1 Oct. 1954, p. 625. See also
       corr. in TLS, R. W. Chapman and S. Tunnicliffe,
       8 Oct. 1954, p. 641.

     (On "the evergreen" and "the tree that sheds
its leaf.")

48   Leavis, F. R.   "The Great Tradition," in The Great
       Tradition. Garden City, N. Y.: Doubleday,
       1954 [London: Chatto & Windus, 1948], pp. 9-41.
       See also 756.

     "Jane Austen is one of the truly great writers,
and herself a major fact in the background of other
great writers. . . . Her relation to tradition is a
creative one. She not only makes tradition for
those coming after, but . . . creates the tradition
we see leading down to her." She inaugurated the
English novel's great tradition, a tradition concerned with form and with technical originality, as
well as "distinguished by a vital capacity for
experience, a kind of reverent openness before life,
and a marked moral intensity."

49   Lewis, C. S.   "A Note on Jane Austen." EIC, 4
       (1954), 359-71. This essay appears also in
       Selected Literary Essays by C. S. Lewis, ed.
       Walter Hooper (Cambridge, Engl.: Univ. Press,
       1969), pp. 175-86. See also 61.

     That JA's novels have a firm ethical base, much
like that of the Rambler and Idler, is evidenced by
the fact that in NA, S and S, P and P, and E "undeception" is the central structural principle. The
very "hardness" and clarity of JA's moral perception
make her comedy possible. In MP, however, Fanny
Price's undeviating rectitude is insipid and unconvincing.

50   Murray, James Gregory. "Measure and Balance in Jane
     Austen's Emma." CE, 16 (1954), 160-66.

     "There are two kinds of measure and balance in
     Emma: what the heroine seeks to impose on the soci-
     ety of Hartfield, and what Jane, through irony,
     brings to Emma." By bringing her management to an
     already ordered society, Emma creates an imbalance.
     But, with Mr. Knightley's guidance, she achieves
     equilibrium by learning that "the truly balanced
     person must have a sense of responsibility" and a
     recognition of his own limitations.

51   Paul, David. "The Gay Apprentice." TC, 156 (1954),
     539-50.

     An examination of JA's minor works reveals
     that, "though the absurd was always to signify
     comedy for her [as for Lewis Carroll], and not de-
     spair, waste or tragedy [as for Camus], she shows a
     decided taste for both kinds" of absurdity. The
     intentions of JA's early work "were quite con-
     sciously to make out of life something that it was
     not; something better, simpler and more satisfying."

52   Robson, M. A. "A Jane Austen Clergyman in Real
     Life." Listener, 25 Nov. 1954, pp. 908-09 and
     913.

     Excerpts from the journal of Charles, later
     Canon, Bellairs show him to be much like JA's Mr.
     Collins.

53   Scrutton, Mary. "Bourgeois Cinderellas." TC, 155
     (1954), 351-63.

     With increasing subtlety Pamela, Evelina, and
     MP chart a young woman's success in marrying above
     her station, a success achieved not by her love or
     wit, but by her virtue. "Yet there is something
     badly wrong with Mansfield Park": by the conclusion,
     JA realized that the events of MP would not have
     occurred as she had written them.

54   Shibata, Akinori. "Two Female Characters Drawn by
     Jane Austen." The Humanities (Journal of the
     Yokohama National University), Sect. II, No. 3
     (1954), pp. 27-35.

Marianne's rebelliousness can best be understood against the background of social conventions
that JA satirizes. P and P, whose merit depends
solely on the witty, playful, and honest character
of Elizabeth, replaces the didacticism of S and S
with psychological subtlety and the satire with
comedy.

55 Sparrow, John. "Jane Austen and Sydney Smith."
       TLS, 2 July 1954, p. 429. See also corr. in
       TLS, F. W. Bradbrook, 16 July 1954, p. 457;
       John Sparrow, 23 July, p. 473; Frank W. Brad-
       brook, 30 July, p. 487; J. D. K. Lloyd, 6
       Aug., p. 501; Cecil Price, 15 Oct., p. 657.
       Sparrow's essay appears also in his Indepen-
       dent Essays (London: Faber and Faber, 1963),
       pp. 88-96.

    Sydney Smith may have been the prototype for
Henry Tilney.

56 Suddaby, Elizabeth. "Jane Austen and the Delphic
       Oracle." NCF, 9 (1954), 235-38.

    "'Know thyself' is an injunction implicit in
all the novels, and in two of them, the heroine's
progress from self-deception to self-knowledge oc-
cupies a central position."

57 Tillotson, Kathleen. "Jane Austen." Corr. in TLS,
       17 Sept. 1954, p. 591.

    (On a nineteenth-century reminiscence of JA.)

58 Tisdale, Cleva. "Would Jane Austen Have Made a Good
       Librarian?" Wilson Library Bulletin, 29
       (1954), 51 and 72.

    "The statement that Jane Austen retained her
faculties, her memory, her fancy, her imagination,
her even temper, her affections, warm, clear, and
unimpaired, and neither her love of God, nor of her
fellow creatures flagged for a moment as long as she
lived would certainly rate her as an unusual librarian. Few in the profession can truthfully boast of
such a full accomplishment."

59 Trilling, Lionel. "Mansfield Park." PR, 21 (1954),
    492-511. This essay appears also in Lionel
    Trilling, The Opposing Self: Nine Essays in
    Criticism (New York: Viking Press, 1955), pp.
    206-30, and, with the title "Jane Austen and
    Mansfield Park," in From Blake to Byron (Vol.
    5 of The Pelican Guide to English Literature),
    ed. Boris Ford (Harmondsworth, Middlesex:
    Penguin, 1957), pp. 112-29. See also 773.

    Concerned with integrity, commitment, and prin-
    ciple, with impersonation, insincerity, and vulgar-
    ity, and employing a profounder irony than that of
    any of her other novels, MP "imagines the self safe
    from the Terror of secularized spirituality. . . .
    When we have exhausted our anger at the offense
    which Mansfield Park offers to our conscious pi-
    eties, we find it possible to perceive how inti-
    mately it speaks to our secret inexpressible hopes."

                        1955

60 Baldwin, James, Frank O'Connor, and Lyman Bryson.
    "Jane Austen: Pride and Prejudice," in The
    Invitation to Learning Reader: Self-Revelation.
    No. 18. Ed. Ralph Backlund. New York:
    Muschel, 1955, pp. 142-50.

    "A supreme moralist," with a passion to teach,
    JA "is always commenting. You're always aware of
    her as a person in the story, and her subject and
    object are beautifully balanced." Dealing with the
    conflict between judgment and instinct, she embodies
    her beliefs in a felt reality and suggests much more
    than she actually says.

61 Bradbrook, M. C. "A Note on Fanny Price." EIC, 5
    (1955), 289-92.

    Contrary to C. S. Lewis' assertion (see 49),
    Fanny does indeed commit errors. She begins as a
    "girlish and unpractised" goose, but finally "learns
    to fear less, and to act."

62 Branton, Clarence L. "The Ordinations in Jane
    Austen's Novels." NCF, 10 (1955), 156-59.

    "Jane Austen's clergymen seem to become priests

without first becoming deacons, and their ordinations occur at uncanonical times."

63 Burchell, Samuel C. "Jane Austen: The Theme of
     Isolation." NCF, 10 (1955), 146-50. See also
     83.

     The isolation evident in JA's novels, as in
     Joyce's, "exists because of misunderstanding, mis-
     interpretation, and distrust. It is the result of
     pride, fear, and weakness." But unlike Joyce, JA
     believes that isolation is remediable (in Mr.
     Knightley's words) through "truth and sincerity in
     all our dealings with each other."

64 Chapman, R. W., sel. and ed. Letters, 1796-1817.
     New York: Oxford Univ. Press, 1955.

     (A selection of about one-third of JA's let-
     ters.)

65 Forster, E. M. "Jane Austen," in Abinger Harvest.
     New York: Meridian Books, 1955 [New York:
     Harcourt, Brace, 1936], pp. 140-56. This es-
     say reprints three separate reviews, pub-
     lished first in 1924, 1925, and 1932, respec-
     tively.

     1. Chapman's 1924 edition of the novels awakens
     the Jane Austenite from his characteristic stupor.
     "The novels continue to live their own wonderful in-
     ternal life, but it has been freshened and enriched
     by contact with the life of facts." 2. Of small in-
     trinsic worth, Sanditon is still interesting for the
     light it sheds on JA's last phase, especially her
     new interest in nature and romanticism. 3. JA's
     letters are characterized by "triviality, varied by
     touches of ill breeding and of sententiousness," and
     "their essential meaning went down with her into the
     grave." Yet they are invaluable in showing that the
     supreme allegiance in her life was the family, "and
     she introduced this faith as the groundwork of her
     six great novels."

66 Grigson, Geoffrey. "New Letters from Jane Austen's
     Home." TLS, 19 Aug. 1955, p. 484. See also
     corr. in TLS, D. Fisher and E. E. Phare, 26
     Aug. 1955, p. 493.

(From members of the Austen family to Anna Lefroy.)

67   Ker, W. P.   "Jane Austen," in On Modern Literature: Lectures and Addresses. Ed. Terence Spencer and James Sutherland. Oxford: Clarendon Press, 1955, pp. 113-20.

JA gives "a lively idea of the action of life as a whole, of the effect of Time carrying on human fortunes and working them out through successive illusions and corrections of illusions. The problem is the problem of all fiction; it is not often that one finds so much variety of characters together with such comprehension of the general movement of life."

68   O'Connor, Frank.   "Jane Austen and the Flight from Fancy." YR, 45 (1955), 31-47. O'Connor's essay appears also, with the title "Jane Austen: The Flight from Fancy," in his The Mirror in the Roadway: A Study of the Modern Novel (New York: Knopf, 1956), pp. 17-41.

JA "who made such fun of romance was chock-full of it. . . . She was a woman afraid of the violence of her own emotions, who rode the nightmare and sometimes rode it on too tight a rein. For it is this fear of herself that makes her the moralist she is, and that very often weakens her finest work." This destructive fear is most apparent in NA, S and S, and MP.

69   Parks, Edd Winfield.   "A Human Failing in Pride and Prejudice?" NCF, 10 (1955), 237-40.

Collins expects a dowry of one thousand pounds at four per cent from Elizabeth, but Mr. Bennet speaks of Lydia's portion as the same amount at five per cent. To determine which of the two men is correct presents an interesting, though apparently insoluble, problem in character.

70   Schoeck, R. J.   "Jane Austen and the Sense of Exposure: Heuristics in Pride and Prejudice." ES, 36 (1955), 154-57.

"This word expose with all its implicit social

force is used at important points in the development
. . . of character, and is carefully integrated into
the plot" of P and P.

71   Spence, D. S.   "White Soup."   N&Q, NS 2 (1955), 488.

White soup is not a "mixture for whitening
footmen's hair," but rather a "refreshment" served
at balls about 1830.

1956

72   Anon.   "Christmas at Pemberley: A Seasonable Theme
from Jane Austen's Pride and Prejudice."
Sphere (London), 9 Nov. 1956, pp. 24-25.

(Illustrations depicting Pemberley, the pleas-
antest place in English literature "in which to find
oneself for the festive season.")

73   Bush, Douglas.   "Mrs. Bennet and the Dark Gods: The
Truth about Jane Austen."   SR, 64 (1956), 591-
96. This essay appears also, with the title
"Mrs. Bennet and the Dark Gods," in New States-
man, 22 Dec. 1956, pp. 820-21, and, with the
title "Mrs. Bennet and the Dark Gods: The Key
to Jane Austen," in Douglas Bush, Engaged and
Disengaged (Cambridge, Mass.: Harvard Univ.
Press, 1966), pp. 20-26, and in The Overwrought
Urn: A Potpourri of Parodies of Critics Who
Triumphantly Present the Real Meaning of Au-
thors from Jane Austen to J. D. Salinger, ed.
Charles Kaplan (New York: Pegasus, 1969), pp.
102-07.

"Who and what is Bingley, the mysterious, ebul-
lient stranger from the north who descends with his
band of followers (his two sisters and Mr. Hurst and
Mr. Darcy) upon a sleepy, conventional society and
whom young people at once look to for providing
dances? Clearly he is Dionysus, the disturbing vis-
itor from northern Thrace."

74   Duffy, Joseph M., Jr.   "Moral Integrity and Moral
Anarchy in Mansfield Park."   ELH, 23 (1956),
71-91.

MP "is not a failure; it is an unachieved masterpiece." Here marriage provides plot complica-
tions, and education the thematic development, "but
the real subject is the corruption of society."
Although the Crawfords are "good tempered," they
lack "good dispositions" grounded in principle by
education and experience. The Crawfords' expulsion
from Mansfield because of their anarchic tendencies,
however, is improbable. Especially in the conclusion, JA's ideas seem illogically to divert the
novel's course of events.

75 Freeman, Kathleen. T'Other Miss Austen. London:
        Macdonald, 1956.

        Rev. in The Times (London), 18 Oct. 1956, p.
13; in TLS, 21 Dec. 1956, p. 763; by Léonie Villard
in EA, 10 (1957), 221-25.

        There are two JA's: one is "Miss Jane Austen,
the Rector's daughter of Steventon, who consciously
wished to be, and tried to be, shaped by the circumstances and conventions of her day"; "t'other Miss
Austen" is the one "chosen for a peculiar destiny,"
possessed of a "daimon," which suggested irrever-
ences and found escape in literary creation. "We
shall find our own Jane, the real Jane, the non
pareil, only in her own words: not in the novels,
except here and there--true novelists are too clever
to give themselves away in direct revelation--but in
the letters."

76 Hackett, Francis. "Northanger Abbey." New Repub-
        lic, 3 Sept. 1956, pp. 21-22.

        In NA, JA "knew imagination for what it was,
the core of her own being, but being aware of
Taine's 'carnivorous and lascivious animal,' she
had her eye on its discipline and its continence."

77 Kondo, Ineko. Jane Austen and Virginia Woolf.
        Tokyo: Kenkyusha, 1956.

        (Not seen.)

78 Lobb, K. M. "Critical Commentary," the introduction
        to his ed. of Northanger Abbey. London: Univ.
        of London Press, 1956, pp. 9-39.

By summarizing the plot we can see that "Northanger Abbey may be . . . read with no suspicion of
its burlesque element, but this knowledge can add
greatly to our enjoyment of one of the best satires
by our greatest woman satirist."

79 Lochhead, Marion. "Literature versus Celibacy."
     QuarterlyR, 294 (1956), 207-17.

Had the Anglican clergy remained celibate,
English literature would have suffered the loss of,
among others, JA. Nor would there have been a Mrs.
Norris or a Mrs. Elton. Further, many of JA's heroines as well as minor characters, who marry clergymen, would have been considerably harder put to find
suitable husbands.

80 Schorer, Mark. "Pride Unprejudiced." KR, 18
     (1956), 72-91. This essay appears also as the
     "Introduction" to Pride and Prejudice (Boston:
     Houghton Mifflin, 1956), pp. v-xxi.

Like JA's other novels, P and P is founded on
the conflict between aristocratic and bourgeois
codes, and on the presentation of "marriage as a
brutal economic fact in an essentially materialistic
society." P and P, which has a "high degree of aesthetic integration," analyzes through its characters
"the discrepancy between social actualities and social sentiment or convention." The plot's main
movement adjusts the social scale with the moral
scale.

81 Seronsy, Cecil C. "Jane Austen's Technique." N&Q,
     NS 3 (1956), 303-05.

JA's method in Chapter Two of S and S "shows
some interesting affinities with a famous scene [II,
iv] in King Lear."

82 Shannon, Edgar F., Jr. "Emma: Character and Con-
     struction." PMLA, 71 (1956), 637-50.

"Analysis of Emma's enlightenment and of the
rhythmic structure of the novel discloses a valid
progression of the heroine from callousness to mental and emotional maturity--a development psychologically consistent and technically consonant."

Emma undergoes "no sudden, unconvincing conversion," but rather one that is "perfectly within the credible limits of her nature as established at the outset and maintained throughout the novel."

83 Wright, Andrew. "A Reply to Mr. Burchell on Jane Austen." NCF, 10 (1956), 315-19.

Contrary to Burchell's assertion (see 63), "Jane Austen's world and thus Jane Austen's subject stand in marked contrast to those of Joyce." The problem in JA's novels is not that social values are no longer viable; rather, for her the humanization of the individual can only be accomplished by integration into the social unit.

1957

84 Amis, Kingsley. "What Became of Jane Austen?" Spectator, 4 Oct. 1957, pp. 439-40. See also corr. in Spectator, Angus Macintyre, 11 Oct. 1957, p. 481; Mary Moorman and Margaret W. Oram, 18 Oct., p. 514; Kingsley Amis, 25 Oct., pp. 544 and 546; Margaret W. Oram, 1 Nov., p. 578; A. Carlton Smith, 22 Nov., p. 687. Amis' essay appears also in his What Became of Jane Austen? and Other Questions (London: Cape, 1970), pp. 13-17.

In MP, JA's "judgment and her moral sense were corrupted." As persons and as embodiments of an ideology, the novel's hero and heroine are defective. "Edmund's notions and feelings are vitiated by a narrow and unreflecting pomposity, Fanny's are made odious by a self-regard utterly unredeemed by any humor." She "lacks self-knowledge, generosity and humility."

85 Bluestone, George. "Pride and Prejudice," in Novels into Film. Baltimore: Johns Hopkins Press, 1957, pp. 115-46.

The 1940 film version of P and P faithfully embodies the intricacies of the novel. It imitates JA's lack of particular detail, the absence of metaphorical language, and her omniscient point of view. Patterned like a dance, the film suggests, as does JA, the identity of physical and psychological movement.

86   Bowen, Elizabeth. "Persuasion." LondonMag, 4 (Apr.
     1957), 47-51.

     JA's "true depth" was not displayed until she
     wrote P. Though it is "a novel about restraint,"
     nevertheless only here does JA "break with her self-
     set limitations" to reach the "depths of emotion."

87   Brogan, Howard O. "Science and Narrative Structure
     in Austen, Hardy, and Woolf." NCF, 11 (1957),
     276-87.

     P and P is "a projection of desire in ratio-
     nalistic terms which reflect Newtonian scientific
     assumptions." JA's universe "exists objectively,"
     independent of "subjective psychological impres-
     sions of it." And for a given distribution of
     characters, a certain set of events must inevitably
     result. Nevertheless, these events always ulti-
     mately conform to "what we would like to happen."

88   Burden, Denis H. "Jane Austen (1775-1817)," in The
     Cambridge Bibliography of English Literature.
     Ed. George Watson. Cambridge, Engl.: Univ.
     Press, 1957. V ["Supplement: A.D. 600-1900"],
     617-19.

     (A selective bibliography of bibliographies,
     editions of the novels and minor works, biography,
     and criticism.)

89   Cecil, Lord David. "A Note on Jane Austen's Sce-
     nery," in The Fine Art of Reading and Other
     Literary Studies. Indianapolis: Bobbs-Mer-
     rill, 1957, pp. 163-75.

     Satirical comedy, such as JA writes, does not
     require elaborate scenic descriptions. The sce-
     nery she does provide illustrates her "human story,"
     and her settings, indoor or out, are convincing and
     economical.

90   Cecil, Lord David. "Sense and Sensibility," in The
     Fine Art of Reading and Other Literary Studies.
     Indianapolis: Bobbs-Merrill, 1957, pp. 149-60.
     This essay appeared originally as the introduc-
     tion to the World's Classics edition of S and
     S, 1931.

In S and S, JA has not yet fully learned that examples work more forcibly than precepts. But several significant traits of her mature fiction are already present and pervasive, including the "exquisite," "good-tempered," "ruthless" irony, the firm grasp of social reality, and the "eye for the essentials of character." Though her range is narrow, she engraves on her bit of ivory "a criticism of life as serious and as considered as Tolstoy's."

91   Church, Richard. "Introduction" to Pride and Prejudice. London: Folio Society, 1957, pp. v-ix.

"The lightest and most lyrical of all her books," P and P is nevertheless wise and mature. Hers is a "pure use of language; what might be called an aristocracy of style."

92   Duncan-Jones, E. E. "Proposals of Marriage in Pride and Prejudice and Pamela." N&Q, NS 4 (1957), 76.

The phrasing of Darcy's first proposal parallels that of Mr. B. in Pamela.

93   Gibbons, Stella. "Introduction" to Sense and Sensibility. New York: Heritage Press, 1957, pp. v-xv.

"How we long to hear some inartistic and unlikely explanation that shall prove the story false or the marriage invalid and see Willoughby restored to Marianne!" "If I have not spoken of Colonel Brandon it is because I do not care to."

94   Gorer, Geoffrey. "The Myth in Jane Austen," in Art and Psychoanalysis. Ed. William Phillips. New York: Criterion, 1957, pp. 218-25. This essay appeared originally in AI, 2 (1941), 197-204; it appears also in Five Approaches of Literary Criticism: An Arrangement of Contemporary Critical Essays, comp. Wilbur S. Scott (New York: Collier, 1962), pp. 91-98, and in The World of Psychoanalysis, ed. G. B. Levitas (New York: Braziller, 1965), pp. 145-51. See also 390.

Reworking fantasies derived from her own actual

life, JA created in her novels a central myth involving "the girl who hates and despises her mother
and marries a father-surrogate." Crucial to this
myth is the debunking of sexual passion. In P she
finally modified this myth.

95 Gorer, Geoffrey. "Poor Honey: Some Notes on Jane
    Austen and Her Mother." LondonMag, 4 (Aug.
    1957), 35-48. Gorer's essay appears also in
    his The Danger of Equality and Other Essays
    (London: Cresset Press, 1966), pp. 248-64.

    "In all the novels except the youthful North-
    anger Abbey the mother, if she is alive, or the
    mother substitute, if the mother be dead, is the
    cause of unnecessary suffering." This fact "sug-
    gests a personal involvement." A review of the
    letters and novels indicates that JA's mother was
    "a domineering old lady, fussy and querulous," a
    "hypochondriac, and possibly also an invalid,
    slightly melancholic, demanding protection."

96 Harding, D. W. "Jane Austen and Moral Judgement,"
    in From Blake to Byron. (Vol. 5 of The Peli-
    can Guide to English Literature.) Ed. Boris
    Ford. Harmondsworth, Middlesex: Penguin,
    1957, pp. 51-59.

    JA depicts the dilemma of the sensitive person
    who must come to terms with a mediocre society.
    "The detachment and autonomy of the individual as a
    centre of self-responsible moral judgement, which
    she maintained unswervingly, was in fact another
    variant of that reaction against submission to
    ready-made social codes which marks Blake, Shelley,
    Wordsworth, and even Byron."

97 Lansdale, Nelson. "Literary Landmark." SatR, 9
    Nov. 1957, p. 31.

    (Illustrated description of Chawton.)

98 Leavis, Q. D. "Introduction" to Mansfield Park.
    London: Macdonald, 1957, pp. vii-xviii.

    Rev. by Kingsley Amis in Spectator, 4 Oct.
    1957, pp. 439-40; see 84.

The product of JA's sustained private life, MP
reveals the influence of Evangelicalism upon the
author. Though unoriginal in its satire and moralism, the book is the first modern English novel,
because it attempts "to work out a psychological
analysis of feeling, which creates a new style."
MP contrasts the pleasures of the Regency world to
more traditional values.

99   Link, Frederick M. "Jane Austen, Mr. Mudrick, and
          Critical Monism." Boston Univ. Studies in
          English, 3 (1957), 60-62.

          "Mr. Mudrick's determined insistence on irony
     as Miss Austen's defense against personal involve-
     ment [see 5] has led him to exaggerate the impor-
     tance of Wickham and Lydia to [P and P]."

100 Mathison, John K. "Northanger Abbey and Jane
          Austen's Conception of the Value of Fiction."
          ELH, 24 (1957), 138-52.

          An examination of Catherine's maturation re-
     veals, first, the similarity of NA to JA's other
     novels, and, second, the value of the novel as a
     genre. In contrast to Gothic fiction, NA, "with
     no sensationalism, no unreality, no sentimentality,
     is no escape from life, but . . . an illumination
     of it." "Jane Austen considers the novel a better
     teacher than history or essays . . . [because] it
     cuts through the surface of things to what is."

101 McKillop, Alan D. "The Context of Sense and Sensi-
          bility." Rice Institute Pamphlet, 44 (Apr.
          1957), 65-78.

          S and S glaringly illustrates the common dif-
     ficulty of combining the tragedy of Clarissa with
     the drawing-room comedy of Grandison. In manipu-
     lating the "convention of romantic fiction and
     romantic taste" and the "convention of disillu-
     sioned common sense," however, JA does show "in-
     dependent power." Willoughby's fate, and the con-
     clusion of S and S in general, constitute JA's
     "disclaimer of the strict pattern of moods, atti-
     tudes, and destinies followed by the conventional
     novelist."

102   Raybould, Edith. "Of Jane Austen's Use of Expanded
        Verbal Forms," in Studies in English Language
        and Literature Presented to Professor Dr. Karl
        Brunner on the Occasion of His Seventieth
        Birthday. (Wiener Beiträge zur englischen
        Philologie, 65.) Ed. Siegfried Korninger.
        Vienna and Stuttgart: Braumüller, 1957, pp.
        175-90.

        JA's "use of verbal forms is determined by
      accurate observation but also by her own need for
      stylistic self-expression." For JA, verbal forms
      serve, among other things, as a means of charac-
      terization.

103   Trilling, Lionel. "Introduction" to Emma. Boston:
        Houghton Mifflin, 1957, pp. v-xxiv. This es-
        say appears also, with the title "Emma," in
        Encounter, 8 (June 1957), 49-59 [and see corr.,
        M. H. Statham, 9 (Sept. 1957), 69-70, and Frank
        W. Bradbrook, 9 (Oct. 1957), 70], and, with the
        title "Emma and the Legend of Jane Austen," in
        Lionel Trilling, Beyond Culture: Essays on Lit-
        erature and Learning (New York: Viking Press,
        1965), pp. 31-55.

        In this, her greatest novel, JA creates an
      idyll and contrasts it to the actualities of society
      and the modern self. She "proposes to us the hope
      of victory in the battle that the mind must wage"
      and "speaks of the expectation of allies in the
      fight." She "represents the possibility of the
      control of the personal life, of becoming acquainted
      with ourselves, of the community of 'intelligent
      love.'"

                              1958

104   Babb, Howard S. "Dialogue with Feeling: A Note on
        Pride and Prejudice." KR, 20 (1958), 203-16.

        (See 182.)

105   Bradbrook, Frank W. "Lord Chesterfield and Jane
        Austen." N&Q, 5 (1958), 80-82.

        JA probably knew of Lord Chesterfield's Letters
      to His Son. His views of men and manners often

coincide with her own; but to JA, Chesterfield represents what is "aimable" rather than "amiable."

106 Church, Richard. "Introduction" to Sense and Sensi-
          bility. London: Folio Society, 1958, pp. v-
          vii.

          S and S comments directly "on the school of
     fiction preceding it, while it points the way to an
     open-minded realism, at least in matters of social
     conscience and conduct." The irony is often savage,
     and the characterization bitter.

107 Coates, John. The Watsons: Jane Austen's Fragment
          Continued and Completed. New York: Crowell,
          1958.

          Rev. by Laura M. Ragg in English, 12 (1958),
     109; in TLS, 13 June 1958, p. 324; by Melvin W.
     Askew in BA, 33 (1959), 356; by Rose Feld in New
     York Herald Tribune Book Review, 22 Feb. 1959, p.
     6; by Joseph Wood Krutch in SatR, 31 Jan. 1959, p.
     17; in Time, 19 Jan. 1959, p. 92.

          (Finishes the fragment.)

108 Daiches, David. "Introduction" to Persuasion. New
          York: Norton, 1958, pp. v-xviii.

          Her "subtlest and most delicately wrought"
     novel, P renders clearly and movingly JA's "sense
     of the limitations which bound all human desires
     and actions." Though JA is aware of the continual
     need for compromise in life, she is no more for-
     giving of folly and vice than earlier in her career.
     With Bath as the moral testing ground, selfishness
     and self-deception still earn her scorn, just as
     generosity and intelligence do her respect.

109 Janković, Danica S. "Beleška o piscu," the after-
          word to Pod tudjim uticajem [Persuasion].
          Trans. Danica S. Janković. Subotica and
          Belgrade: Minerva, 1958, pp. 271-74.

          In P, JA, who believes in all that is rational,
     humane, and social, shows her novelistic skill by
     presenting her characters dramatically. Through
     dialogue they so impress themselves on us, that we

feel them to be alive, close, and convincing.

110   Jenkins, Elizabeth. Jane Austen: A Biography.
         London: Gollancz, 1958 [1938].

         (Biography.)

111   Johnson, Joyce. "Dearest Lizzy." Spectator, 12
         Dec. 1958, p. 875.

         (Report on a competition "to forestall the
      reported musical production of Pride and Prejudice
      by submitting lyrics.")

112   Leavis, Q. D.   "Introduction" to Sense and Sensi-
         bility, with Lady Susan and The Watsons.
         London: Macdonald, 1958, pp. vii-xxiv.

         The "crude satiric base" of S and S is over-
      laid by JA's mature interest in the theme of the
      individual's relation to society. With a plot that
      is dramatic, economic, and original in its use of
      symmetry and surprise, S and S deals with "the
      insubstantiality of first love" and has "a moral of
      Prudence, Reserve and Civility." Lady Susan, "an
      important link between the juvenilia and the pub-
      lished novels," was reworked for MP, and The Watsons
      for E.

113   McKillop, Alan D.   "Critical Realism in Northanger
         Abbey," in From Jane Austen to Joseph Conrad:
         Essays Collected in Memory of James T. Hill-
         house. Ed. Robert C. Rathburn and Martin
         Steinmann, Jr. Minneapolis: Univ. of Min-
         nesota Press, 1958, pp. 35-45.

         NA begins on the plan of a sustained satire of
      novelistic formulas. Catherine, however, is not
      only an anti-heroine but a heroine as well. She is
      intended to "illustrate, not merely to negate roman-
      tic folly," and allusions to other novels are em-
      ployed both for satiric purposes and for charac-
      terization. NA evolves from a blank opposition
      between romance and actuality into a kind of "sur-
      rogate romance in real life."

114   Murrah, Charles.   "The Background of Mansfield

Park," in From Jane Austen to Joseph Conrad:
Essays Collected in Memory of James T. Hill-
house. Ed. Robert C. Rathburn and Martin
Steinmann, Jr. Minneapolis: Univ. of Minnesota
Press, 1958, pp. 23-34.

JA designs the setting of MP for symbolic suggestion as well as for emotional heightening. She
associates good of all kinds with the rural environment of the Mansfield estate and evil with London.
The treatment of light and shade in the descriptions
of Portsmouth provides a clear and natural contrast
to the beauty of Mansfield. And especially in the
Sotherton episode, details of setting convey precisely the moral qualities of each character.

115 Rawson, C. J. "The Sentimental Hero in Fiction and
     Life: A Note on Jane Austen and Fanny Burney."
     N&Q, 5 (1958), 253-54.

     Sir Edward Denham of Sanditon manifests a "rap-
turous sensibility" similar to that of Mr. William
Bunbury in Fanny Burney's Diary.

116 Raymond, John. "Seniority of Mind." New Statesman,
     5 Apr. 1958, pp. 440-41. Raymond's essay
     appears also in his The Doge of Dover and Other
     Essays (London: MacGibbon and Kee, 1960), pp.
     105-09.

     As "one of the world's greatest moralists," JA
"is largely there to remind us that we can be more
than we are. . . . She instructs quite simply by
her 'seniority of mind.'"

117 Shenfield, Margaret. "Jane Austen's Point of View."
     QuarterlyR, 296 (1958), 298-306.

     JA's method is "wholly composed of irony: by
showing an individual's picture of himself (which
is always quite false) and, at the same time, hint-
ing at the true character of the individual, she is
able to give a very clear picture of human isolation." In both NA and E, this isolation and the
humor of the novels derive from the "difficulty of
understanding others and oneself."

118 Southam, B. C. "[Additions and Corrections to the

Index of Characters in the Oxford Jane
Austen]." N&Q, 5 (1958), 458.

(Suggested additions and corrections.)

119 Southam, B. C. "Lady Susan's Husband." N&Q, 5
     (1958), 307-08.

     "Frederic" is probably the first name of Lady
Susan's husband.

120 Ward, A. C. "Introduction" to Pride and Prejudice.
     London: Longmans, Green, 1958, pp. vii-xxvii.

     P and P is noteworthy for its irony, humor, and
characterization. Elizabeth Bennet possesses the
cure for many of the world's problems: laughter.

                        1959

121 Church, Richard. "Introduction" to Mansfield Park.
     London: Folio Society, 1959, pp. v-vii.

     "Mansfield Park is the self-disciplinary work
imposed by Jane to exorcise grief and rebellion.
The general tone, the motive, of the book is di-
rected to this purpose of proclaiming the virtue of
resignation, of patience, of submission."

122 Drew, Philip. "A Significant Incident in Pride and
     Prejudice." NCF, 13 (1959), 356-58.

     Darcy's character is not flawed or split; nor
does he undergo any sudden change. The incident in
which he prevents Georgiana's elopement with Wickham
explains why Darcy is so aware of his own honor in
the first proposal to Elizabeth and also why he can
be credibly sympathetic to Elizabeth's humiliation
over Lydia's seduction.

123 Faverty, Frederic E. "Jane Austen's Pride and Prej-
     udice," in Your Literary Heritage. New York:
     Lippincott, 1959, pp. 94-96.

     The moral of P and P is "fairly obvious and not

too burdensome, stated in the title and borne out in the narrative."

124 Fuentes, Carlos. "Introducción" to Orgullo y Prejuicio. Mexico City: Universidad Nacional Autónoma de México, 1959, pp. 7-22.

In P and P, as in her other novels, JA seeks to adapt the ideals of the eighteenth century to the new bourgeois life of the nineteenth century. A social critic, she tries to find a middle ground between Darcy and Elizabeth, one including courtesy and refinement as well as good sense and imaginative boldness.

125 Gillie, Christopher. "Sense and Sensibility: An Assessment." EIC, 9 (1959), 1-9.

Through the variety of its characters, S and S shows how money influences human virtues. Ideally, for JA, one should neither merely accept nor ignore social standards. "Goodness must often sacrifice charm in order to earn the right to it."

126 Schorer, Mark. "The Humiliation of Emma Woodhouse." LitR, 2 (1959), 547-63.

Employing a style whose metaphors derive from "commerce and property," JA immerses the reader in a "world of peculiarly material value." Her comedy arises from the juxtaposition of this world with that of ostensible or real moral propriety. E's structure reflects JA's double intention of verifying the values of her society and of judging them. Thus, "as the heroine comes into partial self-recognition . . . at the same time [she] sinks more completely into that society."

127 Schorer, Mark. "Jane Austen," the introduction to Pride and Prejudice. New York: Dell, 1959, pp. 5-24. Schorer's introduction appears also in the other JA novels published by Dell in the series called "The Laurel Jane Austen": S and S (1959), P and Lady Susan (1960), E (1961), MP (1961), and NA (1962).

The most profound moral conflicts, those at the center of the greatest human upheavals, are at the core of JA's novels. Her constant subjects are the

harsh economics pertaining to marriage and the vanity pertaining to social class. Her foremost value
and the root of evaluation in all her work is a
generous frankness transcending the motivations of
any one level of society.

128 Selwyn, E. G.   "Jane Austen's Clergymen." Church
       Quarterly Review, 160 (1959), 424-35. This
       essay appears also in Collected Reports of the
       Jane Austen Society, 1949-1965 (London: Dawson,
       1967), pp. 155-65, as the address given to the
       Society's annual general meeting, 1959.

       Like Shakespeare, JA knew that comedy could be
the vehicle of moral truths. The "seriousness"
which characterized Evangelical clergymen underlies
the portrayals of the clergy in her novels, even
those figures who are egregious or servile. MP differs from the other works, not in this element of
"seriousness," but in its "unique concentration upon
the lives and manners of certain clergymen."

129 Southam, B. C.   "Jane Austen: An Early Comment."
       N&Q, 6 (1959), 416.

       A letter dating from 1814 admires JA's work and
compares her to Maria Edgeworth.

                              1960

130 Bradbrook, Frank W.   "Dr. Johnson and Jane Austen."
       N&Q, 7 (1960), 108-12. See also corr. in N&Q,
       H. J. Haden, 7 (1960), 271.

       In all her work, and especially in MP, both
JA's style and subjects evidence her indebtedness to
Johnson.

131 Bramer, George R.   "The Setting in Emma." CE, 22
       (1960), 150-56.

       "Part of Emma's development is her breaking the
abnormal hold which her environment, the novel's
setting, has had on her." "Much of Emma's early
narrowness and foolishness . . . can be attributed
to her seclusion in Hartfield," but finally Emma
"enlarges her vision and simultaneously sheds some

of her small-town snobbery and meddling."

132 Cecil, Lord David. "Jane Austen," in Poets and
       Story-Tellers: A Book of Critical Essays.
       London: Constable, 1960 [1949], pp. 99-122.
       This essay appeared originally in 1935, pub-
       lished by the University Press, Cambridge,
       England.

       True to the general rules of literary art as
well as the particular ones governing the novel, JA
endows her work with universal significance. Inci-
sive, impartial, and profound, employing a "delicate
ruthless irony," she is preoccupied with "essential
human nature," and judges it "before the triple bar
of taste, sense and virtue."

133 Chanda, S. M. "Jane Austen as Novelist: Three
       Stages." CalR, 3rd Ser., 156 (Aug.-Sept.
       1960), 139-44.

       Three stages mark JA's literary career. She
first devotes herself to burlesque (in NA and S and
S) and then turns, in P and P, MP, and E, to the
"dramatic novel," which bears witness to her "craft
as a mature comedian." Finally, in P, descriptive
passages become more important than dialogue.

134 Chanda, S. M. "The New Vein in Mansfield Park."
       Indian Journal of English Studies, 1 (1960),
       96-99.

       MP focuses the reader's attention on the role
of humor and vivacity "as traits detracting from the
good life."

135 Church, Richard. "Introduction" to Northanger Ab-
       bey. London: Folio Society, 1960, pp. 5-8.

       JA's "vigorous, humorous and concise" temper-
ament led her to write NA as a response to the
follies of Gothic romances. And yet JA herself, in
the passionate intensity that is just beneath the
surface of all her work, also shared the age's romantic spirit: "Catherine Morland in love is handled
with abandon, almost with the extravagance that the
book sets out to satirize."

136 Cook, Albert. "Modes of Irony: Jane Austen and
        Stendhal," in <u>The</u> <u>Meaning</u> <u>of</u> <u>Fiction</u>. Detroit:
        Wayne State Univ. Press, 1960, pp. 38-47.

     "Jane Austen's novels posit a central irony be-
tween social status, a kind of appearance, and love,
a kind of reality, between egoism and altruism.
Each of her plots reconciles the contrast, and it
gets into her diction as an interplay between terms
of precision [measurement and intellect] and terms
of what we shall call 'resonance' [feeling]."

137 Daiches, David. "The Novel from Richardson to Jane
        Austen," in <u>A</u> <u>Critical</u> <u>History</u> <u>of</u> <u>English</u> <u>Lit-
        erature</u>. New York: Ronald Press, 1960. II,
        743-65.

     "A novelist of manners with a brilliant ironic
wit, an affectionate understanding of the ordinari-
ness of human life, a mastery of plot structure, a
lively and often subtle sense of character, and a
moral universe within which to set and pattern all
her novels," JA is delicately, precisely, shrewdly
aware "of the differing claims of personality and
society."

138 Elsbree, Langdon. "Jane Austen and the Dance of
        Fidelity and Complaisance." <u>NCF</u>, 15 (1960),
        113-36.

     In addition to complicating the plot, the dance
in JA's novels has the function of announcing a
young girl's nubility. It also reveals a character's sense and vitality. Finally, "dancing is the
ritual expression of group values"--particularly
"the group's unity or discord" and its allegiance to
the gentry or its aspiration to the aristocracy.

139 Gibbons, Stella. "Jane in Space." <u>Punch</u>, 26 Oct.
        1960, 600-01.

     (A science-fiction story told in JA's manner.)

140 Halliday, E. M. "Narrative Perspective in <u>Pride</u>
        <u>and</u> <u>Prejudice</u>." <u>NCF</u>, 15 (1960), 65-71.

     Although in the early chapters of <u>P</u> <u>and</u> <u>P</u>
Elizabeth is not established as the heroine, by

Chapter Ten the "narrative perspective has pene-
trated to Elizabeth's consciousness; the point of
view has become hers not only physically, but psy-
chically." JA organizes the action of P and P
around Elizabeth, and "we are prepared for an essential part of that action to take place in . . .
her mind," rather than in her external behavior.

141 Hubback, John. The Parents in Jane Austen's Novels.
     Kenley, Surrey: The Author [1960].

     (A description of the parents in the novels,
which notes that "the 'plentiful lack' of parents"
in JA's novels faithfully reflects life expectancy
at the start of the nineteenth century, and that the
parents do not produce "unduly diverse offspring.")

142 Kirschbaum, Leo. "The World of Pride and Preju-
     dice," in Twelve Original Essays on Great
     English Novels. Ed. Charles Shapiro. Detroit:
     Wayne State Univ. Press, 1960, pp. 69-85.

     P and P is JA's "attempt to see the real cur-
rents beneath a world she chose to regard as frozen
into immobility. She sees, and yet she does not
see."

143 Koljević, Svetozar. "Razum ili osećanje." Izraz, 4
     (1960), 357-62.

     In S and S, JA pictures a snobbish and selfish
world, where great stress is laid on social obligations and the search for a marriage partner. The
real contribution of the book is its simple and
precise description of a society ruled by money.

144 Laski, Marghanita. "Some Words from Pride and Prej-
     udice." N&Q, 7 (1960), 312.

     P and P provides "examples of words not in
O.E.D. or of earlier date than hitherto recorded."

145 Martin, W. R. "Emma: A Definition of Virtue." ESA,
     3 (1960), 21-30.

     JA dramatizes "the great commonplace that
virtue consists in a harmonious blending of truth

and sincerity with goodwill and humanity, and it is
Mr Knightley who, with his bride, stands four-square
on this basis."

146   Martin, W. R.   "Sensibility and Sense: A Reading of
      Persuasion." ESA, 3 (1960), 119-30.

      The problem of P is the problem of Lady Rus-
      sell, who is "Jane Austen's most penetrating study
      of the gulf that can exist between right conduct and
      virtue." Lady Russell values affluence above affec-
      tion, appearance over reality. "In terms of the
      novel, prudence is worldliness, and at war with
      courage, generosity, love and life itself."

147   Priestley, J. B.   "Afterword" to Pride and Preju-
      dice, in Four English Novels. New York: Har-
      court, Brace, 1960, pp. 254-57.

      Because JA wrote when the class system was
      breaking down, she wrote "comedies of snobbery, so-
      cial pretense and prejudice." She is a great nov-
      elist because of her detachment, "her power of se-
      lection and emphasis and her constant unforced so-
      cial and moral criticism."

148   Stevenson, Lionel.   "Recovery of Prestige (1800-
      1820)," in The English Novel: A Panorama.
      Boston: Houghton Mifflin, 1960, pp. 185-93.

      JA's "incorruptible realism" and "intuitive
      good taste" helped produce novels expressing "the
      very essence of the eighteenth century--its sense
      of permanent social and moral standards, its sus-
      picion of uncontrolled emotion or imagination, its
      precise observation of immediate fact." As a sati-
      rist she is gentle and tolerant, prizing good humor
      and reason.

149   Ward, A. C.   "Introduction" to Northanger Abbey.
      London: Longmans, Green, 1960, pp. vii-xxvii.

      If NA's subject is Catherine's foolishness, the
      novel's import is that life is what actually hap-
      pens, rather than what novels portray it to be.

150   Watson, Winifred.   Jane Austen in London. Alton,

Hampshire: Jane Austen Society, 1960.

(Describes the houses JA stayed in when visiting London.)

1961

151 Booth, Wayne C. "Control of Distance in Jane Austen's Emma," in The Rhetoric of Fiction. Chicago: Univ. of Chicago Press, 1961, pp. 243-66. This essay appears also, with the title "Point of View and the Control of Distance in Emma," in NCF, 16 (1961), 95-116, and, with the title "Control of Distance in Jane Austen's Emma," in Rhetorical Analyses of Literary Works, ed. Edward P. J. Corbett (New York: Oxford Univ. Press, 1969), pp. 115-38. See also 351.

JA's problem in E is to have the reader reprobate Emma's faults and yet wish for her reform. The solution lies partly in the author's "decision to use Emma's mind as a reflector of events," and thereby lead the reader to hope for her good fortune. But our judgments do not rely solely on Emma. Mr. Knightley provides one corrective, and often the narrator guides the reader directly. Thus, JA achieves a perfect balance of involvement and disinterestedness.

152 Bradbrook, Frank W. Jane Austen: Emma. (Studies in English Literature, 3.) Great Neck, N. Y.: Barron's Educational Series, 1961.

Rev. (with other works) by R. P. Draper in CritQ, 3 (1961), 275-77.

With great dramatic skill, with precision and economy, E presents an unconventional heroine who, through the outer world's impingement on her, loses her complacency and is educated into awareness of self and others. Masterly in general psychological realism and discrimination among characters, JA "combines a gift for selecting significant detail with an ability to show the changes and slow, complex development of relationships." She deals with varieties of selfishness and pride, as well as with the conflict between imagination and reason, and between deception and truth. The novel's central

conflict results from the struggle in Emma's mind
between "the graciousness of the eighteenth century
aristocratic code," associated with Frank Churchill,
and "the more rugged, native tradition of morals and
manners, represented by Mr. Knightley."

153   Bradbrook, Frank W.   "Sources of Jane Austen's Ideas
      about Nature in Mansfield Park." N&Q, 8
      (1961), 222-24.

      JA drew on, among others, Shakespeare, Gilpin,
Charlotte Smith, Ann Radcliffe, and Wordsworth.

154   Chapman, R. W.   Jane Austen: Facts and Problems.
      Oxford: Clarendon Press, 1961 [1948].

      (This survey seeks to assemble all the factual
evidence about JA. In addition to the biographical
information about JA and members of her family,
there are chapters on her character and opinions,
the mingling of fact and fiction in her novels, her
critical reputation, the commercial history of the
novels, and the chief sources for the bibliography,
biography, and modern criticism of JA. There is a
chronology of her and her family, and of editions
and translations of her writings, as well as "notes
on the novels"--on such subjects as heredity, plot,
love and marriage, nature, and style--and an appendix on portraits of JA.)

155   Church, Richard.   "Introduction" to Persuasion.
      London: Folio Society, 1961, pp. 5-8.

      P shows signs of JA's flagging vitality: her
usual detachment breaks down, the prose "sometimes
lags into a mild confusion," the artist's commitment to perfection is given up. Yet with all its
weaknesses, P still marks an enlargement of her
powers, a "breaking-away from her previous work,
to a larger and looser method capable of presenting
more desperate and searching themes."

156   Cook, Raymond A.   "As Jane Austen Saw the Clergy."
      Theology Today, 18 (1961), 41-50.

      JA's clergymen are accurate reflections of
eighteenth-century ministers. They are not merely
a backdrop to the novels, but constitute a general

satire of the Established Church. In no other "fiction can we find such inimitably perceptive characterizations of the opportunist, the snob, and the
esthete in whom the message of Jesus is entrusted."

157   Crowder, Tudja. "The Rational Treatment of Emotion:
           An Essay on Jane Austen's Style." Spectrum, 5
           (1961), 91-96.

      As evidenced in P and P, JA does not shrink
from portraying intense emotion. Yet her style
"has an external structure of great formality,
implying that even in moments of crisis, an individual's thoughts and feelings can be described in
a logical manner."

158   Derry, Warren. "Jane Austen." Corr. in TLS, 29
           Dec. 1961, p. 929. See also corr. in TLS,
           B. C. Southam, 19 Jan. 1962, p. 41; Robert
           Gathorne-Hardy, 26 Jan., p. 57.

      (Notes on the novels and letters.)

159   Edge, Charles E. "Mansfield Park and Ordination."
           NCF, 16 (1961), 269-74.

      The sentence in JA's letter to Cassandra which
mentions "a complete change of subject--ordination"
does not proclaim the intention of MP. Rather, it
"is simply Jane Austen's means of getting from one
section of her letter to another, her own characteristic transitional device."

160   Elwin, Malcolm. "Introduction" to Northanger Ab-
           bey. London: Macdonald, 1961, pp. vii-xxii.
           This edition includes the "Biographical Notice
           of the Author."

      There was no reason for JA "to fear that the
satire or the moral of Northanger Abbey might have
lost point during the long interval between the
novel's composition and its publication. . . .
[Her] shrewd recognition of her limitations is as
rare in a young writer as the ability to assess her
contemporaries with the tolerance of humour."

161   Elwin, Malcolm. "Introduction" to Persuasion.

London: Macdonald, 1961, pp. vii-xx. This
edition includes the cancelled chapter.

Unified and intricate, P is JA's most mature
achievement. It offers us a "rich assembly of
satirical portraits," the products of her own shrewd
observations. JA treats Anne tenderly, for her heroine's "romance is the romance that Jane Austen must
have wished for herself."

162   Faverty, Frederic E. "Introduction" to Emma. New
       York: Dodd, Mead, 1961, pp. v-ix.

Notable "for its tightly knit plot, its vivid
characterization, and its ironic delineation of the
social struggle," E is a study in self-delusion.
The heroine is so animated and charming that her
very defects seem to become her.

163   Fryxell, Donald R. "Lovers' Vows in Mansfield
       Park." MidwestR (Spring 1961), pp. 75-78.

"The fact that there are only two important
female roles in Lovers' Vows is the chief reason
. . . for Miss Austen's choice of the play." In
addition to dividing the Bertram sisters, the re-
hearsals bring Mary into close relationship with
Edmund, and Edmund is "attracted by the possibility
of playing a double role which he planned to assume
in life--that of a clergyman and that of Mary Crawford's husband."

164   Heath, William, ed. Discussions of Jane Austen.
       Boston: Heath, 1961.

(In addition to the essays listed below, this
collection reprints several early nineteenth-century
critical comments.)

William Heath, "Introduction," pp. vii-viii.
Regardless of changes in critical vocabulary, the
serious critic of JA "must somehow come to terms
with the 'talk' he finds in the novels--not the
subjects talked about, the congeniality of the
talkers, the history of mankind the talk helps him
to make, but the talk itself."

Reginald Farrar, "Jane Austen" (1917), pp. 19-
24. "The most aloof of writers," never out of date

because "coextensive with human nature," JA is "the
one completely conscious and almost unerring" English novelist. Intent not on stating but suggest-
ing passions, she is merciless, calm, steely, rigor-
ous. "While no novelist is more sympathetic to real
values and sincere emotion, none also is so keen on
detecting false currency, or so relentless in exposing it."

     Virginia Woolf, "Jane Austen" (1925), pp. 25-
31. Evading nothing, slurring over nothing, JA is
"mistress of much deeper emotion than appears upon
the surface." Possessing "an unerring heart, an un-
failing good taste, an almost stern morality . . .
she shows up those deviations from kindness, truth,
and sincerity" which are amusing, delightful, beau-
tiful. The Watsons reveals the preliminary drudgery
she went through before accomplishing her miracles,
and P shows her discovering a "larger, more mysterious, and more romantic" world.

     H. W. Garrod, "Jane Austen: A Depreciation"
(1928), pp. 32-40. Though competent and sometimes
just, JA is "intolerably sensible," parochial,
monotonous, trivial. Limited in materials, unable
to write a story, she finds no room for God or the
poor or nature. "Perhaps it is salutary that it
should sometimes be put to us coolly that the true
grandeur of the soul is its good sense. But I do
not want it put to me by a slip of a girl."

     D. W. Harding, "Regulated Hatred: An Aspect
of the Work of Jane Austen" (1940), pp. 41-50.
"She is a literary classic of the society which
attitudes like hers, held widely enough, would
undermine." JA wrote novels, not to entertain "a
posterity of urbane gentlemen," but to keep alive
her own critical attitudes. Ambivalent to society,
she found an outlet for her conflict in the
Cinderella and the foundling princess themes,
which she at first handled simply, but developed
complexly in her last three written novels.

     Walter Allen, "Jane Austen," pp. 51-57. (See
34.)

     C. S. Lewis, "A Note on Jane Austen," pp. 58-
64. (See 49.)

     Frank O'Connor, "Jane Austen: The Flight from
Fancy," pp. 65-74. (See 68.)

Reuben A. Brower, "Light and Bright and Sparkling: Irony and Fiction in Pride and Prejudice"
(1951), pp. 75-84. Parts of P and P "can be read
as sheer poetry of wit, as Pope without couplets.
The antitheses are almost as frequent and almost
as varied; the play of ambiguities is certainly as
complex; the orchestration of tones is as precise
and subtle." The novel's triumph "lies in combin-
ing such poetry of wit with the dramatic structure
of fiction." This union is achieved fully only in
the central section, and is disturbed toward the
book's conclusion.

Reginald Farrar, "On Mansfield Park" (1917),
pp. 85-86. Though often brilliant, MP "is vitiated
throughout by a radical dishonesty." JA may be torn
between the promptings of morality (deriving from
outside her own nature) and art (originating within), but the reader is not divided: he knows that
Fanny "is the most terrible incarnation we have of
the female prig-pharisee" and Mary "by far the most
persistently brilliant of Jane Austen's heroines."

Lionel Trilling, "Mansfield Park," pp. 87-98.
(See 59.)

Kingsley Amis, "What Became of Jane Austen?
Mansfield Park," pp. 99-101. (See 84.)

Reginald Farrar, "On Emma" (1917), pp. 102-04.
"This is the novel of character, and of character
alone, and of one dominating character in particular. . . . We are to see the gradual humiliation
of self-conceit, through a long self-wrought suc-
cession of disasters, serious in effect, but keyed
in Comedy throughout. . . . To conciliate affec-
tion for a character, not because of its charms,
but in defiance of its defects, is the loftiest aim
of the comic spirit."

Arnold Kettle, "Emma," pp. 105-13. (See 354.)

165 Hickman, Peggy. "The Jane Austen Family in Silhou-
     ette." Country Life, 14 Dec. 1961, pp. 1522-
     23.

(Reproduces several silhouettes of the Austen
family with notes on their composition and artists.)

166 Hughes, R. E. "The Education of Emma Woodhouse."
     NCF, 16 (1961), 69-74.

Challenges to Emma's "unreal and inexperienced
attitude toward society and love" come from two experiences: first, the Elton debacle teaches her
"that money is a factor in society," and, second,
her relationship with Frank Churchill shows her
"that the emotions are not to be ignored." Both
experiences require the human microcosm to assimilate alien experience, and thus "the invasion by the
outside of the inside becomes a dominant theme of
the novel."

167 Jack, Ian. "The Epistolary Element in Jane Austen,"
       in English Studies Today: Second Series. Ed.
       G. A. Bonnard. Bern: Francke Verlag, 1961, pp.
       173-86.

The satire on the epistolary novel in NA and
the revision of S and S mark JA's rejection of the
novel-in-letters as a form. Though she still included letters within her own narrative structure,
as one key to character, JA moved away from Richardson and Burney because, among other things, she
found herself more suited for writing letters from
secondary characters, whom she disapproved of and
treated satirically, than from her protagonists.

168 Levine, Jay Arnold. "Lady Susan: Jane Austen's
       Character of the Merry Widow." SEL, 1 (Autumn
       1961), 23-34.

Lady Susan is the culmination of JA's early
phase of burlesque; it is literary, not personal,
in origin. JA cleverly depicts "the Merry Widow,
a standard minor figure of eighteenth-century fiction, in the major role of an anti-heroine." Lady
Susan is not the intelligent and decorous character
critics have thought her, but rather a vain, overly
self-confident, and ignorant woman.

169 Litz, Walton. "The Chronology of Mansfield Park."
       N&Q, 8 (1961), 221-22.

MP is based on the 1796-1797 calendar and
not, as Chapman argues (see 304), on that of 1808-
1809. This suggests that MP originated in the
Steventon theatricals and the courtship of Henry
Austen and Eliza de Feuillide.

170 Litz, Walton. "The Loiterer: A Reflection of Jane
Austen's Early Environment." RES, 12 (1961),
251-61.

The Loiterer is best viewed "as a record of the
ideas and opinions which prevailed in Jane Austen's
early environment." Authored by James and Henry
Austen, it aimed to correct "moral deformities and
social affectations . . . 'through the exposure of
folly and error.'" In its Johnsonian and Richard-
sonian imitations, its attacks on excessive sensibility and marriages of interest, and its satire of
literary affectation, The Loiterer prefigures the
themes and styles of JA's novels.

171 Logan, Campbell. "Jane Austen and Television."
Folio (July-Sept. 1961), pp. 7-10.

P and P was presented on the BBC in 1952 and
P and E in 1960.

172 Marcus, Mordecai. "A Major Thematic Pattern in
Pride and Prejudice." NCF, 16 (1961), 274-79.

The struggles of Darcy and Elizabeth lead to a
reconciliation of personal and social claims. Collins and Charlotte, however, "demonstrate a complete
yielding to social claims," and Wickham and Lydia
"represent capitulation to personal claims." "Col-
lins-Charlotte and Wickham-Lydia contrast to Darcy
and Elizabeth through lack of integrity, whereas
Bingley and Jane contrast to them through lack of
percipience and strength."

173 Mercer, Caroline G. "Afterword" to Sense and Sensibility. New York: New American Library,
1961, pp. 307-14.

Though much of S and S descends from staples
of eighteenth-century popular fiction, JA here re-
shapes earlier novelistic conventions. Her book
does not try to do away with feeling, but to discover how to accommodate passion to life in the
real social world. Ultimately, the novel demands
that moral judgments be based on both emotion and
intellect. The minor characters are "finely discriminated in their folly."

174 Morse, Joann. "Afterword" to Pride and Prejudice.

New York: New American Library, 1961, pp. 327-32.

With an impersonal narrator, P and P gracefully and judiciously "presents a consistent standard of polite behavior against which the characters are measured, often to fall short." Only Elizabeth is supple and intelligent, her wit "far sharper than the narrator's and her comments more pointed."

175 Schirmer, Duke. "Introduction" to Sense and Sensibility. New York: Washington Square Press, 1961, pp. v-xiv.

JA exposes "sympathetically and satirically the frustration, wrongheadedness, honesty, simplicity and duplicity of human beings." With a playwright's conception of scene, she shows in S and S that, "as morality and sensitivity are conveniently sacrificed to self-interest, shallowness and sham set in."

176 Southam, B. C. "Jane Austen: A Broken Romance?" N&Q, 8 (1961), 464-65.

Sir Francis Doyle in his Reminiscences remarks that JA, while on a European tour, fell in love with a young naval officer, who died before meeting her again. This story, though improbable, vaguely accords with other versions of JA's romance.

177 Southam, B. C. "The Text of Sanditon." N&Q, 8 (1961), 23-24.

There are four significant differences between the manuscript and Chapman's text.

178 Ten Harmsel, Henrietta. "The Villain-Hero in Pamela and Pride and Prejudice." CE, 23 (1961), 104-08.

In both novels, the social and marital "struggle is epitomized in the ambiguous character of the villain-hero--a villain because his hateful assertion of aristocratic privileges makes him all that the heroine abhors; a hero because his good looks, wealth, and aristocracy make him all that she wants."

179   Ward, A. C. "Introduction" to <u>Emma</u>. London: Long-
       mans, Green, 1961, pp. vii-xxv.

       In <u>E</u>, which is both a comedy of errors and a
comedy of manners, JA is passionately concerned with
the portrayal of human personality. Perhaps because
of this concentration, she evinces little interest
in places.

180   Watt, Ian. "On <u>Sense and Sensibility</u>," the after-
       word to <u>Sense and Sensibility</u>. New York:
       Harper, 1961, pp. 229-42.

       The main importance of <u>S and S</u> lies in its de-
velopment of a narrative form fully articulating
the conflict between the age's contrary tendencies.
JA requires us to make complex discriminations between sense and sensibility, and to judge "how far
one can afford to be either intellectually or emotionally sincere, and under what conditions." She
uses verbal brutalities to shock "us into seeing
the disparity between proper norms of conduct and
the actualities of human behavior."

                          1962

181   Adams, Henry H. "Introduction" to <u>Mansfield Park</u>.
       New York: Washington Square Press, 1962, pp.
       v-xii.

       In <u>MP</u> "the love story, the jockeying for so-
cial position, the importance of the trivial, become as intricate as the graceful steps of the
minuet. The dance proceeds towards its conclusion
in inevitable fashion, as the dancers exchange
partners with the utmost of good manners." Based
on sure and penetrating characterizations, the book
might be titled "'Sincerity and Pretentiousness.'"

182   Babb, Howard S. <u>Jane Austen's Novels: The Fabric of
       Dialogue</u>. Columbus: Ohio State Univ. Press,
       1962.

       Rev. by Charles Beecher Hogan in <u>AN&Q</u>, 1
(1962), 63-64; in <u>TLS</u>, 26 Oct. 1962, p. 826; by
Charles Murrah in <u>ELN</u>, 1 (1963), 71-73; by M. Allott
in <u>MLR</u>, 58 (1963), 413-14; by John Hagan in <u>Modern
Philology</u>, 61 (1963), 134-37; (with another work) by

D. W. Harding in New Statesman, 5 Apr. 1963, pp.
494-95; by Wayne C. Booth in NCF, 17 (1963), 395-
99; by Stuart Tave in PQ, 42 (1963), 447-48; (with
other works) by Morse Peckham in SEL, 3 (1963), 602;
(with another work) by Frank W. Bradbrook in BA, 38
(1964), 68; by John K. Mathison in JEGP, 63 (1964),
369-73; by C. J. Rawson in N&Q, 11 (1964), 38-39; by
J. M. S. Tompkins in RES, 15 (1964), 97-99; by Irène
Simon in ES, 51 (1970), 367-71.

Introductory: "Jane Austen's dialogue actually
reveals her characters . . . engaged in the most
fundamental activities of personality." Though her
novels lack physical action, "a sentence is a deed,"
and public "concepts are the real actors." Her
style is marked by her reliance on a conceptual vocabulary, generalization to unify author and audience, avoidance of particulars, and rhetorical balance. By means of these patterns JA renders emotion public and impersonal.

Juvenilia and Fragments: The conversations of
"Catharine or the Bower" approach those of the mature novels in their differentiation of the apparent and the real and in their word play. JA's un-
certainty in The Watsons is manifested by "her
failure to mediate surely between Elizabeth and
Emma" and "her irresolution about Lord Osborne."
The dialogues of Sanditon, though amusing, are un-
interesting technically because they are exaggerated and parodic in intention.

S and S: "The novel contends that the individual can morally engage himself in the social orga-
nism . . . only when he achieves an appropriate
balance between sense and feeling." Marianne's
"emotionally dictated" style displays her deficiency
of both sense and sociability. Conversely, Elinor's
conversation indicates her separation from "the fal-
libilities of private feeling." Each of the "heroes" and minor characters, also, reveals "an individual blend of sense with sensibility and a particular relationship with society that results from
it."

NA: The utterances of both John and Isabella
Thorpe are self-gratifying; they minimize the communal aspects of generalizations and appropriate
them to the service of the individual. General
Tilney, who is "constantly feigning to minimize or
censure himself," seems an inversion of the Thorpes.
"It is through the dialogues between Catherine and

Henry, however, that Jane Austen dramatizes her
theme most richly, rendering in them the very process of education."

P and P: Far from an exclusively proud and unconvincing character, Darcy is three-dimensional and
consistent. He develops "in manner, not in essentials." By limiting our point of view largely to
that of Elizabeth, JA invites us to mistake him.
But, as Elizabeth's dialogue reveals, "warm feeling
rather than cool sense informs many of her deci-
sions." P and P's theme--"judging from behavior and
behaving with judgment"--is illustrated in the multiple connotations of "performance," a focal word in
the novel.

MP: In this attack on the "inability to transcend the purely self-regarding element in feeling,"
only Fanny is not motivated by self-gratification.
Edmund's logic is "unconsciously distorted by his
love for Mary," and Mary's typical style "formulates
her own experience as general truth." In this couple's discussion of the clergy and in their walk at
Sotherton, JA employs the emblematic method of
handling moral principles.

E: Emma's "complete reliance on her own convic-
tions and her ready publication of them mark her
need to dominate." Like her father, Emma "unhesi-
tatingly converts private feelings into principles."
Mr. Knightley's "emotional responsiveness," his fu-
sion of sense and feeling, prevent him from being a
prig. And Emma's progress toward deserving him is
exemplified most clearly in the metaphoric indirection of the proposal scene.

P: "The central issue of Persuasion . . . is
the appropriate quality of feeling in the individual." Contrary to the Elliots' hardheartedness
and the Musgroves' sentimentalism, "the Crofts
personify uninhibited sympathy and basic good
sense." As shown in the metaphoric indirection of
P's climactic scene, Wentworth has moved from pre-
occupation with himself to an ability to transcend
the purely personal. Anne's "greatness of spirit"
is manifest in her intuition, "the union of innate
sense with emotional sensitivity."

183 Beer, E. S. de. "Lovers' Vows: 'The Dangerous In-
      significance of the Butler.'" N&Q, 9 (1962),
      421-22.

Mrs. Inchbald revised the role of Kotzebue's
Butler, making it "sufficiently important to ensure
its being allotted to a competent actor."

184   Bradbury, Malcolm.   "Jane Austen's Emma."   CritQ, 4
        (1962), 335-46.   See also 704.

E is a novel of a particularly "dense moral
atmosphere." Far from insignificant, Emma's faults
are total violations of a worthwhile social and
moral universe. In leading her heroine to rectify
these faults, JA convinces us of the value of involvement and responsibility and the "importance of
true regard of self and others." She persuades us
"to consider every human action as a crucial, committing act of self-definition."

185   Church, Richard.   "Introduction" to Emma.   London:
        Folio Society, 1962, pp. 7-10.

"It is difficult to believe that there can be
any controversy about Emma. . . . It is so consummate purely as a story that again the hard-worn comparison with Mozart's symphonies must be made."
Technically flawless, the book "is a benevolent
comedy."

186   Craig, G. Armour.   "Jane Austen's Emma: The Truths
        and Disguises of Human Disclosure," in In
        Defense of Reading: A Reader's Approach to
        Literary Criticism. Ed. Reuben A. Brower and
        Richard Poirier. New York: Dutton, 1962, pp.
        235-55.

"Society in Emma is not a ladder. It is a web
of imputations that link feelings and conduct. Rank
in this society is what one character stands on when
he defines the motives for the actions of another or
of himself. Rank, in its fullest sense, is dramatic
position."

187   Ebiike, Shunji.   Jane Austen.   Tokyo: Kenkyusha,
        1962.

(Not seen.)

188   Ebiike, Shunji.   "Persuasion: Symptoms of

Romanticism." <u>SELit</u>, 38 (1962), 145-63.

"The outstanding aspect of the author's art is of course irony, and the modification of irony by pathos" in <u>P</u> "implies a Romantic vein." Yet the novel's various weaknesses suggest that JA's new turn toward Romanticism needed "more time than it actually took to express itself completely and harmoniously."

189 Fadiman, Clifton. "An Afterword" to <u>Pride and Prejudice</u>. New York: Macmillan, 1962, pp. 373-74.

"You can read <u>Pride and Prejudice</u> in two ways. You can read it for the story, as rapidly as you care to. . . . The other way is to read it very slowly, to savor the wit, the sly irony and satire and comedy."

190 Fox, Robert C. "Elizabeth Bennet: Prejudice or Vanity?" <u>NCF</u>, 17 (1962), 185-87. See also 270.

Given the circumstances surrounding the titling of <u>P and P</u>, "we should be wary of reading into the title a precise statement of the theme." Elizabeth's fault is not prejudice, but rather vanity--the concern about what others, particularly Darcy, think of her.

191 Kronenberger, Louis. "Introduction" to <u>Sense and Sensibility</u>. New York: Collier, 1962, pp. 7-12.

Though <u>S and S</u> reveals her typical merits--the gifts for scene, character, form, and dialogue--in no other novel does "love burst the dam of Jane Austen's ordered world, a fierce, racing, imperilling torrent of spring. . . . Marianne, who first aroused Jane Austen's comic sense, ultimately thwarted it. Yet what made the book imperfect made it vivid and even haunting as well."

192 Kumar, Anita S. "Jane Austen--The Feminist Sensibility." <u>Indian Journal of English Studies</u>, 3 (1962), 135-39.

Although JA had no affiliations with reformist groups, her novels do manifest a "latent feminism." "There is hardly any novel that does not establish the derivative value of men." Further, JA consistently stresses women's disabilities--"their subordination to men, their lack of education, their economic dependence and the resultant frustration."

193   Kunkel, Francis L.   "Jane Austen." *Critic*, 21 (Dec. 1962-Jan. 1963), 38-41.

Autobiographically, "Fanny is ultimately the antithesis of Jane Austen; Emma is the novelist with her sense of irony extracted." Fanny employs humility, like Pamela, for her own profit, and in Edmund she marries a surrogate William, thus avoiding sexuality. Emma, too, intends marriage without sex, for Mr. Knightley becomes "her father incarnate."

194   Lascelles, Mary.   "Introduction" to her ed. of Northanger Abbey [and] Persuasion. New York: Dutton, 1962, pp. viii-xiii.

Though different, NA and P are alike in being comedies and love stories. "Together they illustrate the range and variety which Jane Austen could achieve within the confines she set herself: in particular, her establishment of the heroine's consciousness as a focal point." Yet though she establishes this point of view, "she never identifies herself with" it.

195   Lascelles, Mary.   "Introduction" to her ed. of *Sense and Sensibility*. New York: Dutton, 1962, pp. ix-xii.

S and S, which is built on "the opposition between hearts and no hearts," has its shortcomings, but they have been exaggerated by readers "impatient to reach the later novels." The book shows, among other things, that JA "has to write herself into equanimity, and she chooses the comic spirit for her ally."

196   Lloyd, J. D. K.   "Jane Austen." Corr. in *TLS*, 2 Feb. 1962, p. 73.

(Suggested emendation for MP.)

197   Lodge, David. "A Question of Judgement: The Theat-
        ricals at Mansfield Park." NCF, 17 (1962),
        275-82. Parts of Lodge's essay appear also in
        "The Vocabulary of Mansfield Park," in his
        Language of Fiction: Essays in Criticism and
        Verbal Analysis of the English Novel (New York:
        Columbia Univ. Press, 1966), pp. 94-113; see
        315.

        "In order to remain faithful to a code of con-
      duct in which social and moral values are so deli-
      cately balanced, in order to preserve one's integ-
      rity," the faculty of judgment is most necessary.
      "The question of whether or not to participate in
      the theatricals is one that pre-eminently requires
      the exercise of judgement." Fanny judges correctly,
      and "Edmund compromises, while the others either
      have no judgement . . . or deliberately misapply
      it."

198   Marshall, Percy. "Jane Austen (1775-1817)," in
        Masters of the English Novel. London: Dobson,
        1962, pp. 94-109.

        A survey of JA's life, works, reading, and
      reputation indicates that she overcame the limita-
      tions typical of nineteenth-century women to assist
      in raising the novel to the status of art. "She is
      . . . a novelist inspired by moral feelings--as were
      Fielding and Smollett; but she lets the moral point
      emerge by itself, relying on the reader to co-oper-
      ate with her."

199   McIlroy, Ellen. "Jane Austen's Families." Thoth,
        3 (1962), 24-31.

        The lives of JA's characters "are centered
      exclusively in their families," and thus "the theme
      of family relationships" is as significant as the
      marriage theme. The "nearly identical" pattern in
      each of the six novels consists of a dead or in-
      significant mother, a father temperamentally op-
      posed to the heroine, and two contrasting sisters.

200   Murrah, Charles C. "Jane Austen in America: Some
        Observations." Polemic, 7 (1962), 12-18.

        JA has never enjoyed as high a reputation in
      America as in England. Americans past and present

have echoed Charlotte Brontë's charge that she lacks
passion. Recently, some critics, notably Mudrick
(see 5), have deprecated her failure to embody the
ideals of modern liberalism. Nevertheless, JA is an
adult artist, who manifests "maturity, wisdom, and
psychological insight, as well as wit and elegance
and formal perfection."

201 Poirier, Richard. "Mark Twain, Jane Austen, and the
       Imagination of Society," in In Defense of Read-
       ing: A Reader's Approach to Literary Criticism.
       Ed. Reuben A. Brower and Richard Poirier. New
       York: Dutton, 1962, pp. 282-309. Poirier's es-
       say, enlarged and revised, appears also, with
       the title "Transatlantic Configurations: Mark
       Twain and Jane Austen," in his A World Else-
       where: The Place of Style in American Litera-
       ture (New York: Oxford Univ. Press, 1966), pp.
       144-207.

       Mark Twain and other American writers antago-
nistic to JA do not recognize that, as in E, "she is
fully aware of the dangers in society which for them
are the dangers of it," and that she fuses natural-
ness and social form. Unlike them, she uses a pub-
licly accredited vocabulary which allows her characters to reveal inner self to others, and she depends, for her basic subject, upon "the act of
choice within society."

202 Rosenfeld, Sybil. "Jane Austen and Private Theat-
       ricals." E&S, 15 (1962), 40-51.

       JA bases her description of the Mansfield Park
theatricals on the actual craze for amateur productions, which began in the 1770's and petered out
after 1810. Though many contemporaries shared her
unfavorable view of this form of entertainment, the
condemnation was far from universal. "In this in-
stance she was going farther than merely subscribing
to the conventions of her time, she was expressing
an inheritance of puritanical prejudice."

203 Simon, Irène. "Jane Austen and The Art of the Nov-
       el." ES, 43 (1962), 225-39.

       "Jane Austen and Henry James are very much
alike. . . . She uses the indirect approach no less
than he does, and . . . her purpose like his is to

make us see." The difference between the two is
that in making us see JA employs multiple points of
view, James only one. Whereas James attempts to
"disappear behind the scenes," JA's self-effacement
is that "of the polite hostess in a civilized society."

204 Sisson, Rosemary Anne. The Young Jane Austen. New
        York: Roy, 1962.

     (Imaginatively rendered biography.)

205 Southam, B. C. "Interpolations to Jane Austen's
        Volume the Third." N&Q, 9 (1962), 185-87.

     The conclusions to "Evelyn" and "Catharine or
the Bower" were not transcribed into the notebook by
JA, and probably were not composed by her.

206 Southam, B. C. "Jane Austen." TLS, 30 Nov. 1962,
        p. 944. See also corr. in TLS, B. C. Southam,
        14 Dec. 1962, p. 980; S. Graham Brade-Birks, 21
        Dec., p. 993; Charles Beecher Hogan, 11 Jan.
        1963, p. 25; B. C. Southam, 25 Jan., p. 59;
        Alberta H. Burke, 8 Feb., p. 93.

     (On the obituary in The Courier, 22 July 1817,
possibly by Cassandra, and evidence for the attribu-
tion of "Venta" to JA.)

207 Southam, B. C. "The Manuscript of Jane Austen's
        Volume the First." Library, 5th Ser., 17
        (1962), 231-37.

     The evidence of literary style, calligraphy,
and spelling suggests that JA was writing the pieces
collected in "Volume the First" before 1790--the
earliest date calculated by R. W. Chapman. Possibly as early as 1787, at age twelve, JA had composed "a considerable number" of childhood tales.

208 Southam, B. C. "Mrs. Leavis and Miss Austen: The
        'Critical Theory' Reconsidered." NCF, 17
        (1962), 21-32.

     (See 258.)

209   Southam, B. C.   "Northanger Abbey."   TLS, 12 Oct.
          1962, p. 800. See also corr. in TLS, Mrs. A.
          H. Burke, 9 Nov. 1962, p. 857.

          On the basis of Cassandra's memorandum, we can
      determine that NA was probably written in 1798-1799.

210   Southam, B. C.   "A Note on Jane Austen's Volume the
          First." N&Q, 9 (1962), 422.

          "A number of misprints, or misreadings," occur
      in Chapman's text.

211   Stevenson, Elizabeth.   "Introduction" to Pride and
          Prejudice. New York: Collier, 1962, pp. 5-9.

          Deep in feeling and sharp in humor, P and P has
      a beautifully articulated plot. Here, as in JA's
      other novels, "small gestures of the spirit count."

212   Urwin, G. G.   "Jane Austen, 1775-1817," the intro-
          duction to "The Fearsome Past of General
          Tilney," an extract from Northanger Abbey, in
          Humorists of the Eighteenth Century. Ed. G. G.
          Urwin. London: Murray, 1962, pp. 275-77.

          "This novel is more than an attempt to poke fun
      at silly tales; it also reveals the gay life of
      Bath, it exhibits forms of vulgarity and gross snob-
      bishness; it describes the slow progress of refined
      affections."

213   Wilson, Angus.   "Evil in the English Novel." Lis-
          tener, 27 Dec. 1962, pp. 1079-80. See also
          corr. in Listener, William L. Fryer and Lila
          M. Gough, 10 Jan. 1963, p. 74; H. H. Hanney,
          17 Jan., p. 127; Angus Wilson and William L.
          Fryer, 24 Jan., p. 169. Wilson's comments on
          JA appear also in KR, 29 (1967), 169-72.

          In JA what Richardson represented as a "really
      titanic struggle" has been reduced to "little more
      than a kind of defence of a social citadel." "The
      transcendental element disappears, the religious
      quality disappears, and it becomes almost entirely
      social: what was evil and good becomes almost en-
      tirely right and wrong." Nevertheless, JA "can

only be understood as an intensely devout religious
writer."

1963

214   Barber, Marjorie M.   "Introduction" to her ed. of
      Persuasion. New York: St. Martin's Press,
      1963, pp. v-xiv.

      In subject and method, P resembles JA's other
novels, but differs in its intensity of emotion.

215   Booth, Bradford A., comp. Pride and Prejudice: Text,
      Backgrounds, Criticism. New York: Harcourt,
      Brace & World, 1963.

      (In addition to the essays listed below, this
edition of P and P includes background material from
the late eighteenth and early nineteenth centuries
and critical pieces from the early twentieth century.)

      Reuben Brower, "Light and Bright and Sparkling:
Irony and Fiction in Pride and Prejudice," pp. 195-
204. (See 164.)

      Andrew H. Wright, "Elizabeth Bennet, from Jane
Austen's Novels," pp. 204-12. (See 33.)

      Dorothy Van Ghent, "On Pride and Prejudice,"
pp. 213-20. (See 31.)

      E. M. Halliday, "Narrative Perspective in Pride
and Prejudice," pp. 221-25. (See 140.)

216   Cady, Joseph, and Ian Watt.   "Jane Austen's Crit-
      ics." CritQ, 5 (1963), 49-63. See also corr.
      in CritQ, B. C. Southam and Alan W. Bellringer,
      5 (1963), 174-75; Joseph Cady and Ian Watt, 5
      (1963), 272-73.

      JA criticism has always revealed as much about
the individual commentator and his own historical
period as about her novels. In the twentieth century, though, much has also been written which allows us to go beyond the critic to a clearer vision
of her art. It is now time "to submit Jane Austen's
social and moral assumptions to an analysis as ex-
acting as . . . [has been] bestowed on the purely
literary side of her achievement."

217 Chillman, Dawes. "Miss Morland's Mind." <u>SDR</u>, 1
     (Dec. 1963), 37-47.

          As is true of the early minor works, "in <u>North-
     anger Abbey</u>, Jane Austen upholds sentiment as the
     true source of ethical action. She attacks the
     Gothic novel, not for its sentimentality, but for
     its failure to present a faithful picture of life."
     "<u>Northanger Abbey</u> reveals its author as a disciple
     of Hume. . . . Her view of life . . . represents
     social order as a product of man's essentially be-
     nevolent nature."

218 Church, Richard. "Introduction" to <u>Shorter Works</u>.
     London: Folio Society, 1963, pp. vii-x. This
     edition includes <u>Lady Susan</u>, <u>The Watsons</u>, and
     <u>Sanditon</u>, as well as much of the juvenilia.

          The shorter works show that even early in her
     career JA knew how to tell a story and could be
     mirthful and savage in her rebellion against current
     literary fashions. Parts of these writings are
     "terrifying" and "unladylike."

219 Drew, Elizabeth. "Jane Austen, 1775-1817: <u>Emma</u>," in
     <u>The Novel: A Modern Guide to Fifteen English
     Masterpieces</u>. New York: Dell, 1963, pp. 95-
     110.

          Penetrating and subtle, <u>E</u> treats, among other
     things, the theme of perception, a theme which every
     personality and action in the novel supports. JA
     illustrates ironic contrasts among Emma as perceived
     by herself, Emma as perceived by others, and what
     she is in actuality. Eventually, through trying
     personal experience, the heroine alters her vision
     of the world, the world itself staying the same.

220 Griffin, Cynthia. "The Development of Realism in
     Jane Austen's Early Novels." <u>ELH</u>, 30 (1963),
     36-52.

          JA moves toward an increasingly complex concep-
     tion of reality in the juvenilia and the first three
     novels, and she develops her techniques accordingly.
     Often unclear and simplistic in the works written
     before <u>P and P</u>, in that novel she presents reality
     from multiple viewpoints, allowing for greater sub-
     tlety, flexibility, and artistic control.

221 Hancock, W. K.   "Jane Austen, Historian."   Histori-
        cal Studies, Australia and New Zealand, 10
        (1963), 422-30.

        Emma Woodhouse would appear to be "an histor-
ian just as much to be relied upon as Anne Elliot,"
who is the paradigm of the patient historian.
Emma's "picture of events corresponds quite as
closely as Anne's does with the evidence of her own
eyes and ears, and it is fully as coherent."   Yet,
unlike Anne, Emma is never puzzled.   "She is too
coherent too soon."

222 Hickman, Peggy.   "Jane Austen's Uncle and Aunt."
        Country Life, 18 Apr. 1963, pp. 842-43.

        (A short illustrated biography of James and
Jane Leigh Perrot.)

223 Lascelles, Mary.   "Introduction" to her ed. of Mans-
        field Park.   New York: Dutton, 1963, pp. viii-
        xii.

        Constantly iterated, finely varied, MP's sub-
ject is the family.   Fanny, who is not merely passive, but a positive force, seeks and finds the
liberty "of free acceptance, of belonging to the
family she alone has fully understood."

224 Lascelles, Mary.   "Introduction" to her ed. of Pride
        and Prejudice.   New York: Dutton, 1963, pp. ix-
        xii.

        "The purest essence of Austenian comedy," P and
P "carries to their utmost limits two principles of
her comic art: selection and symmetry."   Assured and
brilliant, with a "nice adjustment of means to ends"
and wit "never too bright for its context," JA here
showed other novelists "that it was possible to
travel light, to dispense with big pretensions, to
trust comedy."

225 Lascelles, Mary.   Jane Austen and Her Art.   London:
        Oxford Univ. Press, 1963 [1939].

        Rev. by Paul Goetsch in NS, 13 (1964), 596.

        Biography: JA's literary productivity is

divided into two periods. The first, associated with Steventon, includes Elinor and Marianne, First Impressions, and Susan, as well as the juvenilia. But with the move to Bath and later Southampton, JA became depressed--whether because of her ill success with publishers, a disappointment in love, or family deaths is not certain--and her art flagged. Reestablished at Chawton, JA wrote herself back into good humor and produced the mature novels of her final period.

Reading and Response: Far from the "unlearned and uninformed female" she ironically called herself, JA read widely, especially in the novel, and assumed in her readers a general familiarity with conventional "literary illusions." Beginning with burlesque, JA quickly became dissatisfied with its limitations. The dull, sad reality of satire is replaced in her mature novels by a vision of the actual world as prettier and pleasanter than the world of romance.

Style: JA's mature style is marked by its delicate precision. She defines her characters by their peculiarities, yet possesses the tact to refrain from caricature. Unlike Fanny Burney, JA is a master of the middle style, one suited for unemphatic variety of expression and also for plain relation of fact.

Narrative Art: In choice of subject, of mood, and of narrative patterns, JA's limitations are deliberate. It is her "observation of true proportion" that prevents these limitations from falsifying her vision. "No narrower term than incongruity unqualified" can define the comic in JA's novels. Her comedy "allows things alien to itself to be excluded, but refuses to represent otherwise than faithfully what it includes."

At her best JA fulfills the Jamesian mandate for interdependence of character and incident. Even her most comical characters who "might be expected to sit very loosely to the story cannot be studied without reference to it." Regulated by the "practice of forethought," JA's plots are deliberately and symmetrically shaped--so much so that she occasionally verges on a numbing precision.

"An important development in Jane Austen's art is that of the technique of self-effacement." Always tactful, JA rarely speaks directly to the reader; rather, she uses "the consciousness of her characters as a means of communication." In her manipulation of descriptive detail, her character introductions, and balancing of personal and chronological time, JA directs our attention economically and discreetly.

Though JA "habitually establishes the heroine's position as the point of view for the story," she does not employ her heroines merely as mouthpieces. Most important is that JA solves the problem of author-reader rapport by engaging the reader in her own "sympathy with life in its abundance." And she controls this engagement by making her characters specific and concrete--thus preventing the reader's sympathy from degenerating into self-pity or self-love.

226 Lerner, Laurence. "'This Old Maid.'" Listener, 21 Feb. 1963, pp. 340-41. See also corr. in Listener, Frank W. Bradbrook, 28 Feb. 1963, pp. 381 and 383; Laurence Lerner, 7 Mar., pp. 424 and 427; Frank W. Bradbrook, 14 Mar., p. 466; Margaret Southern, 28 Mar., p. 560; Laurence Lerner, 4 Apr., p. 601.

"There is the deepest, and most essential difference between Jane Austen and Lawrence. Lawrence admired a surrender to impulse: Jane Austen admired its restraint." Between these extremes there is no reconciliation, and readers "cannot have both."

227 Liddell, Robert. The Novels of Jane Austen. London: Longmans, 1963.

Rev. by Walter Allen in Listener, 28 Feb. 1963, p. 385; (with another work) by Ray Mathew in London-Mag, NS 3 (Apr. 1963), 81-82; (with another work) by D. W. Harding in New Statesman, 5 Apr. 1963, pp. 494-95; by David Rees in Spectator, 12 Apr. 1963, p. 472; in TLS, 22 Feb. 1963, p. 128; (with another work) by Frank W. Bradbrook in BA, 38 (1964), 68; by Charles Murrah in ELN, 2 (1964), 66-69.

NA: Burlesque has two functions in NA: it assists in the heroine's sentimental education and is used to hide the novel's structural weaknesses. Catherine is both life-like and the butt of JA's burlesque, but General Tilney is only a mechanical and insufficiently developed character.

S and S: Marianne's sensibility is primarily a
joke, and Willoughby is an attractive figure, though
unfortunately unlucky. The novel's primary theme is
reflected in Marianne's lust, which makes her unjust
and neglect her social duties.

P and P: Resembling S and S in pattern and
theme, P and P adopts an ambivalent attitude toward
the Burneyan conventions. Even in the final version there are traces of Elizabeth's original role
as an anti-Cecilia. The heroine's petulance results
from her sexual, social, and intellectual frustration at Longbourn and is removed only as her love
for Darcy blooms. Far from being underbred, as her
niece charged, JA belonged to the society she depicts.

MP: As a reinvestigation (rather than a revision, as Mrs. Leavis would have it--see 396) of the
prominent themes of Lady Susan, MP probably does not
derive from an epistolary prototype. Because JA
here sacrifices art to life, the novel's incidents,
though not impossible, are sometimes improbable.
JA's difficulty in portraying the Crawfords results
from her attempt to make them at once extremely good
and evil. The conclusion of MP is sloppy, betraying
a priggishness which may suggest the influence of
Evangelicalism.

E: Similar in characterization and plotting to
The Watsons, E values marital over brotherly love.
Like MP, the novel concludes with the heroine's marriage to her mentor. JA was not uncritical of her
society (or of Highbury), yet she avoids snobbishness. If E deals at all with the author's personal
predicament, it is in her concern for the problems
of the single woman.

P: No prototype need be predicated for P. Both
Mrs. Smith and her story are unsatisfactory. Mr.
Elliot and Lady Russell, also, are somewhat mechanical and incompletely realized. The genuine feeling
of P is couched in an irony that prevents sentimentality. And this dual tone allows JA to reconcile
sense and sensibility.

Sanditon: Whether we consider this fragment
biographically or as a work of art, Sanditon is
interesting chiefly for the manuscript's corrections.

Letters: Because JA and Cassandra enjoyed a

normal sisterly relationship, their letters are
prosaic. They were rarely separated, and then only
for a short time. The value of the letters consists in their recording JA's background and day-by-
day existence, that is, the world she treats in the
novels.

228 Nichols, Beverley. "On Discovering That Jane Austen
     Was One's Great-Great-Great-Aunt." Saturday
     Book, 23 (1963), 90-100.

     (Humorous sketch.)

229 Pickrel, Paul. "Marriage and Society in Pride and
     Prejudice," the introduction to Pride and Prej-
     udice. Boston: Houghton Mifflin, 1963, pp. vi-
     xvii.

          In P and P marriage "is the expression or in-
     stitutionalization of order," regulating "the rela-
     tions between the individual and society, between
     the sexes, and between the generations." Concerned
     with moral and social rather than strictly intel-
     lectual education, JA believes that experience can
     improve people and that the individual can achieve
     happiness in society. "As balance resolves the
     moral dilemmas of the book . . . so, too, balance
     is the mark of the book's structure as a work of
     art."

230 Priestley, J. B. "Mr. Collins," in The English
     Comic Characters. London: Bodley Head, 1963
     [New York: Dodd, Mead, 1925], pp. 138-55.

          Mr. Collins is JA's only piece of poetry--a
     creation of sublime absurdity whom she enjoyed and
     who always transcends our expectations. He is the
     happiest individual in P and P, a creature of ro-
     mance, "with his snobberies soaring sky-high, lost
     in wonder, innocently and ostentatiously marching
     under the banner of toadyism."

231 Renwick, W. L. "Views of Men, Manners, and So-
     ciety," in English Literature, 1789-1815.
     (The Oxford History of English Literature,
     9.) Oxford: Clarendon Press, 1963, pp. 89-
     100.

JA had the requisite talents for a novelist: "human interest, imagination, and the love of writing, and with them the regulative principles of solid morals, realistic common sense, and artistic discrimination." She deliberately restricted her range, so as "to maintain the authenticity guaranteed by her own observation and--inseparable from it--the aesthetic unity of her artifacts."

232 Southam, B. C. "Jane Austen and Clarissa." N&Q, 10 (1963), 191-92. See also corr. in N&Q, E. E. Duncan-Jones, 10 (1963), 350.

"There may be some significance in the similarities between Mr. Collins and the Rev. Elias Brand" of Clarissa.

233 Southam, B. C. "Jane Austen Documents." Corr. in TLS, 12 Dec. 1963, p. 1031.

(Documents requested for proposed biography.)

234 Southam, B. C., ed. Volume the Second. Oxford: Clarendon Press, 1963.

Rev. by John Gross in New Statesman, 14 Feb. 1964, pp. 256-57; by J. C. Maxwell in N&Q, 11 (1964), 199; in TLS, 5 Mar. 1964, p. 196; (with another work) by G. Müller-Schwefe in Archiv, 202 (1965), 297-99; by E. E. Duncan-Jones in MLR, 60 (1965), 259-60; (with another work) by Philip Waldron in SoRA, 2 (1966), 87-90.

(This edition of one of JA's three notebooks of juvenilia, the notebook never examined in detail by R. W. Chapman, "follows the manuscript as closely as possible in its final corrected and revised form." Volume the Second contains "Love and Friendship," "Lesley Castle," "The History of England," "A Collection of Letters," and "Scraps.")

235 Stern, G. B. "A Most Majestic Novelist." Time and Tide, 7-13 Mar. 1963, p. 23.

"Sir Thomas Bertram, an honourable man with a strong sense of integrity, emerges as the character in this book most worthy of respect."

236 Stern, G. B. "A New Look at Jane Austen's Emma."
     Time and Tide, 28 Feb.-6 Mar. 1963, p. 23.

     "Emma's development shows how she gradually had
     to learn the hard lesson of how not to be intolerant
     and to recognise her own snobbery as being in excess
     of what her period permitted."

237 Watt, Ian, ed. Jane Austen: A Collection of Criti-
     cal Essays. Englewood Cliffs, N. J.: Prentice-
     Hall, 1963.

     Ian Watt, "Introduction," pp. 1-14. (See 216.)

     Virginia Woolf, "Jane Austen," pp. 15-24. (See
164.)

     C. S. Lewis, "A Note on Jane Austen," pp. 25-
34. (See 49.)

     Edmund Wilson, "A Long Talk about Jane Austen"
(1944), pp. 35-40. Her works form a sequence, the
last three written being more psychologically subtle
and realistic in the portrayal of everyday life.
She is almost unique among women in her devotion,
like the great male novelists, to "the novel as a
work of art. . . . The experience behind the relationships imagined by her in her novels is always
an experience of relationships of blood, of which
that between sisters is certainly the most deeply
felt."

     Ian Watt, "On Sense and Sensibility," pp. 41-
51. (See 180.)

     Alan D. McKillop, "Critical Realism in North-
anger Abbey," pp. 52-61. (See 113.)

     Reuben A. Brower, "Light and Bright and
Sparkling: Irony and Fiction in Pride and Prejudice," pp. 62-75. (See 164.)

     Marvin Mudrick, "Irony as Discrimination:
Pride and Prejudice," pp. 76-97. (See 5.)

     Mark Schorer, "The Humiliation of Emma Wood-
house," pp. 98-111. (See 126.)

     Arnold Kettle, "Emma," pp. 112-23. (See 354.)

     Lionel Trilling, "Mansfield Park," pp. 124-40.
(See 59.)

Kingsley Amis, "What Became of Jane Austen? [Mansfield Park]," pp. 141-44. (See 84.)

Andrew H. Wright, "Persuasion," pp. 145-53. (See 33.)

Donald J. Greene, "Jane Austen and the Peerage," pp. 154-65. (See 20.)

D. W. Harding, "Regulated Hatred: An Aspect of the Work of Jane Austen," pp. 166-79. (See 164.)

238   Welsh, Alexander. "Introduction" to Emma. New York: Washington Square Press, 1963, pp. v-xiii.

With the characters who surround Emma reflecting different aspects of the heroine's own situation and personality, JA studies an extreme case of the triangular relationship of fathers, daughters, and lovers. JA maintains that Christian values can and should exist side by side with the distinctions of property and wealth.

239   White, Edward M. "Emma and the Parodic Point of View." NCF, 18 (1963), 55-63.

Emma's illusions "stem largely from the world of books," and her errors illustrate her readiness "to assign novelistic roles" to those around her. Not until Emma fears a match between Mr. Knightley and Harriet are her illusions dispelled by the realization that "life is not a heroic tale, full of romantic matches of unequals, told by an imaginist; but a vibrant struggle for clear perception, which must precede personal fulfillment, and necessitates deep personal commitment."

240   Wright, Andrew. "Introduction" to his ed. of The Castle of Otranto, by Horace Walpole, The Mysteries of Udolpho, by Ann Radcliffe (Abridged), Northanger Abbey, by Jane Austen. New York: Holt, Rinehart and Winston, 1963, pp. xvii-xxi.

Though probably the simplest of all JA's novels, NA "suggests that mere simplicity in the approach to human behavior may be less than enough." "The Gothic world must be rejected as inadequate and false, [but] the real world cannot be apprehended by

good sense alone." The book's happy conclusion is a
triumph, not of common sense, but of character.

1964

241   Church, Richard. "Re-Discovering the Immortal
      Jane." Country Life Annual (1964), pp. 172-73.

      JA's writing is immortal because of "the au-
thority of personal style, clarity of mind, resolute
confinement within and fulfillment of its own
theme." To define the bounds of her own art, she
rejected various literary fashions; and in P she
questioned all that she had already established as a
novelist.

242   Cope, Zachary. "Jane Austen's Last Illness."
      British Medical Journal, 18 July 1964, pp. 182-
      83.

      "Addison's disease of the suprarenal capsules"
probably caused JA's death. This would account for
her "weakness and languor," "severe gastro-intesti-
nal disturbances," and the "black and white appearance" of her skin as death approached.

243   Davie, John, Duncan Isles, and Alastair Stead.
      "Pride and Prejudice." N&Q, 11 (1964), 181-82.
      See also corr. in N&Q, F. W. Bradbrook, 11
      (1964), 272; C. J. Rawson, 12 (1965), 195;
      Kenneth L. Moler, 13 (1966), 182; E. G.
      Stanley, 13 (1966), 226; C. J. Rawson, 14
      (1967), 105; anon., 14 (1967), 310; J. S.
      Szirotny, 14 (1967), 424.

      Occurrences of the phrase in works other than
Cecilia.

244   Duncan-Jones, E. E. "The Misses Selby and Steele."
      Corr. in TLS, 10 Sept. 1964, p. 845.

      The Steele sisters in S and S "began as cari-
catures of the Selbys" in Sir Charles Grandison.

245   Gibbons, Stella. "Introduction" to Emma. New York:
      Heritage Press, 1964, pp. v-xiii.

"All brightness," E "is a story of youth--youth cocksure, silly, vulnerable, light-hearted, and, on the whole, well-meaning." The book displays JA's consummate artistry in realizing minor characters with a few sure words.

246   Harris, Harold J.   "A Note on Snobbishness in Emma."
      Ball State Teachers College Forum, 5 (1964),
      55-57.

      Emma "is simply incorrigibly attached to money and to the kind of life that she knows money alone can buy."

247   Herold, J. Christopher.   "Our Great Favourite, Miss
      Austen."   Horizon, 6 (Spring 1964), 41-48.

      "In her hatred . . . of sentimentality in any form, Jane Austen bordered on Philistinism at one extreme and on cynicism at the other."   As evidenced throughout her canon, "Jane Austen's passion was for truth, and truth to her was comedy. This, of course, is a serious limitation: truth is not always amusing."

248   Hough, Graham.   "Afterword" to Emma.   New York: New
      American Library, 1964, pp. 387-96.

      Like other of JA's novels, E concerns the growth of a central personality, who moves from error to clear-sightedness; but here "the theme is embodied in a more considerable character and worked out with an unfailing patience and fidelity." Pene-tratingly and honestly, the book blends laughter and seriousness, irony and sympathy, showing "that with understanding, goodwill, and a modicum of good for-tune we can expect to come to terms with life."

249   Karl, Frederick R.   "Jane Austen: The Necessity of
      Wit," in An Age of Fiction: The Nineteenth
      Century British Novel.   New York: Farrar,
      Straus and Giroux, 1964, pp. 27-62.

      Stressing what is balanced and genteel, civil and stable, JA makes courtship metaphysical in scope. She values awareness and the comic spirit, for both oppose excess and defend behavioral norms. A novelist of character, with the "theme of the free

individual who acts from choice," she helped make
the English "novel less strictly an entertainment or
a homily and more a way of looking at the world."

250   Lascelles, Mary. "Introduction" to her ed. of Emma.
           New York: Dutton, 1964, pp. ix-xii.

       The culmination of JA's art, E transcends the
conventions on which it is based "by the triumphant
quality of its execution." Rich in detail at the
same time that it is economical, E demonstrates,
among other things, that "an uncritical character
can be a fine instrument in the hands of a critical
author."

251   McCann, Charles J. "Setting and Character in Pride
           and Prejudice." NCF, 19 (1964), 65-75.

       In P and P, JA uses the country house emblem-
atically, to characterize, to create suspense, to
produce irony. There is a constant and subtle correspondence between persons and their setting.

252   Mudrick, Marvin. "Afterword" to Mansfield Park.
           New York: New American Library, 1964, pp. 371-
           81.

       "A belated and highly conscious profession of
faith by a clergyman's daughter," MP is a moralistic
rewriting of P and P. Here, JA establishes a norm
of evangelical complacency, from which love is cast
out and only killing principles admitted. There is
a disjunction between manners and morals, between
personality and character, and there is an attempt
to eliminate "the fundamental illusion which sustains the interest of fiction--the illusion of free
will."

253   Mudrick, Marvin. "Afterword" to Persuasion. New
           York: New American Library, 1964, pp. 241-54.

       In P, "an epilogue of acceptance, a recon-
ciliation," JA distinguishes between true and false
propriety at the same time that she shows that money
is the basis of apparent as of real propriety. Genuine propriety is "discretion still, for discretion
and judgment have nothing to do with mere caution,
conformity, moral sluggishness."

254 Phare, E. E. "Lydia Languish, Lydia Bennet, and Dr.
     Fordyce's Sermons." N&Q, 11 (1964), 182-83.
     See also corr. in N&Q, Frank W. Bradbrook, 11
     (1964), 421-23.

     Lydia Bennet may have been modeled on Lydia
     Languish of Sheridan's The Rivals. Fordyce's Ser-
     mons to Young Women probably "contributed a little
     to the making of Mr. Collins."

255 Porteous, Alexander. "The Beast in the Park: Some
     Features of Jane Austen's Work." CR, No. 7
     (1964), pp. 66-77.

     "What my claim comes down to is that in the end
     Jane Austen sees the world as a divine creation,
     ruled ultimately by divine ordinances; and that
     although in the nature of things the manifestations
     which she treats are almost always social expres-
     sions, their essential nature, and her treatment of
     them, extend far beyond a scheme of merely social
     or ethical right and wrong. Jane Austen's mind is
     in fact basically religious."

256 Rawson, C. J. "'Nice' and 'Sentimental': A Parallel
     between Northanger Abbey and Richardson's Cor-
     respondence." N&Q, 11 (1964), 180.

     Henry Tilney's sarcasm about "nice" may paral-
     lel Lady Bradshaigh's comments on "sentimental" in
     her letter to Richardson.

257 Southam, B. C. "Jane Austen's Juvenilia: The Ques-
     tion of Completeness." N&Q, 11 (1964), 180-81.

     JA wrote a number of early novels which were
     dedicated to her brother Henry, but these "have
     since disappeared."

258 Southam, B. C. Jane Austen's Literary Manuscripts:
     A Study of the Novelist's Development through
     the Surviving Papers. New York: Oxford Univ.
     Press, 1964.

     Rev. by J. I. M. Stewart in Listener, 24 Dec.
     1964, pp. 1017-18; by Brigid Brophy in New States-
     man, 4 Dec. 1964, pp. 879-80; (with another work)
     by G. Müller-Schwefe in Archiv, 202 (1965), 297-99;

by Frank W. Bradbrook in BA, 39 (1965), 458-59; by
John E. Jordan in ELN, 3 Supp. (1965), 20; by
Marilyn Butler in EIC, 15 (1965), 337-41; by
Masahiko Sano in SELit, 42 (1965), 82-85; in TLS, 21
Jan. 1965, p. 48 [and see corr., Frank W. Bradbrook,
28 Jan., p. 72, and B. C. Southam, 4 Feb., p. 87];
(with other works) by Kenneth L. Moler in CE, 27
(1966), 654-55; by John Hagan in Modern Philology,
64 (1966), 83-84; by J. M. S. Tompkins in RES, 17
(1966), 212-13; (with another work) by Philip
Waldron in SoRA, 2 (1966), 87-90.

Introductory: "My purpose in this study has
been to examine the surviving literary manuscripts
of Jane Austen in order to establish the course of
her writing outside the major works and to relate
this to her development in the six novels. The
manuscript works reveal every stage in the formation of the novelist's art."

Juvenilia: Dedications and other biographical
evidence indicate that JA's juvenilia, especially
the satire of popular novels, derive from her own
critical response to reading and from the collec-
tive experience of her highly literate family.
Originally composed between 1787 and 1793, the
youthful productions were transcribed (almost
verbatim) into the three volumes over a long period,
and some fragments were "completed" by family members twenty years or more after JA began them.

Critically considered, the early juvenilia
(1787-1790) are exuberant and farcical. They are
distinguished by their burlesque "manipulation of
style." The middle work (1790-1791), including
"Love and Freindship" and "The History of England,"
satirizes the sentimental novel and popularized
history by comparing them to everyday experience.
The last juvenilia (1792-1793) fail more conspic-
uously than the first because they attempt more;
here JA refines epistolary form, dialogue, ironic
point of view, observation of behavior, and treatment of emotion.

"Lady Susan and the Lost Originals--1795-1800":
Lady Susan's epistolary form and its relative simplicity suggest that it was composed about 1795.
Cassandra's memorandum accurately renders the chronology of the major novels. The epistolary Elinor
and Marianne was begun in 1796, drastically revised
in late 1797, and again at Chawton. First Impressions (perhaps also epistolary) was begun in Oct.

1796 and revised in 1809-1810, 1811, and 1812. NA
was commenced in 1798 and revised little.

The Watsons: JA's only original work between
1799 and 1811, The Watsons is untypical in its as-
perity and bleakness. It was begun, according to
Fanny Lefroy, in 1804 and left unfinished by JA when
her father died in early 1805. Revisions of the
fragment reveal relatively few, though significant,
stylistic and structural changes, even though the
heroine seems to require thorough redesign.

"Plan of a Novel": JA's primary purpose in the
"Plan" (1816) "was to make fun of Clarke and to use
his suggestions in a family entertainment." The
"Plan," like the juvenilia, expresses the author's
"amused contempt for popular fiction"; but, unlike
the early work, it is backed by the experience of
three novels and reaffirms the principle of "fidelity to common experience" that marks JA's mature
productions.

Persuasion: Significant as our most "direct
evidence for Jane Austen's method of composition,"
the cancelled chapters of P demonstrate a relative
failure of tone and of dramatic pattern. The revision (July-Aug. 1816), however, eliminates the "dis-
cordant element of broad comedy" that called into
question the self-control of Anne and Wentworth, and
substitutes a combined climax and resolution that
justifies their marriage.

Sanditon: Begun 17 Jan. 1817, Sanditon is
original in its treatment of place as representative
of "an uneasy spirit of change" and also in its conscious use of caricature, whereby "minor eccentrics
[are] now expanded to take the center of the stage."
The fragment's "air of mystery" is likewise deliberate. Extensive manuscript revision leaves the text
in a state sufficiently finished to be incorporated
in a "completed novel with little change."

Appendix (MP and E): Mrs. Leavis' contentions
(see 396) that MP was a version of Lady Susan,
which, in turn, described the courtship of Henry
Austen and Eliza de Feuillide, and that E derives
from The Watsons are both demonstrably mistaken.
Internal and external evidence shows that Lady
Susan was composed before the courtship. The
purported transformation of Lady Susan into MP is
based largely on guesswork and uncritical source
hunting. And The Watsons shares more elements with
P and P than with E.

259 Ten Harmsel, Henrietta. Jane Austen: A Study in
     Fictional Conventions. The Hague: Mouton,
     1964.

        Rev. by Ian Watt in NCF, 20 (1965), 295; in
     TLS, 22 Apr. 1965, p. 318; by Frank W. Bradbrook in
     BA, 40 (1966), 83-84; (with other works) by Kenneth
     L. Moler in CE, 27 (1966), 654-55; by John E. Jordan
     in ELN, 4 Supp. (1966), 19-20; (with other works) by
     Frederick T. Wood in ES, 47 (1966), 399; by Bert G.
     Hornback in MQR, 5 (1966), 295-96.

        Burlesque Beginnings: Although JA burlesqued
     the Richardsonian conventions of popular fiction,
     she nevertheless did employ them. By analyzing how
     she transforms and adapts the "somewhat degenerate
     fictional 'tradition' of the late eighteenth cen-
     tury," the reader is able to trace JA's artistic
     development and to perceive her novels within their
     historical setting.

        NA: In NA, JA ridicules the stock characters
     and situations of sentimental fiction by creating
     anti-types. For example, Catherine, the anti-
     heroine, is defined as much by what she lacks as
     what she possesses. JA does, however, continue to
     use the sentimental conventions she is satirizing.
     This she is able to do by revitalizing convention
     through "realism, developing character, variety of
     function, and irony."

        S and S: In JA's attempt to "burlesque and
     transform one convention--that of the heroine of
     sensibility--by subjecting it to another--that of a
     didactic opposition of sense to sensibility--the
     author becomes involved in complexities beyond her
     artistic control."

        P and P: Less intent on burlesque in P and P,
     JA interprets the conventions of didacticism, the
     Cinderella-heroine, and the Picturesque, as well as
     those of the "objecting father and the cruel and
     embarrassing chaperone." P and P's greatness de-
     rives from the masterly characterization of
     Elizabeth; but the "merging of villain and hero
     roles in Darcy [after the manner of Pamela's Mr. B.]
     is only partially successful." Weakened by melo-
     drama, the novel's conclusion occasionally lapses
     into mere conventionality.

        MP: Using the Richardsonian "conventions of
     popular fiction--the perfect heroine and hero; the

'black' villain and villainess; the conventional
gallery of minor characters; and the popular motifs
of the love intrigue and the happy ending"--JA
adapts tradition less successfully "than usual because the convention of didacticism influences her
too strongly throughout."

    E: Emma combines the "'perfect heroine' and the
'deluded Quixotic heroine.'" "Jane Austen's use of
delusions--both those of Emma and her associates--
to 'internalize' many of the conventional characters
and situations brings romantic phantasy and the
delusions of everyday life amazingly close together." In its transformation of convention, "Emma
surpasses all of Jane Austen's other novels."

    P: The restraint characteristic of P "creates
a tone of emotional intensity quite new to Jane
Austen. It transforms the conventional role of the
faultless heroine of sensibility so that she becomes
a movingly real and almost tragically noble woman."
Less successful, though, is the extraneous character, Mrs. Smith, and the "scandalous love intrigue"
of Mr. Elliot and Mrs. Clay.

260   Ward, A. C.   "Introduction" to Mansfield Park.
        London: Longmans, Green, 1964, pp. vii-xxv.

        Though a variation on the Cinderella story,
MP is not a fairy tale; rather, it concerns ordinary Englishmen and women in the contexts of decorum and ordination. The book is unusual for JA in
its awareness of nature, but typical of her mastery
of character creation. She gives us individuals
(especially the evil ones) who are puzzles that the
reader is required to solve.

                         1965

261   Austen-Leigh, William and Richard Arthur. Jane
        Austen: Her Life and Letters, A Family Record.
        New York: Russell & Russell, 1965 [New York:
        Dutton, 1913].

        (Biography.)

262   Brower, Reuben A. "Introduction" to Mansfield Park.
        Boston: Houghton Mifflin, 1965, pp. v-xxvii.

Rev. by Edward M. White in <u>CCC</u>, 16 (1965), 185-86.

"An ironic and tender comedy of 'Decorum and Delicacy,'" <u>MP</u> is complex, assured, economical, and eloquent. Only toward the end does JA's narrative art falter, does her moral evaluation seem inadequate to her fictional material.

263 Carroll, David R. "<u>Mansfield Park, Daniel Deronda,</u> and Ordination." <u>Modern Philology</u>, 62 (1965), 217-26.

Common to both <u>MP</u> and <u>Daniel Deronda</u> is the hero's conflict between his public and private roles, specifically between the roles of clergyman and lover. The resemblance in situation, in character (Edmund-Daniel, Mary-Gwendolen), and in ironic tone suggests that Eliot is particularly indebted to JA. But a comparison of the Sotherton episode with Sir Hugo's party reveals that JA could still rely on a fundamental set of values whereas Eliot could not.

264 Chapman, R. W., ed. <u>Pride and Prejudice</u>, Vol. II in <u>The Novels of Jane Austen: The Text Based on Collation of the Early Editions--With Notes, Indexes, and Illustrations from Contemporary Sources</u>. 3rd ed. [with changes and additions to text and notes by Mary Lascelles]. 6 vols. London: Oxford Univ. Press, 1965. This edition was first published in 1932.

(The standard edition.)

Appendixes:

"Chronology of <u>Pride and Prejudice</u>," pp. 400-08. A precise dating of the events in <u>P and P</u> indicates that, although JA followed the almanacs for 1811 and 1812, the action of the novel belongs to the period 1793-1795. [See also 367.]

"<u>Pride and Prejudice</u> and <u>Cecilia</u>," pp. 408-09. "<u>First Impressions</u> owed more to <u>Cecilia</u> than the alteration of its title."

"Modes of Address," pp. 410-13. (A synopsis of formal and informal address, according to JA's usage.)

265 Chapman, R. W., ed. Sense and Sensibility, Vol. I in
     The Novels of Jane Austen: The Text Based on
     Collation of the Early Editions--With Notes,
     Indexes, and Illustrations from Contemporary
     Sources. 3rd ed. [with changes and additions
     to text and notes by Mary Lascelles]. 6 vols.
     London: Oxford Univ. Press, 1965. This edi-
     tion was first published in 1933.

     (The standard edition.)

     Appendixes:

     "Miss Austen's English," pp. 388-421. (A vo-
     cabulary and grammar, according to JA's usage.)

     "Reading and Writing," pp. 422-24. In the
     society of JA's novels "the habit of reading is
     assumed as normal." There are significant "external
     differences between the letters of a hundred years
     ago and those of today."

     "The Early Editions," pp. 425-26. (A brief
     list.)

266 Craik, W. A. Jane Austen: The Six Novels. New
     York: Barnes and Noble, 1965.

     Rev. (with other works) by Gilbert Thomas in
     English, 16 (1966), 22-23; by John E. Jordan in ELN,
     4 Supp. (1966), 18; by Ian Watt in MLQ, 27 (1966),
     480-82; by Howard S. Babb in NCF, 21 (1966), 90-92;
     by Gilbert Ryle in RES, 17 (1966), 336-38; (with
     other works) by John Wiltshire in CQ, 2 (1967),
     184-93; by J. F. Burrows in CambridgeR, 89 (21 Jan.
     1967), 162-63.

     NA: Least satisfactory of JA's novels, NA is
     deficient in plot and character. The novel's two
     intentions--"of literary burlesque and of social
     and moral comment"--clash at the Abbey. Catherine's
     naiveté prevents her revealing "the theme and its
     progress by what she does and thinks," and because
     Henry's "opinion often stands for Jane Austen's," he
     appears an improbable lover. But when JA abandons
     the parody, Henry's judgment and Catherine's sympa-
     thy can combine into a meaningful whole.

     S and S: Serious in manner and theme, S and S
     partly repeats the faults of NA as well as

anticipates the successes of P and P. That Elinor,
as JA's spokesman, must judge others' conduct forces
her to speak "when she would be more effective silent." She appears unfeeling only because her moral
superiority consists in the suppression of feeling.
Less attractive is Marianne, whose near destruction
results from her manipulation of feeling.

P and P: In this novel JA herself appears as a
lively commentator to relay judgments and facts
which her heroine cannot make or know. Serious
without solemnity, P and P employs irony as a mode
of vision rather than as ornament. For the first
time in the canon, hero and heroine are equals in
intellectual powers and narrative significance. P
and P's central theme concerns the moral impact of
financial and family matters in personal affairs.

MP: The action of MP is out of Fanny's control
and "is not capable of much humor." Its subject is
not, as previously, the heroine's reformation--since
Fanny is unheroically passive and unreformably
faultless. From the first, Sir Thomas "embodies the
best principles and authority of his society," and
it is this system of values which the shallow and
cynical Crawfords consistently try to undermine.
MP's "most serious fault lies in the moral insecurity" of the condemnation of the theatricals.

E: Once she has made precise Emma's deficiencies of perception, the narrator either disappears
or merges with Emma's consciousness. The minor
characters, too, can convey facts and judgments
accurately because JA specifies their limitations.
Satire is nearly absent from E, and the heroine,
though often deluded, is always benevolent and thus
never ridiculous. JA's excellence of style "is the
result of clear thinking and firm purpose, not of
consideration of pictorial, rhetorical or musical
qualities."

P: JA agrees so thoroughly with Anne that it is
often both difficult and unnecessary to discriminate
the thoughts of the heroine from those of the narrator. The plot of P is simple and its tone consistent, and thus the novel appears more coherent than
MP. Here JA values frankness over correct conduct,
which is no longer a reliable gauge of character.
But the "really new feature" of P is its use of
locality to group the characters.

267 Demarest, David P., Jr. "Reductio ad Absurdum: Jane

Austen's Art of Satiric Qualification," in <u>Six
Satirists</u>. Ed. Beekman W. Cottrell <u>et al</u>.
(Carnegie Series in English, 9.) Pittsburgh:
Carnegie Institute of Technology, 1965, pp. 51-
68.

"In characters like Mrs. Jennings, Miss Bates,
Harriet Smith, Aunt Norris and Lady Bertram, Austen
manages a double effect—satiric second-looks at her
heroines and at her own positive themes, and a
tolerant insistence that all human beings deserve
acknowledgement. The result of this double effect
is the flexible common sense typical of the neo-
classicists."

268   Dodds, M. Hope. "Daughters of the Clergy." <u>Brontë</u>
       <u>Soc</u>. <u>Trans</u>., 14, No. 5 (1965), 20-24.

A comparison of the early writings of JA and
Charlotte Brontë reveals their almost antithetical
responses to "horrid" fiction. "Jane Austen, even
in her childhood, refused romance because it seemed
to her dull and conventional in comparison with the
ever-varying interest of normal life." "Charlotte
Brontë, on the other hand, knew so much unhappiness
in her early years that she gladly shut out daily
life and became absorbed in first fairy tales and
later romance."

269   Donohue, Joseph W., Jr. "Ordination and the Di-
       vided House at Mansfield Park." <u>ELH</u>, 32
       (1965), 169-78.

"The problem of a disordered society and the
possibility of its being restored to order is . . .
the kind of ordination" that is the subject of <u>MP</u>.
Though the social and moral chaos depicted in the
novel appears more extreme than the comic mode
ordinarily allows, <u>MP</u> concludes with the optimism
basic to comedy. Fanny, the champion of society's
"true principles," preserves her integrity by
remaining faithful to "the guileless heart's dic-
tates."

270   Dooley, D. J. "Pride, Prejudice, and Vanity in
       Elizabeth Bennet." <u>NCF</u>, 20 (1965), 185-88.

Contrary to Fox's assertion (see 190),
Elizabeth's fault is not vanity, but rather, as the
novel's title implies, prejudice.

271 Ebiike, Shunji. "Pride and Prejudice and 'First
     Impressions.'" SELit, English No. (1965), pp.
     31-45.

         P and P's title reflects JA's "response not
     only to Cecilia but also to various other novels of
     the age--in fact, the very tradition of the English
     novel." "First Impressions," both title and idea,
     may derive from Richardson, who uses the phrase in
     his three novels. If JA modeled Elizabeth on
     Charlotte Grandison (or Lady Pemberton of Cecilia),
     she would have significantly raised what had been
     a bystander to the role of heroine.

272 Edwards, Thomas R., Jr. "The Difficult Beauty of
     Mansfield Park." NCF, 20 (1965), 51-67.

         The theme of MP is meddling, which is the moral
     illness of the inhabitants of the Park and its visi-
     tors alike--particularly Henry Crawford, whose "will
     to dominate" repels Fanny. Although Fanny "recog-
     nizes both the difficulty and the impropriety of
     disturbing the existences of other people, however
     bad," she is not perfect. She and Edmund achieve
     peace only by simplification, by ignoring what they
     do not understand.

273 Gillie, Christopher. "The Heroine Victim, 1: Emma
     Woodhouse of Emma, Catherine Earnshaw of
     Wuthering Heights," in Character in English
     Literature. New York: Barnes & Noble, 1965,
     pp. 117-34.

         Until she is shocked into reality, Emma "is
     wrong not because she is superficial, stupid, or
     heartless, but because her social position gives
     her a false perspective both of personal values and
     of her own nature." In E, as in her other profound
     comedies, JA lets us glimpse the tragic alternative,
     and "this looms up before it is made to fade away."

274 Harding, D. W. "Introduction" to his ed. of Persua-
     sion. Baltimore: Penguin, 1965, pp. 7-26.
     This edition includes the cancelled chapter,
     the "Biographical Notice of the Author," and A
     Memoir of Jane Austen. See also 513.

         Rev. (with other works) by R. V. Adkinson in
     RLV, 34 (1968), 543-44.

Anne Elliot is the most mature of JA's Cinderellas. She is not, however, a sufferer of unmerited
wrongs, for she lapsed from her own standard in allowing herself to be dissuaded from marriage by Lady
Russell. The conflict of the novel is between el-
derly prudence and romantic love and JA's focus is
on the survival of the private individual amid the
repressions of a largely despicable society.

275 Hardwick, Elizabeth. "Afterword" to Northanger
        Abbey. New York: New American Library, 1965,
        pp. 213-21.

NA has as subjects avarice, egotism, and social
brutality. "There is wit and balance and proportion, but there is something else between the lines
that speaks of moral rebellion against the ways of
the world."

276 Hellstrom, Ward. "Francophobia in Emma." SEL, 5
        (1965), 607-17.

"The maturation of Emma Woodhouse involves the
choice of good over bad, or . . . a movement from an
early attraction to French 'depravity' to an ultimate total acceptence of English virtue."
"Churchill embodies the depravity of France" and
the desire for revolutionary change; Mr. Knightley
embodies the "goodness of England" and "the stability of the traditional agriculture."

277 Kearful, Frank J. "Satire and the Form of the Nov-
        el: The Problem of Aesthetic Unity in North-
        anger Abbey." ELH, 32 (1965), 511-27.

Because "Northanger Abbey is an illusion about
illusion and delusion, a book about life not being a
book about life," the tension between the satiric
and novelistic aspects of the book is meaningful.
"Its alternation of fictional strategies is an appropriate manner of presenting its action, for that
action is itself a paradox."

278 Kronenberger, Louis. "Introduction" to Emma. New
        York: Collier, 1965, pp. 5-10.

"There is as great mastery of treatment in Emma
as there is maturity of understanding." The novel's

one real artistic deficiency lies in JA's failure
"to fuse the comic and the realistic."

279 Lascelles, Mary. "Mansfield Park." Corr. in TLS,
     21 Oct. 1965, p. 946. See also corr. in TLS,
     Myra Curtis, 28 Oct. 1965, p. 966; Stella
     Pigrome, 4 Nov., p. 981; H. C. Stevens, 11
     Nov., p. 1003.

     (Suggested emendations.)

280 Latham, Jacqueline E. M. "Head versus Heart: The
     Role of Miss Bates in Emma." English, 15
     (1965), 140-43.

     Emma's rudeness to Miss Bates at Box Hill, "a
     revelation of the inadequacy of an intellect unin-
     formed by feeling," "is directed at the woman . . .
     who so conspicuously embodies the generous and un-
     selfish love that Emma lacks."

281 Litz, A. Walton. Jane Austen: A Study of Her Artis-
     tic Development. New York: Oxford Univ. Press,
     1965. See also 452.

     Rev. in Choice, 2 (1965), 227; (with other
     works) by George P. Elliott in HudR, 18 (1965), 433-
     41; (with another work) by P. N. Furbank in Lis-
     tener, 9 Dec. 1965, pp. 967-68; (with other works)
     by Frank Kermode in New York Review of Books, 28
     Oct. 1965, pp. 5-6; by Andrew Wright in NCF, 20
     (1965), 290-95; by W. R. Irwin in PQ, 45 (1965),
     529-30; by Aileen Ward in Reporter, 20 May 1965,
     pp. 45-46 and 48; by Harry T. Moore in SatR, 22
     May 1965, p. 76; in TLS, 23 Dec. 1965, p. 1198;
     (with other works) by Kenneth L. Moler in CE, 27
     (1966), 654-55; (with other works) by Gilbert Thomas
     in English, 16 (1966), 22-23; by John E. Jordan in
     ELN, 4 Supp. (1966), 18-19; (with other works) by
     Frederick T. Wood in ES, 47 (1966), 399; by Brigid
     Brophy in LondonMag, 5 (Mar. 1966), 83-88; by
     Francis Hart in SAQ, 65 (1966), 148-50; by John W.
     Loofbourow in Thought, 41 (1966), 285-86; (with
     another work) by S. F. W. Johnston in AUMLA, No. 27
     (1967), pp. 119-20; by Frank W. Bradbrook in BA, 41
     (1967), 88; (with other works) by John Wiltshire in
     CQ, 2 (1967), 184-93; by Howard S. Babb in Modern
     Philology, 65 (1967), 81-83; by Brian Southam in
     RES, 18 (1967), 107; by J. Delbaere-Garant in RLV,
     36 (1970), 103.

Juvenilia and Lady Susan: Most important to understand in a study of JA is that the early works are not blanket rejections of feeling and sentiment; rather, they are criticisms of the corruptions of these virtues (particularly the selfish foundation of excessive sensibility) in popular fiction of the time. In the juvenilia JA examines the limits of credible human behavior, roughly defining the social relationships that were to be minutely discriminated in her mature fiction. The importance of Lady Susan was overestimated by Mudrick (see 5). It is not the paradigm of JA's dispassionate irony, but rather "a dead end, an interesting but unsuccessful experiment in a dying form based on outmoded manners." The lack of a critical theory that could defend the novel against moralistic objections caused the decline of the genre in the late eighteenth century. JA's implied answer to these objections was that the influence of art "lies not in the matter it imitates but in the forms of expression."

NA and S and S: The sum of Catherine's education in NA is that the sympathetic imagination must be regulated by a knowledge of the real world. In the revision of S and S, JA incompletely liberates herself from the antithetical structure and stereotyped characters of "Elinor and Marianne." Contrary to Mudrick's assertion that in S and S the social mandate represses feeling, JA is here the victim of artistic not social convention.

The Watsons and P and P: The Watsons represents a turning point in JA's artistic development by minimizing authorial intrusion and embodying judgment in dialogue and action. The superiority of P and P over S and S lies in the transformation of the conventions of the Richardson-Burney tradition. Darcy and Elizabeth together represent the conflict between social restraint and the individual will, and in their reconciliation JA expresses her desire to "endow human behavior with the order and symmetry of art."

MP: MP is a full expression of the "shade" JA found lacking in P and P. The puzzle of MP is its bald didacticism, its uncompromising preference of reason over imagination. In the acting of Lovers' Vows JA devises an "artificial polarization" of the characters into defenders and opponents of the neoclassical security of Mansfield Park. In Fanny, the reverse Cinderella, JA elucidates the dangers of wish-fulfilling fiction and shows that "the values of art are not the ultimate ones."

E: Unlike MP, E equally values imagination and reason; fulfillment is realized through total self-knowledge. By accepting Mr. Knightley, Emma unites common sense with imaginative perception and the real with the ideal. In allowing the reader to share Emma's inner life without being limited by it, JA overcomes a problem of the earlier novels: she avoids the dichotomy between sympathetic imagination and critical judgment.

P and Sanditon: In P and Sanditon nature "has ceased to be a mere backdrop; landscape is a structure of feeling which can express, and also modify, the minds of those who view it." Anne's isolation signifies the loss of the sense of community and expresses JA's alarm at contemporary changes in English manners. Sanditon, like the juvenilia, is a private experiment, a defense against JA's final illness and depression.

"Appendix--Chronology of Composition": Contrary to Mrs. Leavis' theory (see 396) that JA continually revised her early fictions, the traditional opinion that divides JA's career into two distinct phases separated by her years at Bath and Southampton is correct.

282 Maniar, U. M. "The Immortal Mr. Collins." Literary Half-Yearly, 6 (July 1965), 46-48.

"Elizabeth and Darcy, Mrs. Bennet and Lady Catherine are lifelike, but Mr. Collins is living."

283 Millgate, Jane. "Introduction" to Sense and Sensibility. New York: Airmont, 1965, pp. 1-4.

Though S and S, as a title, seems to announce lucidly the book's major concern, "the clarity is more apparent than real . . . since the reader must establish for himself the relationship between the two qualities which the novel proposes to present."

284 Moler, Kenneth L. "Fanny Burney's Cecilia and Jane Austen's 'Jack and Alice.'" ELN, 3 (1965), 40-42.

To JA's family, the masquerade in "Jack and Alice" "would have been easily recognizable as a good-humored satire on a similar scene in Fanny Burney's Cecilia."

285 Morkam, R. C. "Austen Editions." Corr. in <u>TLS</u>, 18
     Nov. 1965, p. 1023.

     (Information requested.)

286 Muir, Edwin. "Jane Austen," in <u>Essays</u> <u>on</u> <u>Literature</u>
     <u>and</u> <u>Society</u>. Enl., rev. ed. Cambridge, Mass.:
     Harvard <u>Univ</u>. Press, 1965 [1st ed., London:
     Hogarth Press, 1949], pp. 195-205.

     Evil is present in JA's novels "as a necessary
     part of the picture, and there in proportion as
     everything is in her world." She shows evil to be
     highly attractive but, judging by the outcome, she
     finds the attraction a fraud. Her chief figures of
     evil are charming, irresponsible young men.

287 Nacciarone, Luigi. <u>Jane</u> <u>Austen</u>: <u>Saggio</u> <u>critico</u>.
     Naples: Editrice Intercontinentalia, 1965.

     (This book includes chapters on JA's life, the
     six novels and the minor works, and her art in gen-
     eral. The novels are discussed in terms of plot,
     the liveliness of JA's means of expression, and
     technique, and her art is examined in reference to
     style and content.)

288 Schemm, Mildred Walker. "That Cool and Fastidious
     Attitude," in <u>Wert</u> <u>und</u> <u>Wort</u>: <u>Festschrift</u> <u>für</u>
     <u>Else</u> M. <u>Fleissner</u>, <u>1965</u>. Ed. Marion Sonnen-
     feld, Robert Marshall, Helen Sears, and
     Barbara Kauber. Aurora, N. Y.: Wells College,
     1965, pp. 127-35.

     In <u>E</u>, ironically, JA "puts her own cool and
     fastidious style to the task of stripping preten-
     sion from the pose of detachment" in Emma ("an
     imaginist") and Jane Fairfax ("an illusionist")
     and forces them "deeper into life and closer to
     other human beings."

289 Servotte, Herman. "<u>Emma</u> en <u>Middlemarch</u>: Twee
     auteursromans," in <u>De</u> <u>verteller</u> <u>in</u> <u>de</u> <u>Engelse</u>
     <u>roman</u>: <u>Een</u> <u>studie</u> <u>over</u> <u>romantechniek</u>. Hasselt:
     Heideland, 1965, pp. 27-55.

     <u>E</u> is a "superb" example of the nineteenth-
     century "authorial novel." In this form the nar-
     rator revels "in his absolute powers, showing them

without disguise," and trusts "that the intelligi-
bility and order of his fictional world would arise
from its being a copy of the empirical world which
was in itself meaningful for all."

290   Steeves, Harrison R. "And Jane Austen," in Before
      Jane Austen: The Shaping of the English Novel
      in the Eighteenth Century. New York: Holt,
      Rinehart and Winston, 1965, pp. 332-86.

      In her novels she studies unsentimentally and
with increasing insight, firmness, and finish, "the
subordination of passion to ultimate well-being,"
the theme also of the women novelists who preceded
her. "Her early years were a conscious but not a
passive literary pupilage, not the less serviceable
because she was amused as well as instructed by her
preceptresses." Having paid off her debt to her
predecessors in S and S, she achieved independence
in P and P, and then progressed "to a quite different intellectual order."

291   Tanabe, Masami. The Literature of Jane Austen.
      Kyoto: Apollon-sha, 1965.

      (Not seen.)

292   Tomkins, A. R. "Introduction" to Pride and Preju-
      dice. London: Blackie, 1965, pp. v-x.

      With a narrow range but deep perception, JA
examines, in P and P, the conflict between illusion
and reality. She believes in human beings as free
moral agents and sees human conduct "as public duty
personally interpreted."

293   Wagenknecht, Edward. "Introduction" to Pride and
      Prejudice. New York: Harper & Row, 1965, pp.
      xi-xv.

      JA, who is a great writer because of her at-
titude to experience, is "the most classical of all
English novelists." She treats mating, her basic
theme, as "a serious, realistic business," and the
primary interest of P and P is the romance of hero
and heroine.

294   Walls, A. F. "Miss Austen's Theological Reading."

Anglican Theological Review, 47 (1965), 49-58.

The solidity of JA's Christianity is evidenced
by her knowledge of contemporary theologians. In P
and P Mr. Collins probably reads from Fordyce's Sermons to Young Women, and Henry Crawford's discussion
of homiletics parallels a passage from Blair's lecture on pulpit eloquence.

295 Webb, William. "The Rumford Grate." N&Q, 12
     (1965), 425.

A device for improving chimney conduction mentioned in NA.

296 Wiltshire, John. "Mansfield Park, and Fanny Price."
     CR, No. 8 (1965), pp. 121-28.

Fanny is not the weak prig critics have thought
her, but, on the contrary, is intelligent and coura-
geous, and her strengths exist precisely because she
lacks wit and vivacity. She is imperfect and wholly
convincing. JA's realism fails, however, in the
"moralistic apportionment of punishment" at MP's
conclusion. "Most offensive is the marrying off of
Fanny to Edmund," who does not deserve her.

297 Wright, Andrew. "Introduction" to his ed. of Per-
         suasion. Boston: Houghton Mifflin, 1965, pp.
         vii-xviii. This edition includes the cancelled
         chapter and textual notes.

"Though indubitably a lady, Jane Austen was a
human being of powerful intelligence whose penetra-
tion of the hypocrisies by which people live is
nearly matchless in the history of the English novel; and her willingness to be honest is attested on
every page of everything she ever wrote." In P she
lucidly presents the timeless struggle between love
and duty. The autumnal mood of the book is under-
lined by a feeling of great waste.

298 Zietlow, Paul N. "Luck and Fortuitous Circumstance
         in Persuasion: Two Interpretations." ELH, 32
         (1965), 179-95.

The "dark, menacing quality" of P results from
the numerous chance occurrences (such as Louisa's

accident and Wentworth's survival at sea), which,
though they conclude happily, are potentially tragic. These chance occurrences signify either the
controlling hand of Providence, which ultimately
metes out just rewards to all, or it suggests the
effect of a deus ex machina, by which JA implies
that the felicitous conclusion is only a product of
artistic fantasy.

1966

299 Baker, Sheridan. "The Comedy of Illusion in North-
       anger Abbey." PMASAL, 51 (1966), 547-58. An
       earlier version of this essay appeared, with
       the title "Reality and Romance in Northanger
       Abbey," in Mulberry (Aichi Women's College,
       Nagoya, Japan), English No. (1962).

       JA valued the Gothic parts of NA for their
power to burlesque man's propensity for self-delusion. That Catherine is "comically right about
romance" and about General Tilney is only one in-
stance of JA's deliberate "teasing and outmaneuver-
ing of our expectations" in NA. The final irony is
that NA is not a reality; it is "only a story, an
illusion, a romance." Nevertheless, from romance
we can "learn something valid about life."

300 Blythe, Ronald. "Introduction" to his ed. of Emma.
       Baltimore: Penguin, 1966, pp. 7-32. See also
       513.

       Concerned with the ordeal of marriage and the
moral doctrines governing society, E has "the brilliant surface and the endlessly satisfying depths"
typical of JA's novels. Though her skill results
from "an uncommonly sane mind, a gay heart and a
most dedicated and meticulous workmanship," it is
still true that "something remains indefinable and
must, presumably, always remain so, or others would
have learned her art and written like her."

301 Bradbrook, Frank W. Jane Austen and Her Predeces-
       sors. Cambridge, Engl.: Univ. Press, 1966.

       Rev. by James Walt in BA, 40 (1966), 459; (with
other works) by Derek Hudson in English, 16 (1966),
108-09; by Graham Hough in Listener, 7 July 1966,

pp. 27-28; (with another work) by Margaret Drabble
in Manchester Guardian Weekly, 28 Apr. 1966, p. 10;
by Denis Donoghue in New Statesman, 13 May 1966, pp.
698-99; (with other works) by Geoffrey Hartman in
SEL, 6 (1966), 774; in TLS, 28 Apr. 1966, p. 369
[and see corr., Frank W. Bradbrook and reviewer, 2
June, p. 497]; (with another work) by S. F. W.
Johnston in AUMLA, No. 27 (1967), pp. 119-20; (with
other works) by John Wiltshire in CQ, 2 (1967), 184-
93; by John E. Jordan in ELN, 5 Supp. (1967), 20;
by Stuart M. Tave in JEGP, 66 (1967), 271-74; by
Andrew Wright in NCF, 21 (1967), 387-88; by B. G.
MacCarthy in RES, 18 (1967), 469-71; by R. V.
Adkinson in RLV, 34 (1968), 648-49; by Joseph Cady
in SBHT, 9 (1968), 886-88.

The General Literary Tradition:

(Periodicals) These writings helped show JA how
to combine wit and moral seriousness. Though re-
senting the Spectator's condescension to women, she
shared some of Addison and Steele's aims and subjects. From Johnson she gained a philosophical
depth she otherwise would have lacked.

(Prose Moralists) Concerned with manners and
morals, she is indebted to the type of issues debated in conduct books, collections of sermons, and
other works of advice and instruction. Yet she
consistently modified the seriousness of the moralists by wit and humor.

(The Picturesque) Gilpin's essays show how
"the cult of the picturesque provided Jane Austen
with ideas which were related to the problems she
had to solve as a novelist." Interested in and
knowledgeable about the picturesque, she also
viewed it satirically.

(Drama and Poetry) Her "interest in poetry and
drama may partly explain the comparative sensitive-
ness of her prose, and her ability to select and
concentrate when dealing with intense situations and
moments." Her books are "naturally dramatic," and
Augustan poetry was more directly suited to her
novelistic needs than Shakespeare's poetic plays or
eighteenth-century comedy.

The Tradition in the Novel:

(The Beginnings) JA resembles earlier English
satirists, and shares with Richardson an interest in

detailed psychological analysis (but rejects his
prolixity and is less crude in the treatment of
morals). Her direct debt to Fielding is not great.

(The Feminist Tradition) JA both admired her
predecessors' best efforts and was amused "at the
common level of contemporary achievement." She
could partly accept the world view of earlier women
novelists and turned their inferior work to con-
structive use. She employed "the conventions of the
novel as written by Fanny Burney . . . as a framework for her own fiction."

(Other Influences) She is possibly indebted to
French writers, including Rousseau, and to friends
and neighbors, including the novelist Sir Egerton
Brydges.

Appendixes: (These provide lists from the
eighteenth century of "Books for Young Ladies," as
well as selections from Lady Sarah Pennington's An
Unfortunate Mother's Advice to Her Absent Daughters,
from Mrs. Jane West's Letters to a Young Lady, and
from William Gilpin's An Essay upon Prints.)

302 Brown, Ivor. Jane Austen and Her World. New York:
       Walck, 1966. See also 513.

     (This account of politics, the arts, and man-
ners of JA's contemporaries is illustrated with more
than sixty photographs.)

303 Chapman, R. W., ed. Emma, Vol. IV in The Novels of
       Jane Austen: The Text Based on Collation of the
       Early Editions--With Notes, Indexes, and Illus-
       trations from Contemporary Sources. 3rd ed.
       [with changes and additions to text and notes
       by Mary Lascelles]. 6 vols. London: Oxford
       Univ. Press, 1966. This edition was first
       published in 1933.

     (The standard edition.)

     Appendixes:

     "Chronology of Emma," pp. 497-98. "There seems
to be no clear indication of the date at which the
action is supposed to take place," and thus JA probably "conceived the time to be roughly 'the present.'"

"The Manners of the Age," pp. 499-516. (Observations on contemporary manners, with examples from the novels.)

"Punctuation," pp. 516-18. (Explains the rules of JA's apparently irregular usage.)

304 Chapman, R. W., ed. Mansfield Park, Vol. III in The Novels of Jane Austen: The Text Based on Collation of the Early Editions--With Notes, Indexes, and Illustrations from Contemporary Sources. 3rd ed. [with changes and additions to text and notes by Mary Lascelles]. 6 vols. London: Oxford Univ. Press, 1966. This edition was first published in 1934. It reprints Mrs. Inchbald's translation of Kotzebue's Lovers' Vows.

(The standard edition.)

Appendixes:

"Chronology of Mansfield Park," pp. 554-57. A precise dating of the events of MP indicates that JA probably used the almanacs of 1808 and 1809 in writing the novel. But these events are not conceived as belonging to an actual year. [See also 169.]

"Improvements," pp. 557-60. Excepting her agreement with Marianne's and Fanny's "depredations of the Landscape Gardeners," JA "seems to condone the assumption of her people, that the new is to be preferred."

"On Carriages and Travel," pp. 561-65. (A synopsis of the terminology of modes of conveyance mentioned in the novels.)

305 Cope, Zachary. "Who Was Sophia Sentiment? Was She Jane Austen?" BC, 15 (1966), 143-51.

A satiric letter from "Sophia Sentiment" in the ninth number of The Loiterer (28 Mar. 1789) may be by JA.

306 Donovan, Robert Alan. "Mansfield Park and Jane Austen's Moral Universe," in The Shaping Vision: Imagination in the English Novel from

<u>Defoe</u> to <u>Dickens</u>. Ithaca: Cornell Univ. Press, 1966, pp. 140-72.

<u>MP</u> does not differ very sharply from the other novels, sharing with them a "moral concern with character and incidents." The "dominant moral attribute" of all JA's heroines, including Fanny, is "constancy to whatever ideal of conduct they profess." The world of the novels is ruled by a moral determinism, and neither education nor environment can significantly alter an individual. "Translated into novelistic terms, action is ruled by character, not character by action."

307 Dornberg, Curtis L. "Three Prospects of the Comic Landscape." <u>Mankato</u> <u>State</u> <u>College</u> <u>Studies</u>, 1 (1966), 69-86.

The prospect seen at Donwell Abbey in <u>E</u> (III, 6) focuses our experience and gives us insight into the novel's comic structure. In JA's world there are clearly marked boundaries, and objective knowledge is possible.

308 Duffy, John Dennis. "Introduction" to <u>Emma</u>. New York: Airmont, 1966, pp. 3-6.

<u>E</u> is about the heroine's selfishness, her discovery of it, and subsequent reformation. Emma's education is not basically intellectual, but moral in nature.

309 Duffy, John Dennis. "Introduction" to <u>Persuasion</u>. New York: Airmont, 1966, pp. 3-7.

"Anne Elliot's recovery of her old love is something more than sentimental wish-fulfillment because she possesses particular qualities of character which make it all possible." Though everyone has his own types of persuasions, only the mature characters can overcome their preconceptions and judge objectively.

310 Gomme, Andor. "On Not Being Persuaded." <u>EIC</u>, 16 (1966), 170-84. See also corr. in <u>EIC</u>, Brian Southam and Andor Gomme, 16 (1966), 480-81. See also 381.

"_Persuasion_ is badly flawed." Mrs. Smith, Mr.
Elliot, and Mrs. Clay are less than credible, and
Sir Walter seems "just a target set up for Jane
Austen's scorn." More important, because Lady
Russell did not merit the trust Anne placed in her
advice, doubt is cast on Anne's judgment. Finally,
the narrative focus (centered in the static Anne)
does not coincide with the moral focus (centered in
Wentworth's development).

311   Gooneratne, Yasmine.   "'The Loveliest Medium': The
      New Element in Jane Austen's _Persuasion_." UCR,
      24 (Apr. and Oct. 1966), 1-28.

      That P remained incomplete at JA's death ex-
plains its occasional rough spots. Dick Musgrove
and his mother were left unfinished and probably
would have been revised had JA lived. Sir Walter,
Elizabeth, and Mrs. Clay, however, balance and
fulfill their comic and moral functions. The "dryly
amused" irony of P does not indicate JA's personal
animosity, as Mudrick contends (see 5); rather, it
combines the comic with JA's typical discrimination
of personal and social weaknesses.

312   Gray, Donald J., ed.   Pride and Prejudice: An
      Authoritative Text, Backgrounds, Reviews, and
      Essays in Criticism.   New York: Norton, 1966.

      (In addition to the essays listed below, this
edition of P and P includes selections from the
juvenilia and letters, the "Biographical Notice of
the Author," and several reviews and essays from the
nineteenth and early twentieth centuries.)

      Donald J. Gray, "Preface," pp. vii-xi. P and P
"stands at the entrance to its author's mature practice, preserving some of the lessons and traditions
from which she learned while demonstrating the uses
to which she put them to make for the first time a
fiction unmistakably her own."

      R. W. Chapman, "Chronology of Pride and Preju-
dice," pp. 287-93. (See 264.)

      Q. D. Leavis, "[Pride and Prejudice and Jane
Austen's Early Reading and Writing]," pp. 293-305.
(See 396.)

      Reginald Farrar, "[Truth, Reality, and Good

Sense in Jane Austen]" (1917), pp. 342-45. P and P's "very youthful note of joyousness is also the negation of that deeper quality which makes the later work so inexhaustible."

Mary Lascelles, "[The Narrative Art of _Pride and Prejudice]_," pp. 345-52. (See 225.)

Samuel Kliger, "Jane Austen's _Pride and Preju-dice_ in the Eighteenth-Century Mode" (1947), pp. 352-62. "The purpose of this essay . . . is first to establish the art-nature antithesis as the ground of [P and P's] action and its mode of organization and, second, to show that the doctrine of art and reason is extended to morals, to include, in partic-ular, a concept of class relationships"--specifi-cally, the conceptions of man-in-nature and man-in-society represented by Elizabeth and Darcy, respec-tively.

Dorothy Van Ghent, "On _Pride and Prejudice_," pp. 362-73. (See 31.)

Reuben A. Brower, "Light and Bright and Sparkl-ing: Irony and Fiction in _Pride and Prejudice_," pp. 374-88. (See 164.)

Marvin Mudrick, "Irony as Discrimination: _Pride and Prejudice_," pp. 388-409. (See 5.)

Andrew H. Wright, "[Feeling and Complexity in _Pride and Prejudice]_," pp. 410-20. (See 33.)

Howard S. Babb, "Dialogue with Feeling: A Note on _Pride and Prejudice_," pp. 421-31. (See 182.)

E. M. Halliday, "Narrative Perspective in _Pride and Prejudice_," pp. 431-37. (See 140.)

A. Walton Litz, "[The Marriage of Antitheses: Structure and Style in _Pride and Prejudice]_," pp. 437-47. (See 281.)

313   Henfrey, Norman. "Mansfield Park." _Delta_
        (Cambridge), No. 39 (1966), pp. 4-11.

"If only the moralist could have confronted the Crawfords as fearlessly as did the artist in-stead of bending them to an edifying purpose. The affirmation of Fanny would have been the more

compelling; her weaknesses courageously related to
her strengths, unambiguously allowed their exasper-
ating yet lesser presence."

314 Lane, Margaret. "Jane Austen's Sleight-of-Hand," in
      Purely for Pleasure. London: Hamish Hamilton,
      1966, pp. 95-107. This essay appears also, with
      the title "Jane Austen's Use of the Domestic
      Interior," in Collected Reports of the Jane
      Austen Society, 1949-1965 (London: Dawson,
      1967), pp. 224-34, as the address given to the
      Society's annual general meeting, 1962.

      JA's conjuring trick consists in "the discrep-
      ancy between the extreme spareness of her descrip-
      tions and the lively picture we have of the scenes
      which she has not described." Descriptive details,
      such as Lady Bertram's couch or Mr. Woodhouse's
      gruel, "serve solely to contribute to a character,"
      and by knowing the character we can conjure up his
      environment.

315 Lodge, David. "The Vocabulary of Mansfield Park,"
      in Language of Fiction: Essays in Criticism
      and Verbal Analysis of the English Novel.
      New York: Columbia Univ. Press, 1966, pp. 94-
      113. Parts of this essay appeared originally
      in NCF, 17 (1962), 275-82; see 197.

      In MP, JA schools us "in a vocabulary of dis-
      crimination which embraces the finest shades of
      social and moral value, and which asserts the prime
      importance . . . of exercising the faculty of judg-
      ment. . . . The subtle and untiring employment of
      this vocabulary, the exact fitting of value terms
      to events, the display of scrupulous and consistent
      discrimination" make us "pick up the habit of
      evaluation, and resign, for the duration of the
      novel at least, the luxury of neutrality."

316 Magee, William H. "Romanticism on Trial in Mans-
      field Park." BuR, 14 (Mar. 1966), 44-59.

      Though in MP JA does tolerate feelings, some
      of Fanny's emotions are excessive, and these are
      satirized. But because "irrational Romanticism is
      Fanny's guide to all her reactions, the moral one
      included, the jibes at it have produced the tech-
      nical weakness of the novel. Jane Austen has

undermined the respect for the moral half of Fanny's conduct by deliberately spoofing" her sensitivity.

317   Martin, W. R.   "'Ordination' in Mansfield Park."
          ESA, 9 (1966), 146-57.

          "Edmund's choice of profession is the pivot of
     the plot." Ordination is also the focal device dis-
     criminating the "very different patterns of thought
     and behavior" of Fanny and Mary. Though aware of
     "birth, rank, and wealth," Mary is "almost com-
     pletely blind to the intrinsic being of men. . . .
     In contrast, Fanny's awareness seems to include
     both that of the scholastic, generic quidditas and
     that of Scotus's haecceitas"--both that of private
     and public character.

318   Minter, David Lee. "Aesthetic Vision and the World
          of Emma." NCF, 21 (1966), 49-59.

          The subject of E is Emma herself. By portray-
     ing Emma's insistence that life combine harmony,
     radiance, and beauty, JA renders the significance
     and consequences of forcing an aesthetic ideal on
     the world. This drive toward the impossible lowers
     Emma rather than exalting her, and only when she
     ceases to impose herself on the world by training
     her fancy can she understand and adjust to the
     world as it is.

319   Moler, Kenneth L.   "Sense and Sensibility and Its
          Sources." RES, 17 (1966), 413-19.

          There is no one particular source for S and S,
     and thus the suggestion of Jane West's A Gossip's
     Story as the "starting-point" for JA's novel is
     doubtful. It is probable, however, that Maria
     Edgeworth's story, "Mademoiselle Panache," and
     Jane West's The Advantages of Education "may have
     significantly influenced the conception of Sense
     and Sensibility."

320   Moore, Katharine.   "Jane Austen, 1775-1817," in
          Cordial Relations: The Maiden Aunt in Fact and
          Fiction. London: Heinemann, 1966, pp. 53-62.

          "It is pleasing and fitting that Jane Austen,

herself the most delightful maiden aunt in fact,
should have created [in Miss Bates] the immortal
comic aunt of all fiction."

321 Page, Norman. "Standards of Excellence: Jane
       Austen's Language." Rev. Eng. Lit., 7 (July
       1966), 91-98.

       (See 540.)

322 Phillips-Birt, D. "Jane Austen and Old Portsmouth."
       Country Life Annual (1966), pp. 12-13.

       When, in MP, Fanny visits Portsmouth, "she
registers no impressions of urgent naval occasions,
of the imperial significance of the crowded wooden
warships out in Spithead." Rather, we see through
JA's eyes "as much and no more of the naval scene
and people as such a woman might be expected to
focus on. Hence the fascination."

323 Prescott, Orville, Jan Struther, and Lyman Bryson.
       "Jane Austen: Pride and Prejudice," in Invita-
       tion to Learning: English & American Novels.
       Ed. George D. Crothers. New York: Basic Books,
       1966, pp. 70-79.

       P and P is valuable as a historical document, a
love story, and a social comedy. With "lovely
humor" JA studies people and is "rather malicious
about them, and yet not mean." She believes that
morality must be achieved "within the range of
taste and convention of" one's society.

324 Pritchett, V. S. "Introduction" to Persuasion. New
       York: Fawcett Premier, 1966, pp. 5-18.

       JA's characteristic "gay and militant alert-
ness, in which the small doings of social life and
of the heart are perceived in continual crisis and
change, owes something to the war climate. . . .
The surface is everything to a tense world, where
change is strongly felt." But in P, a post-war novel, "the stress is more on feeling than on the
skirmish."

325 Ryle, Gilbert. "Jane Austen and the Moralists."

OxfordR, No. 1 (1966), pp. 5-18. Ryle's essay
appears also in his Collected Papers (New York:
Barnes & Noble, 1971), I ["Critical Essays"],
276-91, and in English Literature and British
Philosophy: A Collection of Essays, ed. S. P.
Rosenbaum (Chicago: Univ. of Chicago Press,
1971), pp. 168-84.

JA was interested in several general and theoretical problems--such as the relation of sense and
sensibility--that philosophers had examined and was,
"whether she knew it or not, a Shaftesburian." Like
Shaftesbury, JA rejects the Calvinistic dualisms as
a gauge of character; rather, she employs an Aristotelian aesthetic and ethic that represent people
as differing, not in kind, but degree.

326   Schneider, Sister M. Lucy. "The Little White Attic
      and the East Room: Their Function in Mansfield
      Park." Modern Philology, 63 (1966), 227-35.

      At first, the "assignment of the attic as
Fanny's room" symbolizes the Bertrams' "condescend-
ing generosity to her" and Fanny's inferiority as
well. But with the acquisition of the east room,
her consequence and influence increase: Fanny
begins to teach values to her callers--Edmund,
Mary, and Sir Thomas--and to learn them herself.

327   Sherry, Norman. Jane Austen. (Literature in Per-
      spective.) London: Evans, 1966.

      Rev. (with other works) in TLS, 9 June 1966,
p. 516; (with other works) by Frank McCombie in N&Q,
14 (1967), 399-400; (with other works) by Andrew
Wright in MLR, 63 (1968), 462-63.

      Introductory: In her presentation of the
conflict between sense and sensibility, JA stands
between the eighteenth and nineteenth centuries.
She read widely and, though influenced by earlier
novelists, she developed as a writer "in her own
way . . . limiting herself to what she personally
knew of life." "Her insight constantly takes her
beneath the surface of social life."

      The Novels: NA follows the heroine's education
as she distinguishes between life and literature and
then learns the difficulties of ordinary existence.
S and S, which justifies sense at the expense of

sensibility, is weakened by parallel plots. Equally didactic, but with greater irony, P and P has "a dynamic theme and functions by means of conflicts, confrontations and misunderstandings." Suited to its examination of "Christian attitudes to life," MP centers on temptations to the characters' virtue. The highpoint of JA's ironical comedy, E brilliantly unites structure and characterization and "celebrates the vital but deceived heroine." P, treating pride, vanity, and "right quality of mind," presents a Cinderella-type protagonist who both resembles the earlier heroines and differs significantly from them.

General: JA uses the events of courtship and marriage as a vehicle for the consideration of moral and social problems, including the importance and difficulty of right judgment as well as the formation of character by education.

A comic writer, she focuses on inconsistencies and incongruities and uses irony both to raise a smile and to offer serious criticism of people and society.

JA presents her fictional personages, who exhibit either fixed or flexible natures, by means of character sketches and the words and actions of the characters themselves. Among the human traits receiving her continual attention are flattery, vanity, and selfish insipidity.

In her novels gossip and rumor help create a convincing social background full of strong pressures, and the natural setting, "although not obtrusive, is nevertheless of great importance in forwarding character, plot, atmosphere, and theme."

"In its rhythm, its sense of order and decorum, Jane Austen's style is eighteenth-century, based on her favourite Dr. Johnson and . . . capable of many nuances within a narrow range of devices." "Jane Austen was a conscious, if often conventional, stylist."

328 Tanner, Tony. "Introduction" to his ed. of Mansfield Park. Baltimore: Penguin, 1966, pp. 7-36. See also 513.

Rev. (with other works) in TLS, 29 Sept. 1966, p. 901.

In <u>MP</u>, JA depicts a struggle between worlds, speaking "for stillness rather than movement, firmness rather than fluidity, arrest rather than change, endurance rather than adventure." She renders events, such as the Sotherton visit and the theatricals, with "a meticulous surface accuracy" and simultaneously makes them powerfully symbolic. Though as richly comic as the earlier novels, <u>MP</u> shows JA's increased awareness "of the real evils and real sufferings inextricably involved in life in society."

329 Tomlinson, T. B. "Jane Austen's Originality: <u>Emma</u>."
      <u>CR</u>, No. 9 (1966), pp. 22-37.

"Some narrowness and hesitations aside, Jane Austen's originality in <u>Emma</u> is to formulate, almost for the first time in English literature, the sense in which the good qualities in and of a whole society like that of Highbury may actively depend on the bad, or at least on impulses that must also result in foolishness, misjudgment, at times active cruelty."

330 Walcutt, Charles Child. "Jane Austen's Minuet," in
      <u>Man's Changing Mask: Modes and Methods of
      Characterization in Fiction.</u> Minneapolis:
      Univ. of Minnesota Press, 1966, pp. 71-90.

In <u>P and P</u> "character is so perfectly woven into the social fabric that a thread of one is a thread of the other. . . . Every word enriches character, advances the plot, and delights and amuses us with revelations of the wide range of motives, pretenses, maneuverings, and foibles that are possible within this apparently limited social context."

331 Waldron, Philip. "Style in <u>Emma</u>," in <u>Approaches to
      the Novel</u>. Ed. John Colmer. Adelaide: Rigby,
      1966, pp. 59-70.

In <u>E</u>, JA establishes a stylistic norm (indicative of her own values) against which to judge the characters' speech patterns, and so the characters themselves. Relying heavily on nouns and concepts, she does not stress the importance of verbs. She uses figurative language sparingly, constantly generalizes, and seeks balanced and contrasted phrasing.

332   Wiesenfarth, Brother Joseph. "Henry James: Action
          and the Art of Life." Four Quarters, 15 (Jan.
          1966), 18-26.

      "In Pride and Prejudice the meaning of life is
stable and real, and Elizabeth has only to share in
it. In The Portrait of a Lady, Isabel must create a
vision of life and strive to make it actual for herself." P and P is "a novel with a plot," which involves the social determination and fulfillment of
character, whereas James's Portrait is organized
around a central consciousness, which signifies the
individual's isolation.

333   Wildi, Max. "Nachwort" to Anne Elliot. Trans. Ilse
          Leisi. Zürich: Manesse Verlag, 1966, pp. 437-
          59.

      P is JA's most sensitive and introspective
novel. Though Anne Elliot resembles JA, Anne differs in that her life is filled with suffering and
silent observation. The heroine's passivity is the
novel's primary artistic problem. But by her sensitivity and strong moral sense, Anne represents an
ideal JA called "seniority of mind."

                          1967

334   Baker, Ernest A. "[Jane Austen]," in The History of
          the English Novel. New York: Barnes & Noble,
          1967 [London: Witherby, 1929]. VI ["Edgeworth,
          Austen, Scott"], 57-121.

      Though of relatively narrow social experience,
JA never strays beyond her scope. Her genius lies
in a Fieldingesque irony and a dramatic sense reminiscent of Congreve and Molière. By taking "the
morals for granted," she avoids didacticism and
concentrates on manners. "Out-and-out villainy was
not her province"--as shown by the dead end of Lady
Susan. More suited to her ability is the sympathetically drawn Marianne who, like Elinor, "is
half-a-heroine." S and S suffers from its forced
conclusion and satiric tendency, but like P and P,
the most dramatic of the novels, S and S is informed by the idea "that life is a process of education." Least altered of the early novels, NA is
conceived in irony "of an elementary cast," and its
author was "in two minds about Catherine." MP alone
is didactic. Neither Henry nor Mary Crawford is

consistent, since they are betrayed "for the sake of
the moral." Like the Crawfords, Frank Churchill and
Jane Fairfax are "supernumeraries"--technically
necessary but finally inconsistent or vague. Though
less somber, E is not less serious than MP: it up-
holds "an idea of decorum above mere ethics." However rich in sentiment, P "does not abstain from
satire of sentimentalism." It is "the most intimate
and for that reason the most moving of [JA's] love
stories."

335 Bartlett, Lynn C., and William R. Sherwood, eds.
       "Jane Austen: Emma, 1815," in The English Nov-
       el: Background Readings. Philadelphia: Lip-
       pincott, 1967, pp. 119-61.

       (Excerpts from six nineteenth-century accounts
of E, including Sir Walter Scott's review and two
selections by George Henry Lewes, as well as from
five pieces of JA correspondence relevant to E's
publication.)

336 Bel'skij, A. A. "Nravoopisatel'nyj roman Džejn
       Ostin." Učenye zapiski (Perm'), No. 157
       (1967), pp. 44-83.

       (See 378.)

337 Brophy, Brigid. "Introduction" to Pride and Preju-
       dice. London: Pan, 1967, pp. v-xvii.

       Educated by the eighteenth century, JA is pas-
sionate, remorseless, realistic, the inventor of
"the modern English novel of morals, manners and
moods." Her novels are "cogent, dynamic designs,"
with every detail both true-to-life and structur-
ally sound at the same time. Built upon the themes
of economics and sex, her novels center on "the
moral debate in the consciousness and the educational changes in the personalities of her heroines."

338 Brophy, Brigid. "Miss J. Austen," in Don't Never
       Forget: Collected Views and Reviews. New York:
       Holt, Rinehart and Winston, 1967, pp. 249-54.
       This essay appeared originally in New States-
       man, 4 Dec. 1964, pp. 879-80, as a review of
       B. C. Southam's Jane Austen's Literary Manu-
       scripts.

JA is the opposite of the figure the Janeites would make her. "Far from being rather a dear, she is the most sardonic person who ever set pen to paper." "Those who believe great literature to be the outcome of a meeting between sweetness and light are refuted by Jane Austen."

339 Burroway, Janet. "The Irony of the Insufferable Prig: Mansfield Park." CritQ, 9 (1967), 127-38.

The essential irony of MP is that "Fanny Price, who is totally committed to preserving the repose, stability and order of Mansfield Park against the restless, self-assertive and independent forces that threaten it, is required to express this commitment by active, independent self-assertion." The absoluteness of Fanny's commitment to the hierarchy that assigns her its meanest position "brings her to a crisis in which she must place herself mentally and morally above her master."

340 Chew, Samuel C., and Richard D. Altick. "Jane Austen," in A Literary History of England. Ed. Albert C. Baugh. 2nd ed. New York: Appleton-Century-Crofts, 1967 [1st ed., 1948], pp. 1200-06. This edition includes a bibliographical supplement.

Though much is absent from JA's fiction, what she does deal with is based on "so comprehensive a knowledge of human nature as to universalize it." A shrewd moralist and satirist, JA creates "living characters" (the profoundest of whom is Emma) and "firmly integrated" plots. Her style is marked by "delicate precision," "nice balance," "the seeming simplicity which often masks subtlety," "lucidity," "vitality," and "ironic wit."

341 Colby, Robert A. "Mansfield Park: Fanny Price and the Christian Heroine," in Fiction with a Purpose: Major and Minor Nineteenth-Century Novels. Bloomington: Indiana Univ. Press, 1967, pp. 66-104.

MP is rooted in the early nineteenth-century tradition of the religious-didactic novel, a form which treated "female education, courtship, and moral conduct . . . in the light of practical Christianity." Though accepting the evangelical ideals of this tradition, JA applies them to a real, complex, and flawed world filled with dynamic, mixed characters. She seems to be trying "to justify fiction by proving that it can be at once edifying and diverting."

342 Coleman, Terry. "Jane and All That." The Guardian, 15 May 1967, p. 14.

(A description of ceremonies commemorating the one-hundred-fiftieth anniversary of JA's death.)

343 Collected Reports of the Jane Austen Society, 1949-1965. London: Dawson, 1967.

(This volume includes the guest speaker's annual address to the Jane Austen Society, abstracted below for the years 1956 to 1965; the Society has no verbatim record of the speeches given before 1956. In addition to the recorded addresses, this volume contains, among other things, news about the Society's membership, the yearly general meeting, and the development of Chawton Cottage as a showplace and museum, as well as information about the Society's acquisition of JA "relics" and the uncovering of new facts of JA's life. There are, too, many illustrations.)

1956: Sir Harold Nicolson, "Jane Austen and Her Letters," pp. 94-103. Important as a social document, her correspondence, "far from being trivial or dull, introduces us to a more placid, less worldly, and more sensible woman than the student of her novels might suppose."

1957: Roger Fulford, "Jane Austen's Dedication of Emma to the Prince Regent," pp. 117-23. "By the Prince Regent's time a royal dedication was a mark of personal favour, and, accorded to a novel, was a rare proof of both esteem and genius. And . . . in dedicating Emma to His Royal Highness the Prince Regent, Jane Austen made no unworthy choice."

1958: René Varin, "The French Attitude towards Jane Austen's Works," pp. 138-43. The lack of a good biography of JA in French, among other reasons, helps account for the slow increase in France of interest in her. Yet her reputation there seems to be growing, because her classical type of humor is translatable, and she offers all countries a fine

example of a particular English charm, "enchant-
ment."

1959: E. G. Selwyn, "Jane Austen's Clergymen,"
pp. 155-65. (See 128.)

1960: John Gore, "First Impressions . . . and
Last," pp. 179-83. "We should acknowledge her
handicaps and even weaknesses, the better to establish the full miracle of her genius. . . . I am
quite prepared to swallow not only her provincial-
ism but to believe that she lived and died an amateur (as severe literary critics might define that
word), a state which has never appeared shameful to
a great man or woman who possessed the eternal
humility of true greatness."

1961: Andrew Wright, "Jane Austen from an
American Viewpoint," pp. 203-10. JA is "specially
English; and the central quality of her Englishness
lies in being, in a wholly ameliorative sense, insu-
lar: possessed, that is to say, of a sense of proportion; taking for granted a certain harmony in
political, social and individual organization;
assuming not only the desirability but the possibility of consonance."

1962: Margaret Lane, "Jane Austen's Use of the
Domestic Interior," pp. 224-34. (See 314.)

1963: Elizabeth Jenkins, "The Taste of Jane
Austen's Day," pp. 245-58. JA's own epithets for
P and P--"light and bright and sparkling"--are
traits also of her other novels and of the arts
in general during the Regency period. "The very
word Regency calls up the vision of something
bright and elegant, of vigorous, formal simplicity
and natural grace."

1964: David Cecil, "Jane Austen's Lesser
Works," pp. 273-81. JA's lesser works--the
juvenilia, Lady Susan, and the fragments--show us
what in her was innate and what acquired. From
them we learn that she was a deliberate artist,
constantly reworking her materials to achieve the
best effects; that her basic spirit was comic; and
that "the style in which she expressed this comic
vision was with her from the start."

1965: L. P. Hartley, "Jane Austen and the
Abyss," pp. 297-310. Though JA does not stress the
existence of irrationality and evil in human

affairs, her novels (especially S and S) do depict a
great amount of sadness and suffering. If she "does
not take us into the Abyss itself," she at least
lets us glimpse it. [Hartley's essay appears also,
with the title "Jane Austen," in his The Novelist's
Responsibility (London: Hamish Hamilton, 1967), pp.
19-34, and, with the title "Jane Austen and the
Abyss," in EDH, 35 (1969), 85-100.]

344   Crane, R. S. "Jane Austen: Persuasion," in The Idea
       of the Humanities and Other Essays Critical and
       Historical. Chicago: Univ. of Chicago Press,
       1967. II, 283-302.

       In P, "a serious comedy," JA desired "to write
a love story that called for something more positive than merely 'sentimental' acquiescence in its
dénouement," that made us value the protagonists not
only as lovers but as moral persons. Her conception
of her subject involved "various particular problems," including the creation of concrete "occasions" for the psychological "events" of the plot
and a narrative point of view suited to Anne's
feelings and the novel's moral import.

345   Demurova, N. M. "Džejn Ostin i ee roman Gordost' i
       predubeždenie," in Gordost' i predubeždenie
       [Pride and Prejudice]. Trans. I. S. Maršak.
       Moscow: Nauka, 1967, pp. 538-89.

       Rev. by A. Narkevič in NovM, 44 (1968), 260-
62; by L. Arinshtein in PQ, 48 (1969), 330; in SovL,
No. 8 (1969), pp. 188-89.

       In P and P, as in her other novels, JA creates
a precise, harmonious, and finished structure, in
which her protagonists free themselves from error.
Very modern in her objective narration, JA subjects everything to ironic laughter. She is realistic and rational, compact and capacious; focusing
on the internal traits determining character, she
goes much further in the portrayal of mixed characters than most other novelists.

346   Fleishman, Avrom. "Mansfield Park in Its Time."
       NCF, 22 (1967), 1-18.

       (See 347.)

347   Fleishman, Avrom. A Reading of Mansfield Park: An
      Essay in Critical Synthesis. (Minnesota
      Monographs in the Humanities, 2.) Minne-
      apolis: Univ. of Minnesota Press, 1967.

      Rev. (with other works) by Timothy Rogers in
English, 17 (1968), 61-62; by A. Walton Litz in
NCF, 22 (1968), 405-07; by Howard Babb in Novel, 1
(1968), 289-90; (with other works) by Carl Woodring
in SEL, 8 (1968), 740-41; (with other works) in
TLS, 29 Aug. 1968, p. 927; (with other works) by
Lloyd W. Brown in ECS, 3 (1969), 145-48; by John E.
Jordan in ELN, 7 Supp. (1969), 18; by Sister Mary
Alice Muellerleile in Modern Philology, 67 (1969),
201-03; by Angela Smith in Yearbook of English
Studies, 1 (1971), 289-90.

      Introductory: "No single point of view can be
commensurate with the manifold reality of" MP; a
comprehensive reading is possible only through the
application of several different critical approaches. MP requires more precise treatment than
political, historical, or sociological critics in
the past have accorded it.

      History: JA's judgment of Mansfield Park is
ambivalent. A knowledge of topical affairs shows
that MP records the gentry's self-evaluation and
correction of its failings. The Evangelical influence in the book's moral tone exposes religious,
as the episodes involving the theatricals uncover
political, weaknesses. Fanny's commitment to
Romantic ideals implies criticism of accepted class
values, and the development of Sir Thomas' character following his return from Antigua points to
economic peril.

      Psychology: JA sees her heroine as a mixed
character rather than as an ideal: "Fanny exhibits
not only the origins of moral aggression in psychic
needs but also the possibilities of moral awareness
through heightened introspection." Through her
major characters JA presents variations on the
theme of selfhood and illustrates the limitations
of a rigid reliance on morality or feeling.

      Myth: "If the pattern of Mansfield Park is the
accession of a Cinderella to dominance and if the
significance of her victory lies in the conquest of
the chief authority at Mansfield by the life-denying
values she represents . . . the property itself, the

inherited domain," is an Eden redeemed. The inher-
itors must learn of misery and guilt while recognizing "the possibilities of this-worldly salvation--a
feeling of peace after the loss of vitality."

The Literary Tradition: In MP JA creates "a
complex, ambivalent view of the social life of man
and of modern society in particular." "Nineteenth-
century English realism is the tradition founded by
Jane Austen, by virtue of her steady grasp of human
imperfection, her heroic commitment to a world rid-
dled with personal aggression--and touched occasionally by love."

348 Gilson, D. J. "The First American Editions of Jane
        Austen." BC, 16 (1967), 512.

At least one copy exists of the first American
edition of JA (the 1816 E published in Philadelphia).

349 Gornall, J. F. G. "Marriage, Property & Romance in
        Jane Austen's Novels." HibbertJ, 65 (1967),
        151-56; 66 (1967), 24-29. This essay, in
        shortened form, appears also, with the title
        "Marriage and Property in Jane Austen's Nov-
        els," in History Today, 17 (1967), 805-11.

Marriage in JA's novels is governed not only
by love but also by three unromantic factors:
first, the fact that a widow's financial position
"depended to some extent on her own resources, however large her husband's income might have been";
second, "that the landed gentry and their families
voluntarily precluded themselves, within certain
limits, from earning money"; and, third, that the
size of the daughter's marriage portion often
determined who would be her suitors.

350 Grigg, John. "The Best of Her Sex." The Guardian,
        13 July 1967, p. 14.

Though Tolstoy and Dickens are more comprehensive in their view of humanity, JA still possesses the novelist's supreme quality, "the power
to depict human nature with relentless accuracy,
and yet with sympathy."

351 Harvey, W. J. "The Plot of Emma." EIC, 17 (1967),
        48-63.

Wayne Booth's charge (see 151) that "Jane
Austen purchases the maximum of narrative surprise
at the expense of the reader's ironic perspective"
must be tempered by considering that "were the
reader fully aware from the outset of the true facts
then the irony would become ponderous and sche-
matic." Mystification in E heightens the reader's
awareness of the complex and shadowy social pressures on the individual and, also, of his own propensity for mistake.

352   The Jane Austen Society: Report for the Year, 1966.
         Alton, Hampshire: Jane Austen Society [1967].

         (In addition to the guest speaker's address to
the Society's annual general meeting, abstracted
below, this report includes, among other things,
several brief notes.)

         C. V. Wedgwood, "Jane Austen and the Tragic
Muse," pp. 15-25. "Jane Austen is so excellent a
writer of comedy precisely because she has a keen
sense of the tragic threads with which the fabric
of life is interwoven. If these are rarely visible
on the surface of her work, they are present in the
structure."

353   Kawamoto, Shizuko. "North and South: A Victorian
         Pride and Prejudice." TsudaR, No. 12 (Nov.
         1967), pp. 43-54.

         Both P and P and Mrs. Gaskell's North and
South are concerned with the question, "Who is a
gentleman?" The clash of Darcy and Elizabeth in
the first proposal scene is a clash between the
definition of a gentleman by social status and by
character. "If we take North and South as the
social document of admitting industrial capitalists
into the rank of gentlemen," we can see that both
novels achieve a "resolidification of the gentry."

354   Kettle, Arnold. "Jane Austen: Emma (1816)," in An
         Introduction to the English Novel. 2nd ed.
         London: Hutchinson Univ. Library, 1967 [1st
         ed., 1951]. I ["To George Eliot"], 86-98.

         E's strength is ultimately its "rejection of
Life in favour of living, the actual, concrete
problems of behaviour and sensibility in an actual, concrete society. It is Jane Austen's sensitive

vitality, her genuine concern (based on so large an
honesty) for human feelings in a concrete situation,
that captures our imagination. It is this concern
that gives her such delicate and precise insight
into the problems of personal relationships" and
that defeats her limitations.

355 Knight, Richard. "Jane Austen's Bit of England."
     The Field, 6 July 1967, pp. 31-32.

     (Illustrations and description of Chawton.)

356 Knoepflmacher, U. C. "The Importance of Being
     Frank: Character and Letter-Writing in Emma."
     SEL, 7 (1967), 639-58.

     "Jane Austen's creation of Frank Churchill,
     like her subtle exploitation of the letter-writing
     motif, provides the reader of Emma with the guide-
     lines necessary for moral judgment." Frank's
     "persistence in employing the written, rather than
     the spoken word," typifies his irresponsibility and
     his inability to benefit from the "near disaster
     brought about by his previous indirections. Mr.
     Knightley's denunciation of his rival's last letter
     must therefore stand as an irrevocable moral judg-
     ment."

357 Lerner, Laurence. The Truthtellers: Jane Austen,
     George Eliot, D. H. Lawrence. New York:
     Schocken, 1967.

     Rev. by William Kean Seymour in ContemporaryR,
     210 (1967), 278-79; (with other works) by Edward
     Bostetter in SEL, 7 (1967), 759-60; (with other
     works) in TLS, 11 May 1967, p. 400; by George J.
     Worth in JEGP, 67 (1968), 319-21; by Andrew Wright
     in KR, 30 (1968), 420-23; by Frederick P. W. Mc-
     Dowell in PQ, 47 (1968), 335-36; by Miriam Allott
     in MLR, 64 (1969), 408; (with other works) by James
     R. Bennett in DHLR, 4 (1971), 74-89.

     "What Jane Austen most admired was the ability
     to resist impulse; what Lawrence most admired was
     surrender to it. George Eliot . . . did not believe
     there was a clear opposition between impulse and
     reason." But (as evidenced in her conception of
     clergymen) JA's admiration for resisting impulse
     does not indicate a religious view of life.

Though we respond to E with "warmth and anger, grief and fear," these emotions are "never violent enough to run away with our attention." JA does not, however, sacrifice richness of human material to be merely amusing. "Perhaps Emma is as profound as pure comedy can be."

The children in JA's novels act principally as a satirical device for exposing the follies of adults. But the children do not, therefore, represent the moral norm as in George Eliot. They are creatures of impulse, and thus are to be handled with "firmness and severity."

"Jane Austen really believed that every impulse must be submitted to the inspection of the judgment . . . just as she really believed that happiness depended on virtue." The heart is no mystery to JA, for motivation is easily discoverable by common sense. Thus plot explains character; virtue or villainy is at pains to prove itself by some decisive act.

Does JA opt "unequivocally for control and against feeling?" It could be objected against such a view that she "values love more than anything." But some of her characters (Lydia Bennet, for example) "love and are not redeemed by it." Nor does JA advocate love at its most intense: "the forgetfulness of self and even of principle in the intensity of otherness" is absent in the characters she most approves.

JA's alter-ego, the "anti-Jane," who elevates passion over principle, occasionally emerges from behind plain Jane, the old maid. Marianne Dashwood and Mary Crawford "threaten to escape their creator's reign"; their creative energy supersedes their moral purpose. Both S and S and MP are thus divided against themselves because their author is divided against herself.

"Persuasion is the one book in which Jane Austen ceased to see any contrast between sense and passion, and in which what distinguishes the heroine from the other characters . . . is the intensity of her emotions."

358 Litz, A. Walton. "Introduction" to his ed. of Pride and Prejudice. New York: Random House, 1967, pp. v-xvii.

Affirming the worth of what is "light, and bright, and sparkling" without becoming sentimental, P and P achieves greatness in its "easy commerce between a youthful spirit and a mature moral vision." JA pictures the meeting between an older social code and a newer enterprising spirit, and treats both these forces fairly. With irony as her technique and subject, she reconciles "the normally conflicting demands of economics, manners, and aesthetics."

359   Lochhead, Marion. "Jane Austen and the Seven Deadly Sins." QuarterlyR, 305 (1967), 429-36.

"The seven deadly sins are shown in some of her characters with devastating clarity." Evil is not absent from JA's novels.

360   Lynch, P. R. "Speculation at Mansfield Parsonage." N&Q, 14 (1967), 21-22.

The episode of the card game "is a deliberate indication . . . of Fanny's determination" and independence.

361   Mallinson, Anne. An Account of the Commemoration of the 150th Anniversary of the Death of Jane Austen, Chawton, July 14th-18th, 1967. The Wakes, Selborne, Hampshire: The Author [1967].

("An account of the occasion as seen by someone who was closely associated with the Commemoration throughout.")

362   Mansell, Darrel. "Another Source of Jane Austen's 'The History of England.'" N&Q, 14 (1967), 305. See also in N&Q, J. C. Maxwell, 14 (1967), 424-25.

John Whitaker's Mary Queen of Scots Vindicated (1787).

363   Marshall, William H. "The Novel of the Enlightenment," in The World of the Victorian Novel. New York: A. S. Barnes, 1967, pp. 48-57.

"Lying near the center of the Austen world view, a characteristic mixture of traditional

Christian value and eighteenth-century rationalism,
is the privative doctrine of evil, the orthodox
Western position that good is the sole reality and
evil has being to the extent that good is absent."
Her best novels are "those in which the focus is
upon the complexity of human behavior rather than
upon the simplicity of universal structure and moral
value."

364   Martin, W. R.   "The Subject of Jane Austen's Sandi-
       ton." ESA, 10 (1967), 87-93.

       Though we can never know what JA intended in
Sanditon, it appears to deal with a contrast between
an older, stabler society and a newer commercial
one. The work is as fully informed by her moral
vision as the completed novels, but the focus now
seems to have shifted from the individual to his
society.

365   Moler, Kenneth L.   "The Bennet Girls and Adam Smith
       on Vanity and Pride." PQ, 46 (1967), 567-69.

       "Elizabeth's light and deft allusion [to Adam
Smith's Theory of Moral Sentiments] . . . is as
characteristic of her intellect as Mary's ponderous
plagiarism is of hers."

366   Moler, Kenneth L.   "Pride and Prejudice: Jane
       Austen's 'Patrician Hero.'" SEL, 7 (1967),
       491-508.

       (See 401.)

367   Nash, Ralph.   "The Time Scheme for Pride and Preju-
       dice." ELN, 4 (1967), 194-98.

       In P and P "the events of the first autumn
reflect the calendar of 1799, and . . . the events
of spring and summer reflect the calendar of 1802."
This makes it unlikely that, as Chapman asserts
(see 264), P and P underwent extensive revision in
1812.

368   Paulson, Ronald.   "Jane Austen: Pride and Preju-
       dice," in Satire and the Novel in Eighteenth-
       Century England. New Haven: Yale Univ. Press,
       1967, pp. 291-306.

In P and P, as distinct from NA, JA fully sub-
limates satire to her novelistic aims. Indebted to
Fielding for her irony and to Richardson for her
interest in psychology, she treats "the theme of
self-discovery, perhaps derived from Evelina." What
Elizabeth discovers (and what distinguishes the
realism of P and P) is that the failings of one's
acquaintances must be borne as well as judged. To
JA reality "comes to mean a careful description of
how society operates."

369 Rosser, G. C. "Critical Commentary," the introduc-
        tion to his ed. of Pride and Prejudice. Lon-
        don: Univ. of London Press, 1967, pp. 9-59.

        P and P, which deals with self-realization,
perception, and the conflict between appearance and
reality, shows that JA was no "leisurely blotting-
pad scribbler. . . . Discipline, thought, restraint, and a fierce critical intelligence are
always at work in her handling of plot and character. Her work is certainly not a spare-time product: it is craftsmanship and genius of a high
order."

370 Standop, Ewald, and Edgar Mertner. "Jane Austen,
        Scott und der romantische Roman," in Englische
        Literaturgeschichte. Heidelberg: Quelle und
        Meyer Verlag, 1967, pp. 447-58.

        Completely oblivious to the social, political,
and spiritual upheavals of her time, JA lived in
and wrote about a country society securely nestled
between the lower nobility and the upper bourgeoisie. Transcendence and religion play no role
in her novels. Rather, the characters' moral
existence is defined in the forum of society, that
is, by their attitudes and actions toward others.

371 Ten Harmsel, Henrietta. "Emma: Daughter of Anti-
        Romance." EWR, 3 (1967), 137-50.

        An examination of The Female Quixote and The
Heroine as part of E's literary tradition testifies
to the transforming power of JA's imagination and
suggests that "she exposes the falseness of the
world of romance even while she is testifying to
its basic truth." JA surpasses her predecessors by
showing, specifically in Mr. Knightley, that "anti-

romance" (like "romance") represents only a half-truth.

372 Threapleton, Mary M. "Introduction" to Mansfield
        Park. New York: Airmont, 1967, pp. 3-8.

     MP emphasizes the value of a proper education
as the background necessary for committing oneself
to a correct course of action. The book "grants
success and happiness to the good and the dull, not
to the intelligent and the interesting."

373 Wellington, Gerald Wellesley, Duke of. "Houses
        in Jane Austen's Novels." Spectator; rpt. in
        Collected Reports of the Jane Austen Society,
        1949-1965. London: Dawson, 1967, pp. 185-88.

     Though JA "cared nothing for the visual arts,"
she could not "quite get away from domestic archi-
tecture, and her powers of observation were so
extraordinarily acute that the references she
makes to houses are telling enough to enable us to
construct them in our imagination."

374 White, Edward M. "A Critical Theory of Mansfield
        Park." SEL, 7 (1967), 659-77.

     MP is an intentionally querulous and rigid
reaction to the romanticism of Lovers' Vows. JA
"set out to write a novel precisely and centrally
about the need for and value of moral severity,"
and "this central concern developed out of a
desire to reply to an immensely popular play whose
assumptions and effect Jane Austen saw as socially
and artistically destructive."

375 Wiesenfarth, Joseph. The Errand of Form: An Assay
        of Jane Austen's Art. New York: Fordham Univ.
        Press, 1967.

     Rev. (with other works) by Timothy Rogers in
English, 17 (1968), 61-62; by Paul Goetsch in NS,
17 (1968), 407-09; by Carol de Saint Victor in PQ,
47 (1968), 353-54; by Howard S. Babb in SAQ, 67
(1968), 710-11; (with other works) by Carl Woodring
in SEL, 8 (1968), 740; (with other works) in TLS, 29
Aug. 1968, p. 927 [and see corr., Wiesenfarth and
reviewer, 24 Oct., p. 1210]; (with other works) by

Lloyd W. Brown in ECS, 3 (1969), 145-48; by John E.
Jordan in ELN, 7 Supp. (1969), 19; by William D.
Schaefer in NCF, 23 (1969), 489-90; by Frank Mc-
Combie in N&Q, 16 (1969), 79-80; by B. C. Southam in
RES, 20 (1969), 387-88; by John W. Loofbourow in
Thought, 44 (1969), 296-97; by Andrew Wright in Nov-
el, 4 (1971), 275-77.

Introductory: A study of JA outside the ordinary limits of a rigid thesis can solve major problems in the novels still causing disagreement among
critics. These problems "illuminate the errand of
form in Jane Austen's novels because they ultimately
call into question the relationship between patterns
in the novels and the character of the persons who
develop within those patterns."

NA: Possibly indebted to Fielding, NA is a
unified novel. The book's Gothic parody "corre-
lates perfectly with the realism of false friendship and love. In both cases the attempt to substi-
tute a word-construct for real life is exposed."
"Mastery of language becomes the outward aspect of
Catherine Morland's radical human effort to mature."

S and S: S and S insists on solutions involving both sense and sensibility. The novel's structure "attempts to engage and develop the total
personalities of Elinor and Marianne by presenting
them with a series of mysteries that must be
solved." S and S examines the relationship between
esteem and love.

P and P: JA works out P and P in relation to
four obstacles to the protagonists' marriage.
Through the plot she exposes an ideal of conduct
and self-realization that is not subject to irony.
"She disposes the incidents of the plot in such a
way that they shape meaning, direct irony, control
diction, and present themselves as an esthetic fact.
Consequently, Jane Austen makes plot . . . a mold
of values."

MP: Indebted to Richardson, MP has as its
subject "the education of a human being as a total
person and . . . the central issue is the threat to
the integrity of the self that comes from an easy
life lived without principle. Mansfield Park tells
us that the only meaningful human freedom is found
in a self-integrity that is measured by the constant
of principle; therefore, to be truly oneself is to
feel as one ought."

E: Emma's marriage, the book's climactic symbol, is possible only after she has given up her
dominating egoism in favor of true gentility and has
acquiesced in reality as a basis for meaning in her
life. The novel's structure is such that the heroine "encounters the meaning of reality and of person
by seeing how impossible it is to ignore them."

P: Though the episodes involving Dick Musgrove
and Mrs. Smith are not aesthetically satisfying,
they do help to indicate P's main theme--the relationship between dignity and duty. The plot places
Anne in a series of relationships which elicit her
genuine personal dignity and measure that of others
against it.

1968

376   Andrews, P. B. S.   "The Date of Pride and Preju-
      dice."   N&Q, 15 (1968), 338-42.

      There is "possible evidence for some reworking
[of 'First Impressions'] in 1799," and "positive
evidence for probably substantial rewriting in
1802."

377   Apperson, G. L.   A Jane Austen Dictionary. New
      York: Haskell House, 1968 [London: C. Palmer,
      1932].

      (Lists every person, place, and author men-
tioned in JA's works, the titles of her works, the
names of her family and associates, and the places
she lived in or visited.)

378   Bel'skij, A. A.   "Džejn Ostin," in Anglijskij roman
      1800--1810-x godov. Perm': Permskij univ. im.
      A. M. Gor'kogo, 1968, pp. 47-107.

      JA's novels, not published in Russian before
1967, realistically describe the morals and customs
of everyday provincial life. In a penetrating and
economical manner, they show us both the good and
bad in human nature.

379   Bonincontro, Marilia.   "Le ascendenze austeniane del
      Portrait of a Lady di Henry James." PS, 4
      (Jan. 1968), 31-39.

If JA's novels and James's have similar concepts of family relationships, and if they deal in
part with similar characters and events, it is not
necessarily, as Praz has contended (see 733), because her work influenced his; rather, it is probably because they shared the same British tradition
of the high bourgeoisie. What literary affinity
there is, though, exists in style and comes, not
from E, as Praz has said, but P.

380 Borinski, Ludwig. "Jane Austen (1775-1817)," in
     Der englische Roman des 18. Jahrhunderts.
     Frankfurt am Main: Athenäum Verlag, 1968, pp.
     289-323.

JA contemplates the problems of the gentry
against an eighteenth-century social background.
Employing satire as her primary device, she analyzes
the gentry's religion, ethics, and professions.
Although inheriting her social ideals from Richardson, JA surpasses him in novelistic art. And
through Dr. Johnson she developed a moral sensibility based on religion. JA's style is heavily
influenced by Goldsmith; it is without either
metaphorical language or complicated rhetoric.

381 Bradbury, Malcolm. "Persuasion Again." EIC, 18
     (1968), 383-96.

In P, JA created a heroine who, contrary to
Gomme's assertion (see 310), gains in maturity during the course of the novel's action. Anne's growth
consists in her replacement of the values of the
aristocratic class with those of the naval class.
Originally persuaded by Lady Russell "towards a
caution appropriate to rank and security," Anne
evidences in her marriage to Wentworth her acknowledgement of "values having to do with luck, spir-
ited energy and emotional resource."

382 Brogan, Hugh. "Mansfield Park." Corr. in TLS, 19
     Dec. 1968, p. 1440. See also corr. in TLS,
     Brian Southam, 2 Jan. 1969, p. 22; Margaret
     Kirkham and Hugh Brogan, 9 Jan., p. 39; Denis
     Donoghue, 16 Jan., p. 62; Mary Lascelles, 30
     Jan., p. 111.

By 24 Jan. 1813 JA had already advanced beyond
Volume Two, Chapter Seven, of MP. Thus, the mention

of "ordination" in her letter of 29 Jan. refers only
to Edmund's ordination and is not a general statement of the novel's subject.

383   Brown, Lloyd W.   "Jane Austen and the Sublime: A
        Note on Mansfield Park."   SBHT, 10 (1968),
        1041-43.

     Fanny manifests the "ideal taste" that Burke's
Enquiry envisages "as the balanced combination of
sensibility and judgment."

384   Burrows, J. F.   Jane Austen's Emma.   Sydney: Sydney
        Univ. Press, 1968.

        Rev. (with another work) by William D. Schaefer
in NCF, 24 (1969), 248; (with another work) by B. C.
Southam in SoRA, 3 (1969), 281-83; (with another
work) in TLS, 27 Nov. 1969, p. 1357; by Frank Mc-
Combie in N&Q, 17 (1970), 200; (with other works) by
J. Hillis Miller in SEL, 10 (1970), 203-04.

        In E, JA's artistry "is in continual if unob-
trusive motion": "The narrator's function varies
subtly as occasion requires . . . Emma's relationships with her fellows are incessantly in flux . . .
Emma's own moods vary with dazzling rapidity . . .
even the meaning supposedly enshrined in words
like 'reason,' 'imagination,' 'amiable,' and 'elegant' varies significantly as the novel proceeds."
As a result, the usual critical practice of singling
out one part of E as emblematic of the whole over-
simplifies the book's shape and meaning, and makes
static what is essentially dynamic. If we are to do
justice to JA's art, an almost page-by-page analysis
is necessary.

        We may realize how open and flexible is JA's
entire conception in E if we use the character of
Mr. Knightley as a point of reference. Contrary
to prevailing critical opinion, he is not JA's
spokesman, but "one fallible creature among others,"
whose words we may heed yet not bow to. When we
regard him "as a leading but not oracular partici-
pant . . . Emma appears more subtly amusing, more
richly meaningful, and more thoroughly dramatic."

385   Culbertson, Jean.   "Eudora Welty Tells about Jane
        Austen."   The Clarion-Ledger (Jackson, Miss.),
        6 Dec. 1968, p. 16.

In a lecture to a Millsaps College audience, Eudora Welty praised JA's "'genius of originality and genius of comedy.'" JA, who bases what she writes partly on her own experience, makes family relationships the foundation of all other relationships.

386 Emden, Cecil S. "The Composition of Northanger Abbey." RES, 19 (1968), 279-87.

"The main body of the novel was written in about 1794, and . . . the sections burlesquing horror novels, and Mrs. Radcliffe's The Mysteries of Udolpho in particular, were added some four years later." The anti-gothic and the non-gothic Catherines are incompatible, and the horror-burlesque sections of NA exhibit little affinity to the juvenilia. By deleting the later additions (as listed), one can restore the story to its original symmetry.

387 Fahy, Carole. "Introduction" to Sense and Sensibility. London: Heron, 1968, pp. vii-xi.

Of all JA's heroines, Elinor Dashwood most closely resembles her creator--in strength of character, selflessness, and reserve. Elinor lacks only JA's "exquisite sense of humour."

388 Ferns, John. "Neo Classical Structure: The Rape of the Lock and Pride and Prejudice." QQ, 75 (1968), 685-90.

"Both Pope and Jane Austen explore the division between rational morality and unregenerate human nature." "Both authors are prepared to dramatize their beliefs in order, reason and moral proportion through the medium of balanced and symmetrically organized literary structures."

389 Gallon, D. N. "Comedy in Northanger Abbey." MLR, 63 (1968), 802-09.

"'Human comedy' exists in Northanger Abbey as well as the more obvious literary satire." Isabella and John Thorpe are not merely Gothic anti-types, but rather characters who are in themselves and in their relations to the heroine morally complex.

Similarly, "Catherine is not a goose," whose feelings are only ridiculous; she is finally able to
exemplify seriously "the person of feeling."

390   Garnett, Christopher Browne, Jr.   "Psychoanalysis
        and Taste," in Taste: An Essay in Critical
        Imagination. Jericho, N. Y.: Exposition Press,
        1968, pp. 35-42.

        "There is precisely the same relation between
the characters of Miss Austen's novels and Mr.
Gorer's account of them [see 94] as between a treatment of human life with critical discernment and
imagination and the psycho-physiology of hysteria."

391   Green-Armytage, E. L., comp. A Map of Bath in the
        Time of Jane Austen, with Comments and Descrip-
        tions from Her Letters and Novels. Bath: Pit-
        man Press [1968?].

        ("Plan of the City of Bath 1803," with accom-
panying extracts from NA, P, and the letters.)

392   Inglis, Fred. "Persuasion (1818)," in An Essen-
        tial Discipline: An Introduction to Literary
        Criticism. London: Methuen, 1968, pp. 212-24.

        The syntax of P echoes JA's scheme of values--
"energy and balance are held at poise." Because her
values are firm, "when we come up against her firmness, our own standards are shaken into definition,
and redistributed." Not only is the novel about
Lady Russell's initial persuasion, but also the
"subtler kind of persuasion by which Anne overcomes
the understandable pride and distance of Wentworth."

393   The Jane Austen Society: Report for the Year 1967.
        Alton, Hampshire: Jane Austen Society [1968].

        (In addition to the guest speaker's address to
the Society's annual general meeting, abstracted
below, this report includes, among other things,
several brief notes.)

        John Bayley, "Emma and Her Critics," pp. 16-
29. Like Tolstoy, JA "uses the rigidity of society
as a means of liberating her fancy and creative
joy." And it is her "achievement to leave us

sharing rather than judging. Our judgements, like
hers, are contingent on the inability to escape from
the society in which she is writing." [This essay
appears also, in an enlarged form, with the title
"The 'Irresponsibility' of Jane Austen," in Critical
Essays on Jane Austen, ed. B. C. Southam (London:
Routledge & Kegan Paul, 1968), pp. 1-20.]

394 Jones, Evan. "Characters and Values: Emma and Mans-
     field Park." Quadrant, 12 (July-Aug. 1968),
     35-45.

     In E Mr. Knightley is not the spokesman for
JA's values. Rather, an aged bachelor standing in
loco parentis to a girl perpetually fixed at a pre-
adolescent stage of emotional development, Mr.
Knightley becomes the novel's "most deeply ridiculous figure." Frank Churchill is, in contrast,
alert and perspicuous. MP lacks the wit and civility evident in E, and its morality, asserted but not
represented, is "so fragmentary and betrayed that it
is not interpretable."

395 Keynes, Geoffrey. Jane Austen: A Bibliography. New
     York: Burt Franklin, 1968 [London: Nonesuch
     Press, 1929].

     This descriptive bibliography is chiefly con-
cerned with the original editions of the novels, the
first American editions, French translations, collected editions, and separate reprints. There are,
as well, sections on editions of the letters and the
miscellaneous writings, on biography and criticism,
and books from JA's library.

396 Leavis, Q. D. "Jane Austen," in A Selection from
     Scrutiny. Comp. F. R. Leavis. Cambridge,
     Engl.: Univ. Press, 1968. II, 1-80. This
     essay appeared originally in a series of
     articles as follows: (1)--"A Critical Theory
     of Jane Austen's Writings," Scrutiny, 10
     (1941), 61-87; (2)--"A Critical Theory of
     Jane Austen's Writings (II): Lady Susan into
     Mansfield Park," Scrutiny, 10 (1941, 1942),
     114-42, 272-94; (3)--"A Critical Theory of
     Jane Austen's Writings: III. The Letters,"
     Scrutiny, 12 (1944), 104-19. See also 5,
     227, 258, 281.

     So far was JA from writing by miraculous

inspiration, that in her we have "a uniquely docu-
mented case of the origin and development of artistic expression." She wrote unceasingly, in a series
"of thoroughly conscious, laborious, separate draft-
ings. . . . Her novels are geological structures,
the earliest layer going back to her earliest writings, with subsequent accretions from her reading,
her personal life and those lives most closely con-
nected with hers, all recast--and this is what gives
them their coherence and artistic significance--
under the pressure of deep disturbances in her own
emotional life at a given time." Generally, an
early draft becomes in idea the novel subsequently
published at the point when she changes her position
as author from the outside (where she is satirically
above what happens in the fiction) to the inside.

Just as E derives from The Watsons, so does MP
from Lady Susan (via an epistolary intermediary of
1808-1809). MP, though a problem partly because it
does not fully assimilate elements from its precur-
sors, is also greatly superior to them in its richness and polish.

JA's letters destroy the Victorian myth about
her character and novels. The basic fact of her
letters is that "the world of the novels was not
the world of Miss Austen's life but only a selection from it, made in order to facilitate certain
intentions of the novelist."

397   Lodge, David, ed. Jane Austen, Emma: A Casebook.
London: Macmillan, 1968.

Rev. (with other works) in TLS, 29 Aug. 1968,
p. 927; (with another work) by B. C. Southam in
SoRA, 3 (1969), 281-83.

(In addition to the essays listed below, this
collection reprints several early nineteenth-century
comments and various abridged critical pieces from
the later nineteenth and twentieth centuries.)

David Lodge, "Introduction," pp. 11-25. Although the nineteenth century debated JA's status
as a classic, modern critics have accepted her
prominence in English letters and have focused
instead on the precise nature of her achievement.
In E the central issues are: "the character of Emma
and our response to her, the nature of the adjustment she makes to her world, and the relationship of
the world of Emma to the world of actuality. These

are questions of meaning, but they involve at every point questions of form."

Arnold Kettle, "Emma," pp. 89-103. (See 354.)

Marvin Mudrick, "Irony as Form: Emma," pp. 104-29. (See 5.)

Edgar F. Shannon, "Emma: Character and Construction," pp. 130-47. (See 82.)

Lionel Trilling, "Emma and the Legend of Jane Austen," pp. 148-69. (See 103.)

Mark Schorer, "The Humiliation of Emma Woodhouse," pp. 170-87. (See 126.)

R. E. Hughes, "The Education of Emma Woodhouse," pp. 188-94. (See 166.)

Wayne Booth, "Control of Distance in Jane Austen's Emma," pp. 195-216. (See 151.)

Malcolm Bradbury, "Jane Austen's Emma," pp. 217-31. (See 184.)

W. J. Harvey, "The Plot of Emma," pp. 232-47. (See 351.)

398   Manning, Olivia. "Introduction" to Northanger
        Abbey. London: Pan, 1968, pp. 5-20.

NA uses "a multi-narration technique" and an irony that "is a matter of debunking." Though not completely transformed from its burlesque beginnings, NA still shows that JA's "genius haunts our time. Her people are recognizable in our daily lives: her aversion from cheapness, loose emotion, empty rhetoric, heavy handed indifference to suffering, her concern with kindness, honesty, reason, and right conduct, inform her novels with a goodness that we recognize as moral inspiration."

399   Marshall, Sarah Latimer. "Rationality and Delu-
        sion in Jane Austen's Emma." UMSE, 9 (1968),
        57-67.

"Since this umbrella-like atmosphere [of rationality] . . . pervades Emma; since the characters . . . reveal their dependence on common sense and judgment; and since the consequent distortion of judgment or misconstruction of common sense causes the major blunders, the concept of rationality provides, in a sense, the web for Emma."

400 Miyazaki, Koichi, and Shizuko Kawamoto. Shosetsu no Seiki. Tokyo: Kaitaku-sha, 1968.

(Not seen.)

401 Moler, Kenneth L. Jane Austen's Art of Allusion. Lincoln: Univ. of Nebraska Press, 1968.

Rev. (with other works) by Lloyd W. Brown in ECS, 3 (1969), 145-48; (with another work) by William D. Schaefer in NCF, 24 (1969), 247-48; by Howard S. Babb in SAQ, 68 (1969), 434-35; by Alistair M. Duckworth in Modern Philology, 68 (1970), 112-15; by Paul Goetsch in NS, 19 (1970), 582-84; by Jeanne Delbaere-Garant in RLV, 36 (1970), 217-18; (with other works) by J. Hillis Miller in SEL, 10 (1970), 204.

Introductory: JA's borrowings from contemporary authors are "akin to 'allusions,' implied references that she expects to affect her audience." Among the intellectual preoccupations common to her novels are, first, self-knowledge--the knowledge of one's individual propensities to error--and, second, the classification of personality by the relative predominance of art or nature.

NA: In the tradition of Fielding and Burney, NA treats the "young lady's introduction to the world." Catherine develops from an ingenue, who assumes that all others share her natural goodness, through an intermediate stage of "'black and white' moral vision" derived from her Quixotic novel reading, and, finally, she arrives at a state of relative maturity by submitting her "preconceptions to the test of experience."

S and S: The difference between S and S and similar indictments of sensibility by Maria Edgeworth and Jane West is that JA ultimately dramatizes the limitations of Elinor, "the sensible sister," as well as those of Marianne. In her refusal to credit the seriousness of Marianne's decline and in her eagerness to believe Willoughby is only a "callous libertine," Elinor is "not the novel's standard of moral perfection but one of its candidates for self-knowledge."

P and P: "At the beginning of Pride and Prejudice Darcy is a pompous Burney-Richardson aristocrat . . . as well as a representative of 'art' and excessive class pride; Elizabeth is a determined anti-Evelina as well as a symbol for 'nature' and aggressive individualism. The marriage at the end of the story joins a properly humbled patrician hero and an anti-Evelina who has also undergone a partial reformation."

MP: An examination of "the motif of feminine accomplishments" shows that the moral status of the Crawfords is aligned with that of the Bertram family. Sir Thomas advocates and his daughters are products of an education which emphasizes the superficial and the "worldly." The shallow and morally unconcerned Mary also is "merely accomplished." Fanny, though occasionally naive and "schoolmarm-ish," is the "anti-type to the merely accomplished woman" and thus becomes a "representative of more solid and substantial values."

E: Emma's mistakes result from her attempt to deal with the "life around her as if it were the material for an impossibly heightened and perfect 'history.'" However, E not only condemns, but also vindicates the romantic imagination. JA dissolves the antitheses of romance and reality, of imagination and judgment, and in doing so she strikes "a mean between the 'romance' of Mrs. Radcliffe or Charlotte Smith and the 'reality' of Crabbe."

P: Viewed in its historical and literary context, P is not JA's capitulation to "romance." Rather, Anne, who embodies the novel's moral norm, blends prudence with romance. Wentworth, who enters as a "character type of the modern philosopher" in the tradition of Rousseau and Godwin, finally recognizes that the ability to control one's feelings is not weak-mindedness. Thus Wentworth and romance are reconciled, through Anne, to Lady Russell and prudence.

402 Nenadál, Radoslav. "Lyrická komedie empírového salónu," the introduction to Anna Elliotová [Persuasion]. Trans. Eva Ruxová. Prague: Odeon, 1968, pp. 7-16.

Based upon irony and gentle humor, JA's work is a remarkable synthesis of understanding and feeling. She as author is intelligent and witty, truthful and penetrating. In Anne Elliot, JA paints a tender and sensitive self-portrait.

403   Page, Norman. "A Short Guide to Jane Austen Studies." Critical Survey, 3 (1968), 230-34.

(Provides a short history of JA criticism from Scott to B. C. Southam's Jane Austen: The Critical Heritage.)

404   Pevsner, Nikolaus. "The Architectural Setting of Jane Austen's Novels." JWCI, 31 (1968), 404-22.

Having an interest only in people, JA is consistently vague when she comes to describe buildings and their furnishings. Yet still, as regards mansions and parsonages, and various lodgings in London and several resorts, "there is enough to be got out of the novels for anyone eager to know what life was lived by the narrow range of classes" she deals with.

405   Southam, B. C., ed. Critical Essays on Jane Austen. London: Routledge & Kegan Paul, 1968.

Rev. by Margaret Drabble in Manchester Guardian Weekly, 5 Dec. 1968, p. 15; by Julian Mitchell in New Statesman, 6 Dec. 1968, p. 810; (with another work) in TLS, 15 May 1969, p. 526; by John E. Jordan in ELN, 8 Supp. (1970), 19-20; (with other works) by J. Hillis Miller in SEL, 10 (1970), 202; (with other works) by Isabel Rivers in CritQ, 13 (1971), 282-83.

B. C. Southam, "Introduction," pp. xi-xvi. "Any critic convinced of Jane Austen's greatness . . . bears the responsibility of explaining the remarkable phenomenon of such 'limited' greatness."

John Bayley, "The 'Irresponsibility' of Jane Austen," pp. 1-20. (See 393.)

Brigid Brophy, "Jane Austen and the Stuarts,"

pp. 21-38. Like the juvenilia generally, her "History of England" satirizes, and thereby overcomes, "the high-handed absolutism with which daydreaming technique abolishes the obstructions put in its way by time and logic. And in overcoming the absolutism of daydream technique Jane Austen overcame the absolutism of daydream itself and her own nostalgic tendency to go back through her own history and, as it were, re-enthrone the Stuarts."

Denis Donoghue, "A View of _Mansfield Park_," pp. 39-59. JA's "witty and superior voice" dominates _E_ and _P and P_; but in her other novels "there is far less irony, far less 'voice,' the meaning is entrusted to facts which largely speak for themselves." _MP_, approachable by way of the eighteenth-century moralists, focuses on "the bristling relation" among truth (which "charm" and selfishness lay snares for), the moral sense (to which JA "adds" education), and the integrity of the self.

Robert Garis, "Learning Experience and Change," pp. 60-82. JA successfully dramatizes learning experience and change when, as in _P and P_ and especially in _E_, "she is looking directly at the learning character and the learning experience, and seeing the rest of the action from this perspective, through this experience; she fails [as in _S and S_ and _MP_] when this is not the case." She succeeds when learning feels like a gain, fails when it constitutes a loss. As a conscious rewriting of _S and S_, _P_ shows JA's own learning experience.

D. W. Harding, "Character and Caricature in Jane Austen," pp. 83-105. Some of JA's fictional figures "are offered as full and natural portraits of imaginable people; others, while certainly referring to types of people we might easily have come across, are yet presented with such exaggeration and simplification that our response to them is expected to be rather different." The two modes of portraiture can interact, creating special effects, and caricatures, "maintained by concentrating on the outer layers of social behaviour," can develop more normal features.

Gilbert Ryle, "Jane Austen and the Moralists," pp. 106-22. (See 325.)

J. I. M. Stewart, "Tradition and Miss Austen," pp. 123-35. JA "is the mistress of a quaintly confined world, inviolate to ideas and admitting only the most distant reverberations of the passions, and she brings to it a transforming vis comica." But her true status as a novelist depends finally on her creation of personality. What is most important to her "is to understand and convey the play of moral feelings, and of other feelings," within her own area of fiction.

Tony Tanner, "Jane Austen and 'The Quiet Thing' --A Study of Mansfield Park," pp. 136-61. (See 328.)

Rachel Trickett, "Jane Austen's Comedy and the Nineteenth Century," pp. 162-81. "The pitiless perfection of art, the intellectualism of art for art's sake which the nineteenth-century critics found in her was nothing more than the traditional genius of comedy unrecognized in a more solemn period." Whereas P and P and E are successful comic constructions, P fails because its comic form does not suit its content.

Angus Wilson, "The Neighbourhood of Tombuctoo: Conflicts in Jane Austen's Novels," pp. 182-99. The limited range of her art was not a valuable discipline, but "a deforming one; it distorted the balance between the two views of life whose conflict made her art." The dilemma in her books may be called "sense and sensibility; or we may say head and heart, prudence and impulse, rest and motion, or wit and plain speech, or country and town, though . . . the opposing parts are themselves ambiguously represented in her novels."

406   Southam, B. C., ed. Jane Austen: The Critical Heritage. New York: Barnes & Noble, 1968. See also 460.

Rev. by Gene Koppel in ArQ, 24 (1968), 375-76; (with other works) by William D. Schaefer in NCF, 23 (1968), 252; by John Bayley in Spectator, 16 Feb. 1968, pp. 202-03; (with other works) by Carl Woodring in SEL, 8 (1968), 741; in TLS, 1 Feb. 1968, p. 110 [and see corr., Arnold Palmer and reviewer, 22 Feb., p. 189, and Marilyn Butler, 29 Feb., p. 205]; (with another work) by A. Walton Litz in VS, 12 (1968), 259-62; (with other works) by A. O. J. Cockshut in RES, 20 (1969), 514-16; by W. D. Maxwell-Mahon in UES, 7 (May 1969), 94-95; by John E. Jordan in ELN, 8 Supp. (1970), 20.

(This collection of criticism from 1812 to 1870 includes contemporary and posthumous reviews, JA's collected "Opinions," mentions of the novels in early readers' letters, and later critical appraisals.)

"Introduction," pp. 1-33. Between the publication of S and S and the Memoir (1870), "fewer than fifty articles mention Jane Austen at any length and of these only six take her as the principal subject." And because JA was not a widely read novelist, her admirers provided a series of introductory pieces rather than a cumulative body of criticism. Of the contemporary reviewers Scott was alone in recognizing JA as a great writer, indeed, as the progenitor of the "modern novel"--one which imitates ordinary, verifiable reality. Building on Scott's premises, Whately argues that with JA's literary innovation there came a similar advance in criticism: the novel could now be taken seriously as an art form and its criticism as a significant intellectual activity. From 1821 to 1870 JA was overshadowed by the major novelists then publishing, but she nevertheless retained a small following. The readers of the early decades often found JA deficient in romantic idealism, and later readers believed she lacked "high seriousness." Charlotte Brontë's correspondence with G. H. Lewes and W. S. Williams provides the key statements of the Romantic case against JA. Lewes's rebuttal insists on JA's technical mastery and the wide range of experience her admittedly limited fictional world contains. Julia Kavanagh's comments give the impression that the critic is writing out of her enjoyment of JA's novels. Mrs. Oliphant emphasizes JA's "'fine vein of feminine cynicism,'" her reduction of social sins to the level of absurdity. In the outstanding piece of nineteenth-century Austen criticism, Richard Simpson recounts the development of JA's art. He discerns irony as the primary instrument of an all-embracing judgment of society, and he scrutinizes JA's claim to be a historian of society. Simpson's review of the Memoir marks the beginning of the gradual displacement of "dear Aunt Jane" by JA as an ironic and critical genius.

407 Varma, Devendra P., ed. The Northanger Set of Jane Austen Horrid Novels. 7 vols. [Lawrence Flammenberg, The Necromancer; or, The Tale of the Black Forest, trans. Peter Teuthold; The Marquis of Grosse, Horrid Mysteries, trans.

Peter Will; Francis Lathom, The Midnight Bell; Eliza Parsons, Castle of Wolfenbach; Eliza Parsons, The Mysterious Warning; Regina Maria Roche, Clermont; Eleanor Sleath, The Orphan of the Rhine.] London: Folio Press, 1968.

Rev. in TLS, 1 Aug. 1968, p. 826.

(In addition to the introduction to Castle of Wolfenbach, there are introductions to each of the other six novels, which discuss the authors and their works.)

"Introduction" to Castle of Wolfenbach, pp. xiii-xxiv. In the sixth chapter of NA Isabella Thorpe recommends to Catherine Morland seven "horrid" novels which, until Michael Sadleir and Montague Summers verified their existence, early in the twentieth century, many critics believed not to be real books. JA chose these Gothic romances deliberately, picking them "for the quality of the tales rather than for their titles alone. She thus achieved a very representative choice of the typical works of fiction of the period."

408 Wildi, Max. "Nachwort" to Mansfield Park. Trans.
      Trude Fein. Zürich: Manesse Verlag, 1968,
      pp. 649-76.

An experimental novel within JA's canon, MP eliminates the character oppositions of S and S and P and P and replaces the oppositions with variations of a central theme. In the novel's final chapters JA identifies completely with Fanny, the romantic soul who is entirely explicable by her moral feelings and through whom the reader views the virtues of Mansfield.

409 Wilson, Angus. "Jane Austen between the Lines."
      Observer (London), 2 June 1968, pp. 23-24, 26-
      27, and 29.

The tonal change from the early burlesques to the sobriety of the mature novels requires a biographical explanation. Late in her life JA found comfort in her "memory of past love and the Christian religion," which may have influenced her to suppress Marianne and Emma by marrying them to paternal husbands. JA's Evangelicalism and her distrust of cleverness appear also in MP and are

not relieved until P, which combines "risk and wit
. . . with professional duty."

410 Wycherley, H. Alan. "Jane Austen and I." CEA, 30
     (Feb. 1968), 11.

     (Humorous sketch.)

411 Zimmerman, Everett. "Pride and Prejudice in Pride
     and Prejudice." NCF, 23 (1968), 64-73.

     In P and P "the skill shown in using the titu-
     lar qualities to keep the moral framework of the
     novel clear while presenting a novelistic world of
     great complexity is one of the triumphs of Jane
     Austen's developing technique." Pride consists in
     detachment from others, prejudice in a self-inter-
     ested involvement; both distort vision. But finally
     Elizabeth "learns to judge accurately while deeply
     involved."

                         1969

412 Brown, Lloyd W. "The Comic Conclusion in Jane
     Austen's Novels." PMLA, 84 (1969), 1582-87.

     JA's comic conclusion is "basically parodic in
     structure and theme, and is constantly used through-
     out her fiction as the final summary of themes."
     Her typical conclusion presents realistically the
     ultimate development of character and situation and
     allocates appropriate rewards and punishments. In
     MP, as in her other novels, JA employs "the comic
     conclusion as an ironic vehicle for final judgments
     on the individual and his society."

413 Bussby, Frederick. Jane Austen in Winchester.
     The Close, Winchester: Friends of Winchester
     Cathedral, 1969.

     (A booklet on JA's association with Win-
     chester.)

414 Calder-Marshall, Arthur. "Introduction" to Emma.
     London: Pan, 1969, pp. 5-16.

A great novel "not merely for its artistic
perfection, the compression of its interrelated
plots, and the subtlety of its writing, but also
for its ironic wisdom, its passion, and its moral
discrimination," E was, in its use of point of view,
much ahead of its time. The book deals with matchmaking, reconciliation to life, and the problems of
communication.

415 Chapman, R. W., ed. Northanger Abbey and Persuasion, Vol. V in The Novels of Jane Austen: The
Text Based on Collation of the Early Editions--
With Notes, Indexes, and Illustrations from
Contemporary Sources. 3rd ed. [with changes
and additions to text and notes by Mary Lascelles, 1965, and in "this impression Miss Lascelles has replaced the faulty and incomplete 1871
version of the original ending of Persuasion by
reprinting R. W. Chapman's transcript of the
manuscript, with his notes"]. 6 vols. London:
Oxford Univ. Press, 1969. This edition was
first published in 1933.

(The standard edition.)

Appendixes:

"Chronology of Northanger Abbey," pp. 297-301.
By MacKinnon's assumption that JA used the calendar
for 1798, "the Monday of p. 193 would be 26 March,
on which day sunset at Greenwich is at 6 hrs. 21
mins. This may indicate that Mr. MacKinnon's dates
are a week too late."

"Chronology of Persuasion," pp. 302-04. In P,
JA is "as exact as ever; but there is no indication
that she used a calendar."

"Topography of Bath," p. 305.

"The Mysteries of Udolpho," pp. 306-12. (Reprints the passages of Udolpho "by which Miss Austen
was particularly inspired" in NA.)

General Index of Literary Allusions, of Real
Persons, and of Real Places, pp. 317-33. (Collected from the letters and fragments, as well as
from the six novels.)

416 Collins, Thomas J. "Some Mutual Sets of Friends:

Moral Monitors in _Emma_ and _Our Mutual Friend_."
Dickensian, 65 (1969), 32-34.

The significant parallels in the treatment of
Mr. Knightley and John Harmon, morally noble characters who help establish standards by which to measure others, show that JA and Dickens have "a shared
sensitivity to human relationships, a shared insight
into the human character, and a common desire to
create fictional worlds in which moral standards are
clearly, but not obtrusively, enunciated."

417 Corsa, Helen Storm. "A Fair but Frozen Maid: A
       Study of Jane Austen's _Emma_." _L&P_, 19 (1969),
       101-24.

The first line of Garrick's riddle forms a
statement of the theme of the novel as a whole.
Emma avoids an awareness of her own instinctual
needs, retreating behind "her inhibiting defenses,
notably, her infantile narcissism and posture of
omnipotence." The novel moves "from denial to confrontation," and, like Oedipus, Emma finally matures
by becoming aware of, even perhaps accepting, her
erotic desires.

418 Craik, W. A. "Introduction" to _Persuasion_. London:
       Pan, 1969, pp. 7-22. This edition includes the
       cancelled chapter.

"At her most assured and mature" in _P_, JA succeeds, "as usual, in being both comic and serious"
and in portraying "the interior life of her creations." Though all her novels show her to be a
master of economy, _P_ is more compressed than any,
"and is in fact in an intermediate state that she
would later have developed into a full-length
novel."

419 Craik, W. A. _Jane Austen in Her Time_. London:
       Nelson, 1969. See also 513.

Rev. (with another work) in _TLS_, 27 Nov.
1969, p. 1357.

(With more than fifty illustrations, this
account of social conditions, and especially of
middle-class and country life, in the England of
JA's time "attempts to give the reader enough

[information] . . . to enable him to read her novels with the understanding the author assumes he
will possess.")

420   Davis, Earle. "Jane Austen and the Comic Flaw."
          KanQ, 1 (Summer 1969), 23-34.

          "What Jane Austen does best is to portray
characters who have a 'Comic Flaw.'" Her comedy
"operates through the unerring diagnosis of human
weakness, because she, more than other novelists,
had an uncanny sense for portraying human imperfec-
tions and flaws without losing sympathy for her
characters and their comic slips from the normalcy
she admired."

421   Draffan, Robert A.   "Mansfield Park: Jane Austen's
          Bleak House." EIC, 19 (1969), 371-84.

          Interpretations based on Mansfield Park's
being a "promised land" are mistaken. "Mansfield
Park denies life"; "we see it throughout as the
victim of its own inflexibility." Both Sir Thomas
and his wife are pompous fools, "obsessed by the
desire to be comfortable." Their elegance and
refinement crumble under pressure and finally are
demonstrated to be worthless, hollow, and incapable
of assimilating even so innocuous an outsider as
Fanny.

422   Ellis, David. "The Irony of Mansfield Park." CR,
          No. 12 (1969), pp. 107-19.

          Most critics severely underestimate the extent
to which irony is important to MP. Every character
in the book, including Fanny, is presented with JA's
typical complicating irony. And it is, finally, the
coexistence of warmth and tenderness with the
author's "ingrained scepticism which makes Mansfield
Park such a great novel."

423   Farnham, Anthony E.   "The Engagement of Elizabeth
          Bennet and Fitzwilliam Darcy," the introduction
          to an extract from Pride and Prejudice, in A
          Sourcebook in the History of English. Ed.
          Anthony E. Farnham. New York: Holt, Rinehart
          and Winston, 1969, pp. 139-40.

"Though the language of civil conversation
enables us to envision the scene only indirectly
. . . the reader should not fail to encounter a
twinkle in the eye of Jane Austen--an awareness
that civility is itself half hope and half terror,
at once a means of approach to the ineffable and a
defense against too sudden exposure."

424 Fergusson, Sir James, of Kilkerran. "Scots in Jane
        Austen," in The Man behind Macbeth and Other
        Studies. London: Faber and Faber, 1969, pp.
        174-84.

        JA's use of Scottish names in her novels
indicates her fidelity to contemporary English life.
Foremost among the Scots in her canon are the Elliots of Kellynch Hall, and the Crawford group in
MP (from the Admiral to Lord Stornaway) seems also
to be of Scottish descent.

425 Freeman, Jean. Jane Austen in Bath. Alton, Hamp-
        shire: Jane Austen Society, 1969.

        (This illustrated booklet describes Bath and
JA's association with it.)

426 Gilson, D. J. "The Early American Editions of Jane
        Austen." BC, 18 (1969), 340-52. See also
        497.

        JA was probably unaware of "the American edi-
tion of Emma, published by Mathew Carey of Philadelphia in 1816." Of this edition two copies are
extant. "No other American edition of any of
Jane Austen's novels is known before the publication of all six novels in 1832 and 1833 by Carey &
Lea of Philadelphia."

427 Gilson, D. J. "Jane Austen Bibliography." Corr.
        in TLS, 17 Apr. 1969, p. 415.

        (Proposed updating of Keynes's bibliography.)

428 Ishizuka, Torao. Jane Austen Kenkyu. Tokyo:
        Kobunsha, 1969.

        (Not seen.)

429 The Jane Austen Society: Report for the Year, 1968.
Alton, Hampshire: Jane Austen Society [1969].

(In addition to the guest speaker's address to
the Society's annual general meeting, abstracted
below, this report includes, among other things,
several brief notes.)

B. C. Southam, "Jane Austen and Her Readers,"
pp. 22-32. JA, who was concerned for what was said
of her novels, knew two kinds of contemporary
readers: first, the ordinary novel-reader, who might
not appreciate her realism; and second, "the relation or friend whose interests and tastes were close
to her own, who . . . contributed a particular quality to her writing: an intimacy of tone and address
which somehow involves us with the author herself."

430 Kroeber, Karl. "Perils of Quantification: The
Exemplary Case of Jane Austen's Emma," in
Statistics and Style. Ed. Lubomír Doležel and
Richard W. Bailey. (Mathematical Linguistics
and Automatic Language Processing, 6.) New
York: American Elsevier, 1969, pp. 197-213.

(See 505.)

431 Kronenberger, Louis. "Jane Austen: Lady Susan and
Pride and Prejudice," in The Polished Surface:
Essays in the Literature of Worldliness. New
York: Knopf, 1969, pp. 127-50.

JA's basic theme is the conflict between human
and social values. Lady Susan presents an unhumor-
ous form of worldliness, P and P a comic one. JA
wisely chose the latter as her prevailing form.

432 Laski, Marghanita. Jane Austen and Her World. New
York: Viking Press, 1969.

Rev. by Claire Tomalin in New Statesman, 25
July 1969, pp. 117-18; in TLS, 28 Aug. 1969, p. 948.

(This biography contains more than one hundred
pictures depicting the Austen family, various contemporaries, and different aspects of the life of
the period.)

433 Lawry, J. S. "'Decided and Open': Structure in
Emma." NCF, 24 (1969), 1-15.

Emma's misuse of fancy is "so fixed that it
constructs a paradigm, seemingly repetitive and un-
alterable, within the action." Opposed to the pattern of her imaginative faults is the stronger and
more natural "pattern of rational marriage . . .
reached by means of Emma's contrition." But not
until she is brought to believe that her fault has
cost her the love of Mr. Knightley can Emma fulfill
the ideal of rational marriage.

434   Loofbourow, John W.   "A Critical and Biographical
        Profile of Jane Austen," the introduction to
        Pride and Prejudice. New York: Watts [1969],
        pp. vii-x. This essay appeared originally in
        The Encyclopedia Americana, 1968.

"Her novels are poised in time between the
neoclassicism of the eighteenth century and the
lyricism of the romantic movement. Her spare, witty
style and satiric insight are in the eighteenth-
century tradition; her imaginative values share the
sensitivity of the romantic poets."

435   Mansell, Darrel, Jr.   "The Date of Jane Austen's
        Revision of Northanger Abbey." ELN, 7 (1969),
        40-41.

Possible borrowings from Gilpin's Observations
on Several Parts of the Counties of Cambridge, Nor-
folk . . . suggest that NA may have been revised in
1809 or later.

436   Matache, Liliana.   "Metoda narativă oblică şi stilul
        indirect liber în romanul Emma de Jane Austen."
        Analele Universităţii Bucureşti. Literatură
        universală şi comparată, 18, No. 2 (1969), 63-
        70.

JA presents Emma's maturation through the use
of "free indirect speech (die Erlebte Rede). This
stylistical innovation allows the direct transposi-
tion of thoughts, the faithful recording of feelings, being a perfect tool for a dramatic novel,
concerned with changes and psychological analyses."

437   Matache, Liliana.   "Stilul indirect liber în romanul
        Emma (1814) de Jane Austen." Analele Univer-
        sităţii Bucuresti. Limbi Germanice, 18 (1969),
        159-68.

E, which hinges on the heroine's mystification and misunderstanding, is presented dramatically, through the subtle interplay of dialogue and free indirect speech (die Erlebte Rede). "The unity of the novel is worked out by the effacement of the author resulting in a vivid bracing atmosphere, which reflects the dialectics of life, where knowledge is reached after chaotic, erroneous apprehensions."

438 Mews, Hazel. "Women Awaiting Marriage (1): Fanny Burney, Maria Edgeworth, Jane Austen," in Frail Vessels: Woman's Role in Women's Novels from Fanny Burney to George Eliot. London: Athlone Press, 1969, pp. 47-68.

The guidelines JA lays down for women's behavior are the same as those of her contemporaries, but she portrays them more profoundly. She requires her female characters "to govern themselves, control their tempers, master their feelings, exercise fortitude, cultivate sound understanding, be realistic, clear-sighted and considerate in personal and social relationships, avoid excesses of sensibility for sensibility's sake, cultivate taste and elegance of mind and manners, and, with all this, have tenderness of heart."

439 Moore, E. Margaret. "Emma and Miss Bates: Early Experiences of Separation and the Theme of Dependency in Jane Austen's Novels." SEL, 9 (1969), 573-85.

JA's novelistic preoccupations with dependency and with devaluating mother-figures require a biographical explanation. "The early separation experiences to which Jane Austen was exposed" incapacitated her from relating to her mother or to anyone else. It is for this reason that Emma's ridicule of Miss Bates (a mother-figure) is so poignant.

440 Page, Norman. "Categories of Speech in Persuasion." MLR, 64 (1969), 734-41.

In P, JA uses at least four categories of speech: narrative, authorial comment, direct speech, and free indirect speech. Most important, this last category combines the "advantages of direct and indirect speech," thereby bringing "the reader close

enough to the character's consciousness" to approxi-
mate a sense of interior monologue, yet preserving
an objectivity that renders overt authorial commentary possible.

441 Page, Norman. "Jane Austen and 'The Best Chosen
        Language.'" WascanaR, 4, No. 2 (1969), 67-76.

        (See 540.)

442 Pérez Martín, María Jesús. "Jane Austen y la Utopía
        de Tomás Moro." FMod, Nos. 33-34 (1969), pp.
        115-20.

        There are many similarities between JA and Sir
Thomas More, but a crucial difference also. They
are alike as writers, in their elegance, sustained
good taste, irony, assured control, and sharp insight into human weakness; and they resemble each
other, too, in their desire to preserve individual,
familial, and social calm. They differ, however, in
that she lacks any transcendental element.

443 Phillipps, K. C. "Jane Austen's English." NM, 70
        (1969), 319-38.

        (See 482.)

444 Phillipps, K. C. "Lucy Steele's English." ES,
        Anglo-American Supp. (1969), pp. lv-lxi.

        Lucy Steele's faulty use of language was
acceptable by the criteria established before the
work of grammarians like Lowth and Priestley.

445 Rubinstein, E. "Jane Austen's Novels: The Meta-
        phor of Rank," in Literary Monographs. Ed.
        Eric Rothstein and Richard N. Ringler.
        Madison: Univ. of Wisconsin Press, 1969. II,
        101-93 and 218-25.

        Rev. (with other works) by J. Hillis Miller
in SEL, 10 (1970), 203; by John E. Jordan in ELN,
9 Supp. (1971), 25-26.

        JA employs "English social history as one of
her principal sources of metaphor, using birth and
rank" as the means of dramatizing "the interplay

between the old and the new, the tension between the
established classes and those armed mainly with
their own attainments."

NA, S and S, and The Watsons: Although a significant theme of S and S is the contest between the
middle class and the aristocracy, the social issues
of neither NA nor S and S are fully accommodated to
their fictional structures. Beginning with The
Watsons JA focuses specifically on the conflict of
"older hierarchic social values and newer democratic
ones."

P and P and MP: In P and P the confrontation of
the middle class and the nobility receives a classic
formulation. But JA portrays the "merger" of the
two classes in Elizabeth's discovery that the traditional "perquisites and obligations of social rank"
are indeed worthy of respect. In MP tradition becomes almost cultish. "The baronetcy emerges in
this novel as the last bastion of English country
tradition, surrounded by a grasping lower bourgeoisie and by an aristocracy which no longer partici-
pates (if it ever did) in the country traditions."

E and P: The ideals of MP are critically examined in both E and P. In E Highbury replaces
Mansfield as the representative of country and
middle-class tradition. Highbury, a microcosm of
English society, is characterized by freedom of
social intercourse among its several ranks.
Emma's error is to misinterpret this freedom as a
denial of all hierarchic social arrangements. P
completely repudiates the ideals of MP. Pride in
rank is reduced to vanity, while individual achievement, as represented by the naval class, is consistently held up for approval.

446 Rubinstein, E. "Northanger Abbey: The Elder
         Morlands and 'John Homespun.'" PLL, 5 (1969),
         434-40.

NA "is concerned with two radically different
ways of perceiving the world: the first, embodied
by Catherine before Bath and the Abbey, and embodied
no less dramatically by her 'proverb'-loving mother
[as illustrated in John Homespun's letter to The
Mirror], derives from the inclination to accede to
doctrinaire authority of one kind or another; the
second, embodied by the educated Catherine, derives
from the willingness to submit to the greater truths
of individual awareness."

447 Rubinstein, E., ed. Twentieth Century Interpreta-
     tions of Pride and Prejudice: A Collection of
     Critical Essays. Englewood Cliffs, N. J.:
     Prentice-Hall, 1969.

          Rev. by T. J. Verster in UES, 8 (Mar. 1970),
     52-53.

          E. Rubinstein, "Introduction," pp. 1-18. The
     charge that JA is trivialized by the absence of a
     view of mortality, man's destiny, and sexuality is
     refuted by acknowledging, first, that romantic
     comedy always excludes death, second, that JA does
     depict the dissolution of the aristocracy and the
     rise of the middle classes, and, finally, that a
     novel whose dénouement depends upon seduction (for
     example, P and P) is hardly prudish. She chooses
     courtship as the crucial moment of a young adult's
     life.

          Dorothy Van Ghent, "On Pride and Prejudice,"
     pp. 19-30. (See 31.)

          Reuben A. Brower, "Light and Bright and
     Sparkling: Irony and Fiction in Pride and Preju-
     dice," pp. 31-45. (See 164.)

          Samuel Kliger, "Jane Austen's Pride and Preju-
     dice in the Eighteenth-Century Mode," pp. 46-58.
     (See 312.)

          A. Walton Litz, "Into the Nineteenth Century:
     Pride and Prejudice," pp. 59-69. (See 281.)

          Mary Lascelles, "Narrative Art in Pride and
     Prejudice," pp. 70-77. (See 225.)

          E. M. Halliday, "Narrative Perspective in
     Pride and Prejudice," pp. 77-83. (See 140.)

          Mordecai Marcus, "A Major Thematic Pattern in
     Pride and Prejudice," pp. 83-87. (See 172.)

          Charles J. McCann, "Setting and Character in
     Pride and Prejudice," pp. 87-96. (See 251.)

          Andrew H. Wright, "Heroines, Heroes, and
     Villains in Pride and Prejudice," pp. 97-110. (See
     33.)

          Douglas Bush, "Mrs. Bennet and the Dark Gods:
     The Truth about Jane Austen," pp. 111-15. (See
     73.)

448 Sørensen, Knud. "Johnsonese in Northanger Abbey: A
       Note on Jane Austen's Style." ES, 50 (1969),
       390-97.

       "Johnsonese modes of expression are distinctly
     traceable in Jane Austen, as regards both form and
     content." Both Johnson and JA have an inclination
     to three-member sentence structures, whose third
     member receives most stress.

449 Southam, Brian C. "Jane Austen: 1775-1817," in The
       New Cambridge Bibliography of English Litera-
       ture. Ed. George Watson. Cambridge, Engl.:
       Univ. Press, 1969. Vol. III ["1800-1900"],
       cols. 692-700.

       (A selective bibliography of bibliographies,
     collections and editions of the novels, minor works,
     and letters, and criticism.)

450 Spector, Robert Donald, ed. Emma, with an Introduc-
       tion, Notes, Biographical Sketch, and a Selec-
       tion of Background Materials and Commentaries.
       New York: Bantam, 1969.

       (In addition to the essays listed below, this
     edition of E includes various critical comments from
     the nineteenth and early twentieth centuries.)

       Robert Donald Spector, "Introduction: Creating
     a Masterpiece," pp. vii-xiii. In E, JA shows that
     she "fully understood the nature of her art: how to
     convey moral sense through the characters and their
     actions; how to adapt point of view to the needs and
     purpose of a particular novel. At the same time,
     those things that she had always done well, she was
     now doing at her best."

       Q. D. Leavis, "How The Watsons Became Emma,"
     pp. 454-59. (See 396.)

       B. C. Southam, "Why The Watsons Did Not Become
     Emma," pp. 460-63. (See 258.)

       Joseph M. Duffy, Jr., "Emma: The Awakening from
     Innocence," pp. 479-83. (See 43.)

       Edgar F. Shannon, Jr., "Rhythm in Emma," pp.
     484-88. (See 82.)

451   Strauch, Gérard. "Jane Austen's Response to Fanny
        Burney." BFLS, 47 (1969), 217-31.

      From "the point of view of Jane Austen's man-
agement of her narrative material, Fanny Burney's
influence appears at once to have been vaster in
extent, and to have elicited a response more uni-
formly critical in nature, than has hitherto been
assumed." Especially in S and S, P and P, NA, and
P, "the theme and plot are developed from Burneyan
precedents by means of . . . critical rewriting."
JA thereby transcends the techniques, psychological realism, and moral significance of her predecessor.

452   Tanner, Tony. "Introduction" to his ed. of Sense
        and Sensibility. Baltimore: Penguin, 1969,
        pp. 7-34. See also 513.

      Rev. (with other works) by J. Hillis Miller
in SEL, 10 (1970), 203.

      The matters of abiding concern S and S treats
are "obscured if we regard it as an early casualty
in an evolving genre." S and S is not simplistic,
as Litz and others would have it (see 281), but
complex--in the handling of sense and sensibility,
property and marriage, secrecy and illness. The
book's action, taking place at that point where the
forces of private and public worlds impinge on each
other, reveals the difficulties and paradoxes of
life in society.

453   Welty, Eudora. "A Note on Jane Austen." Shenan-
        doah, 20 (Spring 1969), 3-7.

      JA ardently believed "that the unit of every-
thing worth knowing in life is in the family, that
family relationships are the natural basis of every
other relationship and the source of understanding
all the others." Her "work at its best seems as
nearly flawless as any fiction could be."

454   Zimmerman, Everett. "The Function of Parody in
        Northanger Abbey." MLQ, 30 (1969), 53-63.

      NA is a unified novel. Its parody creates "a
response consonant with the nonparodic elements,"
and "the reader implied by the parody [is]

consistent with the reader implied elsewhere." JA
both attacks the conventions of sentimental fiction
and appeals to the taste for them.

455 Zimmerman, Everett. "Jane Austen and Mansfield
      Park: A Discrimination of Ironies." SNNTS, 1
      (1969), 347-56.

      "Consistent with the later stage of Jane
      Austen's development," MP differs from the earlier
      novels "not because of the absence of irony but
      because of the pervasiveness of the irony." This
      ubiquitous irony is clearest in JA's attitude toward
      her heroine. None of Fanny's judgments can be ac-
      cepted unequivocally, and her marriage to Edmund
      represents neither "complete satisfaction nor . . .
      resounding defeat."

                          1970

456 Aldington, Richard. "Jane Austen," in Richard
      Aldington: Selected Critical Writings, 1928-
      1960. Ed. Alister Kershaw. Carbondale:
      Southern Illinois Univ. Press, 1970, pp. 103-
      13. This essay appeared originally as the
      introduction to the Chawton edition of JA's
      novels (London: Wingate, 1948).

      Macaulay, Saintsbury, and Arnold Bennett, like
      many of JA's admirers, have carried their praise too
      far. Her art "may be perfect, but with the perfec-
      tion of a Tanagra statuette compared with a temple
      and cathedral." JA's triumph is that, despite her
      renunciation of great deeds and splendid settings,
      she created novels of enduring value.

457 Bellot-Antony, Michèle. "Pride and Prejudice:
      Comédie des erreurs?" LanM, 64 (Jan.-Feb.
      1970), 67-74.

      JA's comedy of errors results from her lucid
      analysis of the human condition and her faith in
      man's ability to surmount his mistakes and adapt
      to life.

458 Bradbrook, Frank W. "Introduction" to his ed. of
      Pride and Prejudice. New York: Oxford Univ.

Press, 1970, pp. vii-xvi. This edition includes textual notes and bibliography by James
Kinsley. See also 513.

Rev. (with other works) by A. Dwight Culler in
SEL, 11 (1971), 770; (with other works) in TLS, 19
Nov. 1971, p. 1438.

Consideration of P and P's sources does not
explain its achievement. JA's wit is manifest
partly "in the neatness of the patterns and antitheses formed by the various combinations, comparisons, and contrasts of characters and situations."
"The story of Pride and Prejudice is genuinely romantic, as well as realistic, with a powerful vein
of poetry beneath the surface."

459 Copeland, Catherine H. "Pride and Prejudice: A Neo-
      Classical Work in a Romantic Age." CLAJ, 14
      (1970), 156-62.

"A critical look at Pride and Prejudice . . .
leads one to the conclusion that [JA] was certainly
more neo-classic in her inclinations than romantic."
The novel is "a satire of village life, depicting in
humorous fashion, but in polished, dignified language, the constant conflict between marital aspira-
tions and neo-classic conventions." Among P and P's
weaknesses is JA's tendency "to expound her philos-
ophies" in dialogue.

460 Draffan, Robert A. "Jane Austen and Her Time."
      History Today, 20 (1970), 190-97.

Recent critics have tended to exaggerate JA's
early reception. Contrary to the contention of
Southam and others (see 406), "Jane Austen was
largely unappreciated during her life and in the
years immediately following her death." Nor is
"the smallness of Jane Austen's early audience
. . . compensated for by its undue perceptive-
ness."

461 Ehrenpreis, Anne Henry. "Northanger Abbey: Jane
      Austen and Charlotte Smith." NCF, 25 (1970),
      343-48.

Both Camilla Stanley of "Catharine or the
Bower" and Isabella Thorpe of NA may derive from

Clarinthia Ludford in Charlotte Smith's Ethelinde.

462 Emmett, Victor J., Jr. "Jane Austen's Plots." MQ,
11 (1970), 393-409.

Plot in JA's novels, as all fiction, is the
prime agent of meaning. In NA "the peer ex machina
by means of which Catherine's husband is secured to
her complete with fortune suggests that it is the
business of Providence to provide such husbands for
such girls." This formula, with few variations,
also holds true for the later novels.

463 Gooneratne, Yasmine. Jane Austen. Cambridge,
Engl.: Univ. Press, 1970.

Rev. (with another work) in TLS, 30 July 1971,
p. 920; by John E. Jordan in ELN, 10 Supp. (1972),
30.

Introductory: Intense, subtle, critical, discriminating, JA penetrates "through the externals
of the social customs and behaviour she knew so
well, to the bases of human conduct." Her ironic
vision is relevant and faithful to our life to-
day.

Letters: "Through their successful evocation
of a personality and a milieu, by their definition
of Jane Austen's moral and artistic standards, her
letters provide a background of fact against which
we may trace" her progress as a novelist.

Minor Works: "A steady determination to see
and present life in true perspective gives a moral
strength to Jane Austen's earliest satires at the
expense of romanticism and sentimentality." In
their themes and techniques the minor works reveal
stages in her novelistic development.

NA: Though it began in literary satire, NA
gives evidence of JA's growing interest in the
psychological motivation of her characters. A
technical masterpiece, probably revised late in
her career, "the novel traces Catherine's progress
from immaturity and social unease to an adult
ability to discriminate between the valuable and
the worthless, in literature and in life."

S and S: With increasing moral seriousness

underlying her satiric treatment of money, marriage, and the doctrine of sensibility, JA insists on the need for balance and proportion in the healthy human personality. Despite structural weaknesses, the novel clearly shows her ability to create mixed character, to allow her people to reveal themselves through their own language, and to make minor figures necessary to the plot and illustrative of her themes.

P and P: For the first time completely successful in tracing the progress of a young woman's education, JA here provides an excellent example "of her habit of gazing through the social interminglings of the community to the moral standards they fulfil, or deny and betray." She is serious but playful, and stresses the need for self-respect, high principles, and commitment to life.

MP: JA's deepening moral vision and maturing novelistic technique "can be seen in the confidence with which a large number of complex characters are . . . kept in motion; in the replacement of purely comic or satiric interests by an accurately observed psychological motivation of character; in the symbolic use of a wide range of interior and outdoor settings; and in the way each of these contributes to the exploration of serious themes" like selfishness, discipline, and endurance.

E: "In a spirit of pure comedy" and with "confident ease" E treats, among other themes, selfish irresponsibility, moral education, the unity of village life, and the unmarried woman's situation in society. At the center of the novel is "the human, everyday problem of disciplining oneself to meet the demands of ordinary life."

P: JA here subordinates all her earlier interests, "notably her talent for satire and her inclination towards didacticism, to a new artistic problem, the psychological exploration of character." She sympathetically presents, in Anne Elliot, a personality which weds disciplined intelligence to intense feelings. P has striking weaknesses, owing probably to incomplete revision.

464 Gould, Gerald L.   "The Gate Scene at Sotherton in Mansfield Park." L&P, 20 (1970), 75-78.

The locked gate separating the wooded garden

from the hunting grounds is an explicit sexual image, rare in JA. In this scene she "not only prefigures crucial actions but places her key characters in illuminating typical stances."

465   Green, Maria. "Snobbery as a Pursuit and Disease in Proust and Jane Austen," in Proceedings: Pacific Northwest Conference on Foreign Languages, Twenty-First Annual Meeting, April 3-4, 1970. Ed. Ralph W. Baldner. Victoria, B. C.: Univ. of Victoria, 1970. XXI, 255-62.

JA's requirements for a peaceful social life are that one be aware of self and others, and be ready to accept others' faults. In E she shows that snobbery, more than making one ridiculous, "prevents individual self-development and, if at all common, leads to a sickness in society."

466   Harding, D. W. "Two Aspects of Jane Austen's Development." Theoria, 35 (1970), 1-16. See also corr. in Theoria, J. V. Crewe, 36 (1971), 67-68.

JA's "increasing technical command of dialogue . . . allowed facets of character to be displayed more tellingly, states of mind to be put more convincingly, and comedy effects to be achieved more swiftly and without being laboured." And as she matured, too, she developed subtler and bolder means of mingling tones of comedy and tones of seriousness.

467   Hayter, Alethea. "Xanadu at Lyme Regis." ArielE, 1 (Jan. 1970), 61-64. See also corr. in ArielE, Brian Southam, 3 (July 1972), 79.

"Jane Austen's description of Lyme Regis in Persuasion is unlike any other landscape of hers." This uniqueness may derive from the echoes in this passage of Coleridge's "Kubla Khan," around whose phrases JA's memories of the scene seem to have coalesced.

468   Hough, Graham. "Narrative and Dialogue in Jane Austen." CritQ, 12 (1970), 201-29.

JA employs five kinds of discourse in E:

authorial voice, objective narrative, colored narrative, free indirect style, and dialogue. "Her
novels reflect the social consciousness of the
feminine half of the upper bourgeoisie of her
time," but they also "point backwards" to the
world of Johnson and the mid-eighteenth century.
JA's moral values are always limited by their
application to and derivation from a closed and
insulated class, one immune from internal strains
and ultimate conflicts.

469 The Jane Austen Society: Report for the Year, 1969.
     Alton, Hampshire: Jane Austen Society [1970].

     (In addition to the guest speaker's address to
the Society's annual general meeting, abstracted
below, this report includes, among other things,
several brief notes.)

     Elizabeth Bowen, "Jane Austen and Charm," pp.
21-28. "Alert to the susceptibilities people have
with regard to each other," JA treats charm in two
ways: there is the charm one fictional character
exercises on another, and the charm of a fascinat-
ing fictional character that works on the reader.
"Evil can tarnish charm--and that is a tragedy, which
the novels lament."

470 Kaul, A. N. "Jane Austen," in The Action of English
     Comedy: Studies in the Encounter of Abstraction
     and Experience from Shakespeare to Shaw. New
     Haven: Yale Univ. Press, 1970, pp. 193-249.

     "Jane Austen's novels are the central achieve-
ment of English comedy." "She is a classic of
bourgeois comedy": JA does not question the basic
structure of society, but rather "is concerned only
with those values--love above all--which she con-
siders attainable in her society even as it stands."
Especially in NA, S and S, P and P, and P, JA medi-
ates between the view of love as possible only in
the fantasy world of sentimental fiction and the
view of love and marriage as a prudential bargain.

471 Kauvar, Elaine M. "Jane Austen and The Female
     Quixote." SNNTS, 2 (1970), 211-21.

     From Charlotte Lennox' The Female Quixote JA
borrowed "both the quixotic formula and the coming-

of-age theme." "She used what she found there in
several of her novels," notably NA, S and S, and E,
and "consistently refined it until human delusions
spring from personal quirks instead of fictional
ones."

472 Kissane, James. "Comparison's Blessed Felicity:
     Character Arrangement in Emma." SNNTS, 2
     (1970), 173-84.

     E is "a novel whose characters are revealed
and given significance primarily by the way they
stand with reference to one another." Emma's
progress from self-deception to self-awareness is
imaged in her relation to Elton, Frank, and Mr.
Knightley; her relation to Harriet, Jane, and Mrs.
Elton establishes her "essential human qualities
and worth." She is "involved with men" and "compared to women."

473 Knight, Charles A. "Irony and Mr. Knightley."
     SNNTS, 2 (1970), 185-93.

     Though Mr. Knightley represents "the highest
values" of E, he is nevertheless "an ironic character." His kindness to Harriet fosters her illusions about him and creates a relationship ironically parallel to that between Churchill and Emma.
Further, Mr. Knightley's admonitions to Emma probably stimulate, rather than curb, her matchmaking
tendency.

474 Lamont, Claire. "Introduction" to her ed. of Sense
     and Sensibility. New York: Oxford Univ. Press,
     1970, pp. vii-xxi. This edition includes tex-
     tual notes and bibliography by James Kinsley.
     See also 513.

     Rev. (with other works) by A. Dwight Culler in
SEL, 11 (1971), 770; (with other works) in TLS, 19
Nov. 1971, p. 1438.

     Despite its occasional clumsiness, S and S is
remarkable for its picture of violent emotion and
the "devastating precision" with which even minor
characters are drawn. Though JA prefers sense to
sensibility, sense itself is also criticized. "The
novel is full of quiet echoes and parallels [between
the characters] which do not press themselves on the
reader."

475 Lauber, John. "Minds Bewildered and Astray: The
        Crawfords in Mansfield Park." SNNTS, 2 (1970),
        194-210.

        "To admire the Crawfords 'properly' is to enjoy
their undeniable wit and charm, their unsurpassed
agreeability, while bearing in mind their deficiencies." "If our response to the Crawfords is 'proper,' as discriminating as Jane Austen's presentation, then . . . our response to Mansfield Park as a
whole is likely to be favorable whatever our feelings toward Fanny Price may be."

476 Lock, F. P. "Jane Austen: Some Non-Literary Manu-
        scripts in the Fitzwilliam Museum and the
        University Library Cambridge." TCBS, 5 (1970),
        145-48.

        (Prints and comments on several letters and a
fragment.)

477 Lucas, John. "Introduction" to his ed. of Mans-
        field Park. New York: Oxford Univ. Press,
        1970, pp. vii-xviii. This edition includes
        textual notes and bibliography by James
        Kinsley. See also 513.

        Rev. (with other works) by A. Dwight Culler
in SEL, 11 (1971), 770; (with other works) in TLS,
19 Nov. 1971, p. 1438.

        Though, in MP, JA "seems to be writing from a
position of evangelical earnestness which we may be
ready to find oppressively humourless and morally
priggish," in this novel actually "her moral attitudes emerge with a new complexity and authority."
She deals with conduct as a judge of character, and
the effort, focused on love, to reconcile private
and public behavior. Fanny's values are "put to
unremitting pressure and do not break under it."

478 Mays, J. C. C. Persuasion, Jane Austen: A Critical
        Introduction. Dublin: Scepter, 1970.

        JA's most "poetic" novel, with as many affini-
ties to contemporary Romantic poetry as to her own
earlier work, P retells the fairy tale of the Sleep-
ing Beauty. The story records Anne's movement from
bondage to various evil forces, including an

uncongenial environment and the past, to liberation
into an ideal society (represented by the Navy),
which can reconcile both private and public needs.
"The thematic pattern of growth, of cancellation of
one state of being by another, of loss followed by
retrieval," has its counterpart in the pervasive
autumnal mood, which is in turn dependent on the
cyclical rhythm of the seasons. Solidly embodying
its vision in a specific social framework, and
subtly intermingling tones of ironic detachment and
subjective involvement, P deals also with persuad-
ability and weakness, firmness and obstinacy.

479 McMaster, Juliet. "The Continuity of Jane Austen's
        Novels." SEL, 10 (1970), 723-39.

        JA maintains balance and proportion not only
within her novels but between them--each work qual-
ifies its predecessor or prepares for what follows.
P and P develops the superiority of head to heart
found in S and S, but finds it perverse; and Sir
Thomas' benevolent adoption of Fanny in MP becomes
in E the heroine's desire to dominate other human
beings. The social liberalism of P and P is
qualified in P, where the Romantic hero must be
chastened.

480 Myers, Sylvia H. "Womanhood in Jane Austen's
        Novels." Novel, 3 (1970), 225-32.

        Critics have overstressed the educative func-
tion of JA's heroes. Seen in terms of Erik Erik-
son's psychological distinctions, JA's novels deal
with the specifically female concerns of "inner
space"--the security of enclosure and, conversely,
the fear that "inner potential will never be ful-
filled." "Even in the narrow world of Austen's
women" is visible the pressure of mediating among
"soma, psyche and polis," that is, "the physical
life cycle, the ego and the community."

481 O'Neill, Judith, ed. Critics on Jane Austen.
        (Readings in Literary Criticism, 5.) Coral
        Gables, Fla.: Univ. of Miami Press, 1970.

        Rev. by J. W. Blench in DUJ, 33 (1971), 74-
75; by Frank McCombie in N&Q, 19 (1972), 314.

        (In addition to the essays listed below, this

collection reprints various abridged critical pieces
from the nineteenth and early twentieth centuries.)

Judith O'Neill, "Introduction," pp. vi-vii.
The student of JA needs to be wary both of the
Janeites and of those offering more sophisticated
and extreme readings of the novels.

Mary Lascelles, "Jane Austen's Style," pp. 35-
41. (See 225.)

D. W. Harding, "Regulated Hatred: An Aspect
of the Work of Jane Austen," pp. 42-49. (See 164.)

Leonard Woolf, "The Economic Determination of
Jane Austen" (1942), pp. 50-51. Though JA's environment was that of the country gentleman of the
eighteenth century, her social and economic standards are those of a capitalist bourgeoisie--money
and snobbery.

R. A. Brower, "The Controlling Hand: Jane
Austen and Pride and Prejudice," pp. 52-61. (This
essay, originally published in 1945, is an earlier
version of the one published as "Light and Bright
and Sparkling: Irony and Fiction in Pride and Prejudice"; see 164.)

Marvin Mudrick, "Persuasion: The Liberation
of Feeling," pp. 62-71. (See 5.)

C. S. Lewis, "Two Solitary Heroines," pp. 72-
77. (See 49.)

Malcolm Bradbury, "Jane Austen's Emma," pp. 78-
89. (See 184.)

Thomas R. Edwards, Jr., "The Difficult Beauty
of Mansfield Park," pp. 90-96. (See 272.)

Laurence Lerner, "Sense and Sensibility: A
Mixed-Up Book," pp. 97-101. (See 357.)

482 Phillipps, K. C. Jane Austen's English. London:
      Deutsch, 1970.

Rev. (with another work) in TLS, 30 July 1971,
p. 920; by Knud Sørensen in ES, 53 (1972), 365-67;
by Margaret Kirkham in EIC, 22 (1972), 192-95; (with
another work) by J. F. Burrows in SoRA, 5 (1972),
172-76.

A cataloguing of JA's vocabulary, sentence
structure, and modes of address that demonstrates,
first, her precise awareness of the uses and possible misuses of language; second, her careful
discrimination among the different meanings of words
and phrases, among various grammatical constructions, and between correct and substandard usage,
so as to reveal character, rank, age, and, generally, to achieve a wide range of effects; and,
third, her reliance "on eighteenth-century abstractions, the assured manipulation of conventional
terms like liberality, propriety, delicacy," as well
as "the best spoken English she heard about her."
Further, there is explanation of changes in meaning
and usage that have occurred between her time and
ours.)

483   Rohmann, Gerd. "Jane Austen: Pride and Prejudice:
          Auktorialer Kommentar und Perspektivtechnik."
          NS, 19 (1970), 455-61.

P and P's central theme, the problem of human
understanding, is reflected in JA's narrative technique. Seen from Elizabeth's perspective, Darcy
undergoes a considerable change in the second half
of the novel. But by balancing the heroine's per-
ceptions with authorial comment, JA allows the
reader to surpass Elizabeth's limitations and
recognize Darcy's consistency.

484   Ryals, Clyde de L. "Being and Doing in Mansfield
          Park." Archiv, 206 (1970), 345-60.

"In the last analysis Fanny Price . . . is
Jane Austen's embodiment, in Pater's words, 'of
those whose ideal is rather in being than in
doing,' and Mansfield Park is her working out of
'those manners which are, in the deepest as in the
simplest sense, morals.' In none of her other works
does Jane Austen point so clearly to the essential
concerns of nineteenth-century literature."

485   Soye, Brigitte de. "Bath dans Northanger Abbey."
          EA, 23 (1970), 83-86.

In NA, JA successfully captures the atmosphere
of Bath as it actually was toward the end of the
eighteenth century.

486   Stone, Donald D.   "Sense and Semantics in Jane
         Austen." NCF, 25 (1970), 31-50.

      JA's "similarity with Wittgenstein in the
matter of language and reality" consists in their
agreement that "the limitations of one's language
necessarily mean the limitations of one's world."
Throughout her canon JA depicts people at the
"mercy of jargon-ridden patterns of language and
conduct." "Hers is a warning against the atrophy
of word and deed by any form of verbal and emotional manipulation."

487   Watson, J. R.   "Mr. Perry's Patients: A View of
         Emma." EIC, 20 (1970), 334-43.

      In E "the comedy about health is able to illu-
minate character in a significant way." By its
combination of the serious and the amusing, the
health theme fulfills the ethical potential of
comedy.

                         1971

488   Arbasino, Alberto. "Jane Austen," in Sessanta
         posizioni. Milan: Feltrinelli, 1971, pp. 43-
         45. This essay appeared originally in Il
         Giorno in 1963.

      JA is as innocent as a satyr offering candy.
Belonging to the eighteenth century, JA, who is the
first modern novelist, deals with money, marriage,
inheritances, and class conventions, in a language
without emotions and scruples.

489   Banfield, Ann. "The Moral Landscape of Mansfield
         Park." NCF, 26 (1971), 1-24.

      The neoclassic analogy between art and morals
underlies the structure of MP and is reflected in
its use of place. As the protagonist of the novel,
"Mansfield wavers between the extremes of un-
principled adherence to rules (Sotherton) and
unruled feeling (Portsmouth)." But Mansfield
ultimately balances reason and feeling, art and
nature, society and the individual. MP also
dramatizes the physical, psychological, social,
and moral "coming-out" of Fanny and the parallel
emergence of Edmund.

490 Barnett, George L., ed. "Jane Austen (1775-1817),"
in Nineteenth-Century British Novelists on the
Novel. New York: Appleton-Century-Crofts,
1971, pp. 21-28.

(Reprints three defenses of fiction taken from
NA--which "point up the hesitation of the early
nineteenth century to recognize the novel as a
serious art form"--and the "Plan of a Novel, According to Hints from Various Quarters"--which
shows "her innate sense of comedy.")

491 Corringham, Mary. I, Jane Austen: A Re-Creation in
Rime Royal Based on the Letters of Jane Austen,
Her Novels and the Comments of Her Biographers.
London: Routledge & Kegan Paul, 1971.

Rev. (with other works) in TLS, 19 Nov. 1971,
p. 1438; (with other works) by Gilbert Thomas in
English, 21 (1972), 72-73.

(Biography.)

492 Cowley, Malcolm, and Howard E. Hugo, comps. "Afterword [to 'The Ball at Netherfield']," in The
Lesson of the Masters: An Anthology of the Novel from Cervantes to Hemingway. New York:
Scribner's, 1971, pp. 95-97.

"The ball at Netherfield, with its ceremony
and decorum, its comic blunders and savagely wounded
sensibilities, epitomizes much that is characteristic
of this novel in particular and of Austen's writing
in general."

493 Davie, John. "Introduction" to his ed. of Northanger Abbey and Persuasion. New York: Oxford
Univ. Press, 1971, pp. vii-xix. This edition
includes the "Biographical Notice of the
Author," an appendix with "The Original Ending
of Persuasion," and textual notes and bibliography by James Kinsley.

Rev. (with other works) in TLS, 19 Nov. 1971,
p. 1438; (with other works) by U. C. Knoepflmacher
in SEL, 12 (1972), 824.

Though in NA she has problems with the handling
of characters, JA executes surely and integrates

neatly the serious story--the relationship between
hero and heroine--with her burlesque of popular fiction. More profound and more finely organized, P
achieves its effects subtly and delicately.
Catherine Morland's reward derives from her increased self-knowledge, Anne Elliot's from stoicism
and integrity.

494 Devlin, D. D. "Mansfield Park." ArielE, 2 (Oct.
        1971), 30-44.

        The crucial irony of MP is that "Fanny alone is
free," and "the stress is always on the difficulty
of achieving such freedom against the formidable
pressures of time and place and circumstance."
Freedom achieved through moral education is "possible only where there is love." But everyone at
the Park, and the Crawfords also, have been "corrupted by a false education." Lacking love, they
are bound by "conventional social and economic
pressures."

495 Duckworth, Alistair M. The Improvement of the Es-
        tate: A Study of Jane Austen's Novels. Balti-
        more: Johns Hopkins Press, 1971.

        Rev. by Howard S. Babb in NCF, 27 (1972), 238-
40; (with other works) by U. C. Knoepflmacher in
SEL, 12 (1972), 823; in TLS, 14 Apr. 1972, p. 412.

        Introductory: A transitional figure between
the "divinely structured" world of the eighteenth-
and the unstructured world of the nineteenth-century
novel, "Jane Austen affirms society, ideally considered as a structure of values that are ultimately founded in religious principle, at the same
time as she distinguishes it from its frequently
corrupted form." Typically, her plots chart the
individual's course from an initial inherited
security through an intermediate estrangement and
finally to a reintegration with society.

        MP: Rather than the "counter-truth" it is often
considered, MP is "fundamental to Jane Austen's
thought." Henry Crawford's Reptonian urge for
"improvement" in landscape, in houses, and in
preaching indicates his willingness to destroy inherited social, moral, and religious norms. Against
this self-serving and revolutionary attitude, JA
establishes Mansfield Park as the symbol of an

imperfect but fundamentally sound system of traditional values, which ironically is preserved not by
the estate "trustees" but by Fanny Price.

NA and S and S: The partially successful NA and
S and S resemble MP in demonstrating the need to
ground individual action in a social context. While
voicing the author's fear that economic will overcome moral considerations in determining conduct,
S and S exposes the insufficiency of an attractive
individualism as a guide to social response. NA, as
a novel of education, brings the reader (if not
Catherine) to recognize the necessity of balancing
judgment and sympathetic imagination.

P and P: In a movement whose final effect is to
reduce the distances between people and between
classes, Elizabeth emerges from an individualist and
thus relativist ethic and Darcy from a too strict
attention to the duties of his station, and both
approach a reconciliation whereby the "claims of
spontaneity" inform and are informed by "cultural
discipline." Thus viewed, "Pride and Prejudice is
no contradiction of the meaning of Mansfield Park."

E: Employing the same basic elements as MP,
E investigates the cultural dangers of "excessive
individualism." As an heiress, Emma's freedom is
matched by her responsibility. But because she is
a victim of snobbishness or, epistemologically, of
"subjective idealism," Emma threatens the cohesive-
ness of Highbury society. Likewise, her desire to
"improve" reality and Churchill's game-playing
involve a secrecy which destroys social unity.

P: "Persuasion addresses itself to the predicament of the isolated self responding to social
deprivation." The Elliots' abandonment of Kellynch
signals the heroine's alienation from a viable
social context, which adversity she faces with a
Christian Stoicism. The union of Anne and Wentworth
does not bring about a thematic reconciliation or
social reconstitution as in JA's previous novels.
Rather, their private love subsists despite and
outside of social disintegration.

Sanditon: Like Mansfield Park, Sanditon is a
"place endangered by 'improvements.'" But in the
case of Sanditon, the reader cannot be certain that
innovation will be resisted. Mr. Parker, a false
trustee, views his estate as an object of "speculation." And Charlotte Heywood, like Anne Elliot, is

divided from her social context and "can no longer
be an agent of social renewal."

496 Duckworth, Alistair M.   "Mansfield Park and Estate
        Improvements: Jane Austen's Grounds of Being."
        NCF, 26 (1971), 25-48.

     (See 495.)

497 Gilson, D. J.   "The Early American Editions of Jane
        Austen." BC, 20 (1971), 388-89.

     (A list of early American editions that have
     come to light since 1969; see also 426.)

498 Higuchi, Kinzo.   "The Comic Structure of Emma."
        SELit, 48 (1971), 57-66.

     (Not seen.)

499 Ivaševa, V. V.   "Dva romana Džejn Ousten (Ubeždenie
        i Mensfild Park [Persuasion and Mansfield
        Park])." Vestnik Moskovskogo universiteta,
        Ser. 10 (Filologija), No. 6 (1971), pp. 17-29.

     Perfect in its realistic analysis of character
     and filled with a sparkling irony, MP is a novel
     about the power of money. P, whose subject is
     similar, is written in a different manner and its
     emotional coloring is new. In her last novel JA
     is more satiric and more sarcastic and evaluates
     her characters much more directly than in MP.

500 Izubuchi, Keiko.   "Northanger Abbey and Its Fic-
        tional Convention." Pursuit, 11 (May 1971),
        1-36.

     NA, as well as being indebted to the Gothic
     novel and the anti-romance tradition is an original
     work. It treats "the theme of a young heroine's
     entrance into the world and her deception and
     awakening," not only to the nature of fictional
     romances, but "to the reality of the human world
     and then that of her own mind."

501 The Jane Austen Society: Report for the Year, 1970.

Alton, Hampshire: Jane Austen Society [1971].

(In addition to the guest speaker's address to the Society's annual general meeting, abstracted below, this report includes, among other things, several brief notes.)

Rachel Trickett, "Jane Austen's Imagination," pp. 11-28. "For all her clear-sighted, relentless observation of folly, her love of the ridiculous, her delight in the absurd, she is perfectly aware of pain and suffering, of the complexity of human experience, of the impossibility of contriving neat solutions to problems of human conduct. Like all great comic artists she is under no illusion about the unresolved conflicts, the imperfection of life."

502 Kestner, Joseph A., III. "Intimacy in the Novels of Jane Austen." Iowa English Bulletin Yearbook, 21 (Fall 1971), 52-59.

The gradations of friendship are carefully demarcated in JA's novels. She distinguishes among acquaintance, "attachment, friendship, intimacy, familiarity, and sexual love. Since intimacy is the point from which marriage may result, this particular relationship when practiced by men with women is carefully studied." Besides its benefits of greater understanding, intimacy tends to obscure judgment and reduce objectivity.

503 Kestner, Joseph A., III. "Silence and Shyness in the Novels of Jane Austen: 'The Quietness of It Does Me Good.'" Descant, 16 (Fall 1971), 40-47.

JA uses the themes of silence and shyness "as an ethical force explicit in the presentation of the characters, and as an artistic force implicit in the method of presentation. As ethical forces, silence and shyness are presented as aspects of sense in one's personal conduct." As artistic forces, they reveal JA's technique of "understatement and exclusion."

504 Krieger, Murray. "Postscript: The Naïve Classic and the Merely Comic," in The Classic Vision: The Retreat from Extremity in Modern Literature. Baltimore: Johns Hopkins Press, 1971, pp. 221-43.

In P and P the obstacles the individual must overcome are slight; the communal sense is never seriously challenged; and the inner life of the characters is not very complex. "The deck has been stacked in favor of the moderate victory of this hardly impressive set of social values, which Austen at once sees through and cherishes." "All comes out right-side-up for those who are on their way to a little bourgeois future."

505 Kroeber, Karl. Styles in Fictional Structure: The Art of Jane Austen, Charlotte Brontë, George Eliot. Princeton: Princeton Univ. Press, 1971.

Rev. by Bert G. Hornback in JEGP, 70 (1971), 680-82; (with another work) in TLS, 20 Aug. 1971, p. 986; by George Levine in VS, 15 (1971), 245-47; by Mary Ellmann in YR, 61 (1971), 132-34; by G. B. Tennyson in Criticism, 14 (1972), 192-94; by David V. Erdman in ELN, 10 Supp. (1972), 30; by David Lodge in Novel, 5 (1972), 260-62; by Priscilla Jenkins in RES, 23 (1972), 514-15; (with another work) by J. F. Burrows in SoRA, 5 (1972), 172-76; by Alistair M. Duckworth in ELN, 10 (1973), 233-36.

Words in Fiction: In the attempt to place JA in a "history of fictional styles," a statistical analysis of E's vocabulary would probably not reveal "how Jane Austen's simple, lucid, even formally 'correct' language can overlie a deeper complexity of meaning contained within it." The study of both E's "surface and depth" is necessary, for JA uses "conventional form to conceal true form."

Characterization: "One might summarize Austen's form of characterization as being the depiction of representative figures as unique individuals." Her characters are largely static; they unfold rather than change. And each is defined as a "special nexus of interpersonal relations," rather than as an autonomous and discrete individual.

Point of View: JA's omniscience is based on a static community linking author and reader. This community is less comprehensive than that of Fielding, for it is limited to the "genteel novel-reading public of her day." And because her community is "so purely an aesthetic one, Jane Austen's most topical novel [NA] retains its charm and vitality."

Style and Change: "A focus on 'disappointed-

lover' scenes reveals a consistent development from
rational to' passional presentation." While Elinor
"reflects alone or explains her past feeling," "the
action of the disappointment scene in Pride and
Prejudice is immediate, even violent." Finally, in
P, JA "probes deeply into the sentiments which defy
the resources of the rational."

Resolutions: Of Shirley, Felix Holt, and MP,
"the happy resolution of Mansfield Park is plainly
the most conventional." It is "presented in a cool,
generalized, summary fashion because it does not
simplify. The difficulties which make up the action
of Mansfield Park are really less subtle and complex
than the union which resolves them."

Total Design: "Austen concentrates the time
covered by her action more than do Eliot and
Brontë," and she consistently adheres to "an underlying pattern of temporal continuity." JA prefers
"'internalized' narration" to description or exposition, and uses "fewer settings than Brontë or
Eliot."

Contrast of Passages: The contrast of a passage
from E (II, ix-xii) with one from Villette and one
from Middlemarch reveals that "Austen is not as concerned with vitalizing her characters by exposing
hidden psychic drives." "Instead she characterizes
with a lucid rendering of a purely conscious mind."
JA rarely depicts isolated characters, and "we find
the temporal ordering of the Emma passage surpris-
ingly regular."

Narrative and Dialogue: JA "employs more variety of narrative sentence form" and more often
clusters dialogue and narrative than Brontë. Both
her narrative and dialogue sentences are usually
declarative, and her dialogue displays less variety than Brontë's or Eliot's. "At word level
Austen's essential focus is on what is said, not on
the manner of speech."

Appendixes: These include tabulations of, among
other things, JA's vocabulary in selected passages,
time distortions, setting changes, number of characters, chapters, sentences, nouns, verbs, and adjec-
tives.

506   Lauber, John.   "Heroes and Anti-Heroes in Jane
          Austen's Novels." DR, 51 (Winter 1971-1972),
          489-503.

JA's heroes and anti-heroes are not conventional and simplistic figures, but complex, seriously presented individuals, who "are precisely
adapted to the heroine of each novel, and comple-
ment each other as well."

507   Linder, C. A.   "The Ideal of Marriage as Depicted
      in the Novels of Jane Austen and Charlotte
      Brontë."   Standpunte, No. 96 (Aug. 1971), pp.
      20-30.

"Jane Austen considered marriage to be the
only means for a woman to obtain independence within an established social circle, stressing always
the social rôle of marriage; while Charlotte Brontë
recognised the need for a woman's emotional fulfil-
ment through marriage and emphasised its psychological effect."

508   Lodge, David.   "Introduction" to his ed. of Emma.
      New York: Oxford Univ. Press, 1971, pp. vii-
      xvi.   This edition includes textual notes and
      bibliography by James Kinsley.

Rev. (with other works) in TLS, 19 Nov. 1971,
p. 1438; (with other works) by U. C. Knoepflmacher
in SEL, 12 (1972), 824.

"On first reading, Emma is a comedy of mysteries and puzzles," and the second time through
it "becomes a comedy of ironies."   "Perhaps we read
Emma first mainly for the presentation, and subsequently mainly for the assessment."   Before the
heroine can commit herself to "intelligent virtue,"
she must stop imposing fictional forms on actual
persons.

509   Moran, Leila.   "Jane Austen Is Alive and Well!"
      ABC, 22 (Nov.-Dec. 1971), 11-14.

(A description of the author's expedition to
Lyme and other places associated with JA.)

510   Ørum, Tania.   "Tidens kvinde: Billeder fra Jane
      Austens romaner."   Selvsyn (Copenhagen), 11,
      No. 4 (1971), 73-80.

JA omits much from her fiction, depicting a

"microcommunity," provincial and closed. Yet because it is unhistorical, it remains timeless. In
her novels both men and women strive for the security and repose of matrimony.

511   Page, Norman. "'The Best Chosen Language': Styl-
         istic Modes in Jane Austen." ArielE, 2 (Oct.
         1971), 45-51.

      (See 540.)

512   Pilgrim, Constance. Dear Jane: A Biographical
         Study of Jane Austen. London: Kimber, 1971.

         Rev. in TLS, 27 Aug. 1971, p. 1020.

      Through a re-examination of the novels, "to-
      gether with background reading of one kind or an-
      other, and much pondering over actual places and
      scenes described," we can "explore a little known
      period of her life, the period of 'exquisite
      felicity,' the meeting with the unknown admirer."
      JA's admirer was John Wordsworth, the poet's
      brother.

513   Southam, B. C. "General Tilney's Hot-Houses: Some
         Recent Jane Austen Studies and Texts."
         ArielE, 2 (Oct. 1971), 52-62.

      What is needed in Austen scholarship is
      "critical interpretation . . . informed by a
      thorough and detailed understanding of the
      historical-cultural relationship" between JA and
      her time. Recent studies by Ivor Brown (see 302)
      and W. A. Craik (see 419) purportedly placing JA
      in a historical context are inadequate. Gener-
      ally, the new Oxford (see 458, 474, 477) and
      Penguin (see 274, 300, 328, 452) editions of the
      novels repeat Chapman's deficiencies in respect to
      annotation. Critics, also, emphasize too exclusive-
      ly JA's literary heritage, to the neglect of her
      general cultural heritage.

514   Wade, Rosalind. "The Anatomy of Jane Austen (1775-
         1817)." ContemporaryR, 218 (1971), 132-36.

      The real JA is to be found amid "failure in
      love and authorship," a woman "whose personal and

professional life went devastatingly wrong due to a
variety of circumstances and through no one's
fault."

515 Walls, A. F. "Miss Austen on Sunday." _Trivium_, 6
       (1971), 92-102.

       Bishop Beilby Porteus' restrictions on Sunday
activities coincided with JA's attitudes. "For most
of the people in the novels . . . even the smart and
worldly, church going is a normal . . . Sunday
activity." Bad weather might prevent attendance,
but attendance at two Sunday services was not unusual. "Curiously enough, the best attested feature
of Sunday after morning service is the morning
walk."

516 Warner, Sylvia Townsend. "An Introduction" to
       Northanger Abbey. Baltimore: Printed for the
       Members of the Limited Editions Club by the
       Garamond Press, 1971, pp. v-xi.

       "It was as a young iconoclast, a representative
of a _nouvelle vague_, that she assumed the mannerisms
of Fielding in order to deride the unreality of the
Romantics." For JA, reality meant, in part, "the
ordinary human failings of cupidity, credulity,
boasting, and bad temper."

517 Wiesenfarth, Joseph. "_Persuasion_: History and
       Myth." _WC_, 2 (1971), 160-68.

       From the beginning of _P_ to its close, "the new
order meets the old, Cinderella affronts Narcissus,
Eros challenges Thanatos in a world touched by history. To the very end history provides the realistic context in which Jane Austen works out the myths
of _Persuasion_."

518 Wiltshire, John. "A Romantic _Persuasion_?" _CR_,
       No. 14 (1971), pp. 3-16.

       _P_ is JA's first novel whose resolution is "also
its highest and deepest point of truth." Imagination, dream, poetry are not merely self-indulgent:
"Anne Elliot's dream is not to escape from, but to
recover her life, and the resolution which Jane
Austen undertakes is one that includes rather than
evades sorrow." The conclusion is not

"conventionally 'Romantic,'" since its poignancy
derives "from a deeply-felt discipline of moral and
social decorum."

519 Wolfe, Thomas P. "The Achievement of Persuasion."
        SEL, 11 (1971), 687-700.

        The distinctiveness of P within JA's canon
results from the fact that the narrator and the
heroine are so closely allied in point of view and
tone. Thematically, this narrative technique op-
poses personal and mental to social values. The
problem of P is clearest in the last half of the
novel, where the narrator is dissociated from
Anne and often becomes melodramatic.

1972

520 Auerbach, Nina. "O Brave New World: Evolution and
        Revolution in Persuasion." ELH, 39 (1972),
        112-28.

        Like The Tempest, P suspends "the iron law
of consequences," and "the seeds of apparent
tragedy produce unexpected joy." JA unequivocally repudiates "the attempt of 'sense' to
counsel feeling." The created world of the
novel is "governed by nature and by human desire,"
and the unnatural Elliots are therefore rendered
powerless. Among JA's novels, "only Persuasion
endows the representatives of nature and feeling
with the superior social power income symbolizes
and bestows."

521 Corwin, Laura J. "Character and Morality in the
        Novels of Jane Austen." RLV, 38 (1972), 363-
        79.

        Of two types of character JA uses as the
vehicle of her moral vision, one is "protean"--
not caring about moral implications and locating
and defining "the self through the techniques of
theatrical performance." The other type is
"stable"--viewing the self through the idea of
decorum, seeing the social world as "a reflection
of significant moral structures in which to locate
the self."

522 Craik, W. A.   "Introduction" to Sense and Sensi-
        bility. London: Pan, 1972, pp. 5-15.

        In S and S, JA examines not only the two quali-
ties of the title, but taste, decorum, and morals,
and uses money as a touchstone of character. Indebted to the novel of manners, the epistolary novel, and the drama, JA, the "most self-effacing of
narrators," here reveals her typical abundance,
variety, and competence.

523 Dickens, Monica.   "Introduction" to Mansfield Park.
        London: Pan, 1972, pp. v-xiii.

        "Mansfield Park is a long book, filled with the
details of day-to-day life, but all of it is fasci-
nating. This is the essence of Jane Austen's art.
She made great creations out of a very small and
inhibited world in which many people, especially
women, wasted most of their lives on trivia."

524 Edge, Charles.   "Emma: A Technique of Characteriza-
        tion," in The Classic British Novel. Ed.
        Howard M. Harper, Jr., and Charles Edge.
        Athens: Univ. of Georgia Press, 1972, pp. 51-
        64.

        E deals with varieties of teachers and stu-
dents, rulers and subjects, good and bad health.
These sets of contrasts and comparisons help us
understand some of the book's basic subjects, including egotism, power, and commitment.

525 Ehrenpreis, Anne Henry.   "Introduction" to her ed.
        of Northanger Abbey. Baltimore: Penguin, 1972,
        pp. 7-24. This edition includes the "Biograph-
        ical Notice of the Author."

        Though the structure and characterization often
seem weak, NA still incisively criticizes the arti-
ficiality of fiction popular at the end of the eighteenth century. As in her other novels, here JA
uses her characters' literary tastes as a guide to
their morality and shows the danger of fancy not
controlled by reason.

526 Gullans, Charles B.   "Jane Austen's Mansfield Park
        and Dr. Johnson." NCF, 27 (1972), 206-08.

(Proposed punctuation of the MP crux, "And,
alas! how always known" [III, ii], by analogy to a
similar passage in Boswell's Life.)

527 Hodge, Jane Aiken. "Jane Austen and the Pub-
         lishers." Cornhill, No. 1071 (Spring 1972),
         pp. 188-94.

     "Jane Austen's early experience with pub-
lishers was unlucky," and later, in the second
decade of the century, she experienced many risks
in publishing her books. "She earned less than
£700 in her lifetime and there is no pretending
that this does not compare miserably with the prof-
its other people were making."

528 Hodge, Jane Aiken. Only a Novel: The Double Life
         of Jane Austen. New York: Coward, McCann &
         Geoghegan, 1972.

     Rev. by Dorothy L. Parker in Christian Science
Monitor, 5 July 1972, p. 7; in TLS, 23 June 1972,
p. 704; by Andrew Wright in NCF, 27 (1973), 495-97.

     JA led a double life: she was both the beloved
family member, seldom saying an unkind thing, and
the author who plumbed the "depths of intellectual
and moral despair" to achieve an "extraordinary
ironic moral vision. . . . While she sat there,
every inch the maiden aunt, she was doubtless
wrestling, like every other artist who has created
something that endures, with her vision of the
universe. . . . Peering, in my turn, through the
mists of a hundred and fifty years, I have tried
for my own picture of the person who could write
those" extraordinary books.

529 The Jane Austen Society: Report for the Year, 1971.
         Alton, Hampshire: Jane Austen Society [1972].

     (In addition to the guest speaker's address
to the Society's annual general meeting, abstracted
below, this report includes, among other things,
several brief notes.)

     Filippo Donini, "Jane Austen in Italy," pp.
13-25. "How can something which is the negation
of opera be popular in Italy?" The critical attention paid her by Mario Praz helps make up "for all

the disregard and the censure Jane Austen has suffered in Italy."

530   Jordan, Ellen. "Mansfield Park." Corr. in TLS, 23
        June 1972, p. 719. See also corr. in TLS,
        Claire Lamont, 7 July 1972, p. 777; William
        Empson, 14 July, p. 819.

        A newly discovered biographical detail sug-
gests that "only two years before she began Mansfield Park Jane Austen was prepared to 'act a part'
herself."

531   Kestner, Joseph A., III. "The 'I' Persona in the
        Novels of Jane Austen." SNNTS, 4 (1972), 6-
        15.

        The "I" of JA's novels includes three separate
identities: JA in propria persona criticizes literature and society directly; in auctoris persona she
controls the characters and ethic of a work; and in
a combination of the above two she invokes "reality
and actuality as interdependent verifications of
one another in reconciling life and art."

532   Kiely, Robert. "Northanger Abbey: Jane Austen,
        1803," in The Romantic Novel in England.
        Cambridge, Mass.: Harvard Univ. Press, 1972,
        pp. 118-35.

        "As a display of the disciplined mind and the
well-chosen word," NA deflates the excesses of romanticism. Yet JA directs her parody, not only at
the world of subjective fancy, but the realistic
world of social convention. Not completely rejecting either realm, JA explores "the same division of
mind which is at the core of romantic fiction."

533   Lascelles, Mary. "Jane Austen and Walter Scott:
        A Minor Point of Comparison," in Notions and
        Facts: Collected Criticism and Research.
        Oxford: Clarendon Press, 1972, pp. 230-46.
        See also corr. in TLS, Mary Lascelles, 9 Feb.
        1973, p. 153.

        "Novelists who employ the law in the further-
ance of their designs fall into several groups.
There are those who write from the inside--chief

among them, Scott . . . and one who accepts it with inscrutable detachment: Jane Austen. Only in so far as the law concerns itself with inheritance is Jane Austen concerned with the law."

534   Lauber, John.   "Sanditon: The Kingdom of Folly."
       SNNTS, 4 (1972), 353-63.

"Sanditon is a state of mind. It is the kingdom of folly, of debased imagination." "Sanditon represents everything that is new, showy, and insubstantial, in contrast to the solid sense and security of the older England, represented by the description of the Heywoods and their way of life, and of Mr. Parker's now abandoned family estate."

535   Lock, F. P.   "Jane Austen and the Seaside."   Country
       Life Annual (1972), pp. 114-16.

Although Sanditon is an imagined town, "Bognor was certainly the kind of resort Jane Austen had in mind." When completed, Sanditon "would very likely have been the most penetrating study in our literature of the social kaleidoscope of the seaside resort."

536   Lock, F. P.   "'The Neighbourhood of Tombuctoo': A
       Note on Sanditon."   N&Q, 19 (1972), 97-99.

"Tombuctoo is an image of Sir Edward's mind: a mirage of riches and sexual freedom concealing a mean and sordid reality."

537   Measham, D. C.   "Sentiment and Sentimental Psychol-
       ogy in Jane Austen."   RMS, 16 (1972), 61-85.

In many matters, including attempted definitions of love, Richardson, "the principal novelist whom she read and re-read," influenced JA directly. In her early work she gives a behavioristic account of love similar to his in Grandison. "Emma is the first of Miss Austen's novels to look critically at interpreters of behaviour, though it still sees falling in love as purposive in character."

538   Morgan, Alice.   "On Teaching Emma."   JGE, 24 (1972),
       103-08.

Among freshmen E aroused "two kinds of difficulties." "One sort was a matter of information--social facts, physical facts--needed to understand the setting and even the events of the novel."
The other was the development of a relationship between the students and what seemed to them such a
conservative work.

539 Moss, Howard. "Jane Austen." SatR, 9 Sept. 1972,
     p. 37.

     (Humorous sketch.)

540 Page, Norman. The Language of Jane Austen. (Language and Style Series, 13.) Oxford: Blackwell, 1972.

     Introductory: Though her language has been
generally neglected, "style is a component of
exceptional importance in Jane Austen's work, and
. . . it is only through an unremitting alertness
to her language in action that her meaning can be
fully understood."

     Style: Innovative and traditional both, JA's
style accounts for her ability to convey "the far-
reaching importance of the local and the ephemeral."
Her early novels "are to a striking extent about
language." NA is characterized by its focus on the
ambiguity of language, and in S and S style is an
index of social behavior. P and P's use of dialogue
and stage conventions renders it the most dramatic
of JA's novels. The absence in MP of "witty dialogue and ironic commentary" accounts for its
uniquely grave tone; here "fluency becomes suspect."
Like NA, E shows language to be "a highly equivocal
medium." P abandons Johnsonian periodicity and
combines narrative and dialogue into a whole that
prefigures the twentieth-century novel.

     Language: JA's belief in absolute and general
standards of conduct is reflected in her use of
abstract nouns that denote the public and accepted
values upheld by the novels. Because many of these
"key-words" have lost or changed meaning since JA
used them and because they convey the matrix of her
vision, a "real effort of linguistic imagination" is
required of the reader.

     Syntax: The influence on JA of Johnson's formal

(and often tripartite) syntactic structures wanes
appreciably during her artistic maturation. His
formality becomes a device of parody and mock-heroic
inflation. Consistently, JA moves toward a style
which, though not colloquial, is patterned on
speech. Analysis of JA's sentence length and
paragraph rhythm reveals the variety of styles,
accommodating a variety of intentions, she employs.

Conversation: JA "displays an impressive
versatility" in dialogue and "offers a wider range
of speech-varieties than has sometimes been suggested." Few novelists use dialogue more organ-
ically, for in JA's novels "language itself . . .
carries the burden of meaning and suggestion."
Particularly important are JA's development of
"free indirect speech," which combines authorial
comment and drama with economy, and her use of
distinctive speech patterns to signal both the
social and moral qualities of her characters.

Epistolary Art: Though JA used the epistolary
mode early in her career, she gradually abandoned
it "in favor of other narrative techniques, though
important traces remain even in the later novels."
The original epistolary form remains discernible in
S and S, and P and P may also derive from an earlier
draft told in letters. Letters in JA's novels, as
in Richardson's and Smollett's, "provide precious
opportunities for 'exercises in style.'"

Conclusion: What differentiates JA from novelists contemporary with her and renders her a great
writer is style. Her works display "a consistently
scrupulous attention to verbal values, a sensitive-
ness to nuances of vocabulary and phrasing, and a
flexibility of approach to syntax which can combine
the strengths of an inherited tradition with a
readiness for innovation."

541   Parrish, Stephen M., ed. Emma: An Authoritative
      Text, Backgrounds, Reviews, and Criticism.
      New York: Norton, 1972.

      (In addition to the essays listed below, this
      edition of E includes selections from JA's letters
      and The Watsons, from the "Biographical Notice of
      the Author" and the Memoir of Jane Austen, as well
      as from critical pieces of the nineteenth and
      early twentieth centuries.)

Stephen M. Parrish, "Preface," pp. vii-ix. "If
the conventions within which she worked were limited . . . the world of human feeling that opens out
inside her novels is complex and vital, and the
sensitivity and taste that created this world stand
unparalleled in English."

Mary Lascelles, "The Narrator and His Reader,"
pp. 388-92. (See 225.)

Arnold Kettle, "Jane Austen: Emma (1816)," pp.
393-400. (See 354.)

Wayne Booth, "Control of Distance in Jane
Austen's Emma," pp. 400-19. (See 151.)

G. Armour Craig, "Jane Austen's Emma: The
Truths and Disguises of Human Disclosure," pp. 420-
27. (See 186.)

A. Walton Litz, "The Limits of Freedom: Emma,"
pp. 427-35. (See 281.)

W. A. Craik, "Emma," pp. 435-51. (See 266.)

W. J. Harvey, "The Plot of Emma," pp. 451-57.
(See 351.)

542 Pikoulis, John. "Jane Austen: The Figure in the
     Carpet." NCF, 27 (1972), 38-60.

In P and P "the very real virtues Jane [Bennet]
enacts are the unstated ideal which governs the
novel." Though Jane's views, compared with
Elizabeth's, sometimes appear spineless, the older
sister's "'sanguine hope of good' is eventually
justified. Every crisis in the novel seems designed
to test the sisters' opposing views and eventually
to justify Jane's." Elizabeth's development toward
self-knowledge--toward Jane's "spirit of love"--is
paradigmatic of similar situations in JA's other
novels.

543 Pirani, Alix. "Northanger Abbey and the New Fifth."
     The Use of English, 24 (1972), 117-21 and 126.

Though NA "is in many respects well suited to
adolescents," "pupils may be put off, even repelled
by Jane Austen (and her mouthpiece Henry), whose
cynicism is often scornful and intolerant--and much

resembles that of many teachers. She is indeed a
teachers' author: the lone, articulate, sensitive
and responsible voice crying in a wilderness of
apparent stupidity and vulgarity."

544 Swift, J. A. "Scanning Electron Microscope Study
        of Jane Austen's Hair." Nature, 238 (1972),
        161-62.

        "Within the last three years of her life Jane
Austen did little to tend her hair."

545 Tanner, Tony. "Introduction" to his ed. of Pride
        and Prejudice. Baltimore: Penguin, 1972, pp.
        7-46.

        In its treatment of the problem of knowledge
and in its "respect for limits, definition, and
clear ideas," P and P is a book nourished on
eighteenth-century philosophy. Other concerns of
the book include the individual's development from
performance to reflection on performance, and the
differences between the socially restricted and
free personality. In the protagonists' marriage,
which unites playfulness and regulation, JA represents "a society in which the individual can experience freedom as well as commitment."

546 Ward, William S. "Three Hitherto Unnoted Contem-
        porary Reviews of Jane Austen." NCF, 26
        (1972), 469-77.

        (Reprints unsigned reviews of Emma from the
Champion, the Augustan Review, and the British
Lady's Magazine, and Monthly Miscellany.)

547 Watts, Mary. "God and Jane Austen." New Black-
        friars, 53 (1972), 15-22.

        Through her interest in human behavior, JA
expresses a deeply religious outlook on life. The
key to MP is "principle," and by this term JA
intends "not merely a knowledge of what is socially
or humanly right, but such a knowledge based on
religious belief." And, by their emphasis on
extra-rational charity, E and P also demonstrate
the "inadequacy of humanism alone to the good
life." In all three novels, comic conventions of

ultimate order coincide with traditional Christian
belief.

548   Weinsheimer, Joel.   "Chance and the Hierarchy of
        Marriages in Pride and Prejudice." ELH, 39
        (1972), 404-19.

        In P and P "the characters' responses to chance
are significant criteria for the evaluation of their
relative merits . . . and each married couple illustrates a double view of one position in the novel's
scale of imperfect responses to chance." The moral
superiority of the marriage of Elizabeth and Darcy
is manifested by the couple's movement from self-
ignorance and the consequent domination by chance
to an awareness of their finite understandings and
to "determining probabilities."

                            1973

549   Brown, Lloyd W.   Bits of Ivory: Narrative Tech-
        niques in Jane Austen's Fiction. Baton Rouge:
        Louisiana State Univ. Press, 1973.

        Introductory: Investigations of JA's style must
elucidate the relation of language not only to particular characters but to the thematic concerns of
the whole work. Word usage, as JA was completely
aware, is intrinsic to her "definition of moral
and intellectual values." And, as "an eighteenth-
century novelist," JA framed her diction and the
ideas it conveys within the moral, philosophical,
and literary traditions she inherited from that
century.

        Irony: JA's conceptual terms (as in the titles
S and S, P and P, and P) comprehend the "ambiguous
usages that juxtapose multiple, even contrary, meanings." As shown by passages in Burke, Hume, Locke,
Shaftesbury, and Johnson, these titular ambiguities
"are rooted in the philosophical assumptions of the
novelist's background" and go far to explain the
novels' ironies.

        Imagery: "Far from being 'unmetaphorical,'
Jane Austen's style is remarkable for the aptness
of figurative epigrams that illuminate the essence
of situation or personality." Though she "ridi-
cules excessive or inappropriate imagery" because it

fails to communicate meaning, JA's comments on metaphor echo those of "the most ardent supporters of figurative language in the eighteenth century."

Symbolism: JA's characters "interpret and react to the significance of names; and their evaluation, or misinterpretation, of each symbol is symptomatic of personal morality and feeling." Throughout her canon, but especially in MP and the later novels, JA analyzes "the individual's instinct to symbologize, to project objects or incidents as the embodiment of his feelings or status." This instinct and its particular manifestations are in themselves modes of characterization.

Conversation: "The real import of 'conversation' [that is, personal style] in Jane Austen's novels is the definition of individual tastes and ethics as they are evinced by social intercourse." But the conversation of major and (equally important) of ancillary characters is not limited to self-revelation; "it is integrated with the total development of each novel's theme and structure."

Letter Writing: "On the basis of her knowledge of Richardson, and as a result of her own experiments in the juvenilia, Jane Austen's epistolary structures serve to dramatize emotional crises," to characterize both a letter's author and reader, and to present the events of the novel as filtered through a mind other than that of the narrator.

Dialogue: In the tradition of Fielding and Sterne, dialogue among JA's characters "tends to be an exercise in noncommunication. It dramatizes all the psychological and moral barriers to meaningful human relationships." Dialogue can, however, act as an "emotional catalyst," making comprehension possible.

Parody: JA's parodies are based on "the exploitation of the diverse standards represented by her readership." This diversity allows her "to juxtapose and challenge a set of conflicting reactions to a literary or moral viewpoint." Increasingly throughout her development JA combines parody and characterization, and in E the integration is complete. JA's happy endings are marked, first, by their "self-consciousness" and "transparent inevitability," and, second, by their reappraisal of the realism of poetic justice.

550 Hamilton, Jack. "A Conversation with Jane Austen."
     Intellectual Digest, 3 (May 1973), 16-18.

     (An imaginary interview.)

551 Pinion, F. B. A Jane Austen Companion: A Critical
     Survey and Reference Book. London: Macmillan,
     1973.

     Rev. in TLS, 26 Jan. 1973, p. 99.

     (This illustrated review of JA's life and
     writings includes, among other things, a background
     of her times, bibliographical and critical notes on
     the novels, letters, and minor works, a discussion
     of writers who influenced JA and of her literary
     reputation, a list of people and places she men-
     tions, a glossary of her diction, a select bibliog-
     raphy, and appendixes on the chronology of composi-
     tion, the "Plan of a Novel," the Mirror, and the
     Austen family.)

II. Doctoral Dissertations

1952

552 Brown, Walter Lee. "The Function of the Family in
          Jane Austen's Novels." Unpub. Doct. Diss.,
          1952 (Calif., Berkeley).

     JA portrays family life "quite unlike that in
her own life, her own security and self-realization
contrasting with insecurity and frustration in her
novels." Through the use of Cinderella-type figures, JA stresses the need for renunciation before
marriage. JA is morally realistic: she comprehends
both the real nature of her society and what her
society should become.

553 Ullmann, Helga. "Charakterzeichnung und Komposi-
          tionskunst in den Romanen Jane Austen's."
          Unpub. Doct. Diss., 1952 (Kiel).

     An examination of each of the major and ancil-
lary characters of JA's novels and minor works
reveals that, despite the limitations of her
experience, she was nevertheless able to create a
wide variety of characters. Indeed, JA is a novelist of character.

1953

554 Daniel, Maggie Browne. "A Study of William Dean
          Howells's Attitude toward and Criticism of the
          English and Their Literature." Unpub. Doct.
          Diss., 1953 (Wis.), pp. 203-20 and *passim*.

     Howells praised JA highly as a realistic nov-
elist, "'the first and last of the English novelists to treat material with entire truthful-
ness.'"

1954

555 Sanders, Helen Morse. "Jane Austen's Novels: A

Study in Narrative Method." <u>DA</u>, 14 (1954), 2059-60 (Syracuse).

JA's novelistic skill "manifested itself in establishment of a relationship between herself as author and her principal figure--always the hero-ine--as central intelligence, a relationship which worked to remove the presence of the 'omniscient' author from the story altogether."

1955

556   Babb, Howard S.   "Techniques of Conversation in Jane Austen's Novels."   Unpub. Doct. Diss., 1955 (Harvard).

(See 182.)

557   Duffy, Joseph Michael, Jr.   "Jane Austen and the Nineteenth-Century Critics of Fiction, 1812-1913."   Unpub. Doct. Diss., 1955 (Chicago).

There are four basic periods in JA's critical reputation in the nineteenth century: first, the initial favorable reception and the posthumous decline of interest (1812-1832); second, the gradual establishment of her reputation, with limited recog-nition by "cultivated" readers (1833-1866); third, a notable increase of publishing and critical activity (1867-1883); and fourth, her achievement of the position of "great novelist" (1884-1913).

558   Murrah, Charles.   "Jane Austen's Treatment of Back-ground and Setting."   Unpub. Doct. Diss., 1955 (Harvard).

JA treated background and setting economically and realistically.   Her descriptions, blending the imaginative and factual, are pervaded by her "love of the country, her knowledge of the picturesque, and her sensitive appreciation of nature."   In her later novels JA intimately relates background descriptions to her other artistic elements, in-cluding plot and character.

559   Neubert, Albrecht.   "Die Entwicklung der 'Erlebten Rede' im bürgerlichen englischen Roman von Jane

Austen bis Virginia Woolf." Unpub. Doct.
Diss., 1955 (Leipzig), pp. 13-27.

JA introduced to the novel the technique of
erlebte Rede, defined as the narration of a character's inner experience in a mode of narration
colored by that experience. JA stimulates the
reader's empathy by revealing her characters'
motives and feelings without direct authorial
intrusion and thus prefigures the twentieth-century
disappearance of the author from his story.

560 Wright, Andrew Howell. "Irony in Jane Austen's
        Novels." Ohio State University Abstracts of
        Doctoral Dissertations, No. 66 (1955), pp. 405-
        10.

     (See 33.)

                        1956

561 Gleason, George Donald. "Dramatic Affinities in
        the Life and Work of Jane Austen." DA, 16
        (1956), 956 (Iowa State).

     JA participated to some extent in all forms
of the contemporary theatrical mania, and she uses
the theatre in all her novels. "Love and Freindship" shows heavy borrowing from Sheridan's The
Critic, and MP was probably based on the Steventon
experiences with private theatricals.

562 Holznagel, Siegfried. "Jane Austen's Persuasion
        und Theodor Fontanes Der Stechlin: Eine
        vergleichende morphologische Untersuchung."
        Unpub. Doct. Diss., 1956 (Bonn).

     In P the relationship between the time imi-
tated (erzählte Zeit) and time as represented
(Erzählzeit) is the fundamental morphological
principle. Both time and space proceed linearly
without interruption. Dialogue, too, moves
directly toward the reunion of Anne and Wentworth.
In contrast to the stasis of Fontane's Der Stechlin,
P is a novel of expansion and activity.

1957

563 Loomis, Emerson Robert. "The Anti-Gothic English
        Novel." DA, 17 (1957), 3003 (Fla. State).

        NA belongs to the genre of the anti-Gothic
     novel, a genre characterized by exaggerated imita-
     tion of the stock characters, plots, themes, set-
     tings, and language of the Gothic novel. Like other
     anti-Gothic novelists, JA supports the tradition of
     the realistic novel.

564 Sandstrom, Glenn Arthur. "Deception and Undeception
        in the Novels of Jane Austen." DA, 17 (1957),
        1086-87 (Ill.).

        All of JA's heroines and a few of her heroes
     at first suffer from deception, undergo a process
     of undeception, and finally arrive at a norm of out-
     look and conduct. Improvement depends on factual
     enlightenment. Because "one trend in the novels
     is a movement toward greater completeness of unde-
     ception," they appear increasingly realistic.

1958

565 Bersani, Leo. "Jane Austen: Emma," in "Point of
        View in Fiction: Studies in Narrative Tech-
        niques." Unpub. Doct. Diss., 1958 (Harvard),
        pp. 113-72.

        We experience E both from the heroine's point
     of view and the narrator's. The narrator makes
     Emma an object of irony "simply by exposing with
     unrelenting thoroughness the moral naïveté implicit
     in her vanity." JA "made expert use of narrative
     techniques that we identify with a much later stage
     in the development of modern fiction."

566 Edge, Charles E. "Jane Austen's Novels: A Study
        of the Theme of Isolation." Unpub. Doct.
        Diss., 1958 (Duke).

        One of JA's basic themes is the individual's
     isolation from others, a condition which may be
     owing to a variety of factors--to a character's
     personality, to social institutions, to the nature
     of existence itself. Stressing the difficulty of

establishing adequate personal relationships, JA
allows her protagonists, by virtue of their ultimate
generous and intelligent awareness of self and
others, to remove the barriers initially separating
them. Through interaction with other concerns, the
theme of isolation contributes to our sense of the
novels' complexity.

1959

567 Link, Frederick Martin. "The Reputation of Jane
        Austen in the Twentieth Century with an
        Annotated Enumerative Bibliography of Austen
        Criticism from 1811 to June, 1957." DA, 19
        (1959), 1742-43 (Boston).

        JA's initial reception was favorable but her
reputation declined after her death. Interest
revived with the publication of the Memoir (1870)
and Brabourne's edition of the letters. Early
twentieth-century criticism was largely "appre-
ciative," but criticism in the thirties scruti-
nized and reevaluated the tradition in which she
wrote. In the fifties most JA criticism came from
academic environments.

568 Widmer, Eleanor Joan Rackow. "Love and Duty: The
        Heroines in Jane Austen and Charlotte Bronte."
        DA, 19 (1959), 3297-98 (U. of Wash.).

        In JA destiny is knowledge of self and so-
ciety, "joined in an honest and loving rapproach-
ment." Like other nineteenth-century novelists, JA
creates heroines who fulfill themselves in ways
never at odds with duty.

1960

569 Fryxell, Donald Raymond. "The Patterns of Jane
        Austen's Novels." DA, 20 (1960), 4110 (Ky.).

        Analyses of the patterns of the novels reveal
that JA's art "fails more frequently than is com-
monly supposed." The novels are dramatic, and
a five-act structure is discernible in all six. In
her best work the satirist and humorist predominate,
and in her poorest the moralist takes charge.

570   White, Edward Michael.   "Jane Austen and the Art of
         Parody." Unpub. Doct. Diss., 1960 (Harvard).

         In JA's writings parody starts as criticism of
literature and progresses to a criticism of life.
Though the juvenilia are almost completely parodic
in nature, they foreshadow JA's later use of satire.
In NA and S and S parody is subordinate to satire
and irony; and in her major novels, "although the
exaggerated imitation that is parody becomes rare,
the parodic way of examining the problem of reality
becomes infused into the [novels'] very texture."

                          1961

571   Binkley, William O.   "Comic Self-Discovery in Jane
         Austen's Novels." DA, 22 (1961), 1992-93
         (Wis.).

         Self-discovery, which determines both plot
structure and patterning of characters, develops in
the novels from a conventional and theory-ridden
theme to one "treated with individuality and
artistry." JA recognizes both the chaotic and
ordered worlds, and this double vision enables her
to combine the exposure of comic self-deception
with the portrayal of the progress of a sensitive
individual from the chaotic world to an acceptance
and understanding of the values of the ordered
world.

572   Estey, George Fisher.   "The Constituted Scene in
         Certain English Novels: 1813-1872." DA, 21
         (1961), 3097 (Ill.).

         Because "it is limited in time, in social
level, and in theme, and is almost as limited in
space," P and P is congenial to the novelist's
dramatization of issues. JA's careful use of
"constituted scenes," or meetings between characters in which an issue important to the book is
resolved, helps make P and P "one of the most
'scenic' of novels."

                          1962

573   Servotte, Father Herman.   "Emma and Middlemarch--Two

Authorial Novels," in "The Narrator in English
Fiction: A Contribution to the Literary History
of the Novel." Unpub. Doct. Diss., 1962
(Louvain), pp. 116-76.

In E "the unobtrusive narrator using the general categories of his public, the perfect character embodying the values of polite society, and the
reliance upon the reader's acceptance of those same
values and categories all reflect [JA's] basic
conservatism and parochialism. In other words, her
technique and her conception of life are closely
related."

1963

574 Chillman, Dawes. "Jane Austen's Juvenilia as a
          Key to the Structure of Her First Three Mature
          Novels." DA, 24 (1963), 724-25 (Texas).

JA's juvenile works have features in common
with NA, S and S, and P and P. These similarities
include satire on the novel of sentiment and the
philosophy of sensibility, and the exploration of
the mental processes of an inexperienced young
woman who is both intelligent and imaginative.

575 Craik, Wendy Ann. "Pattern in the Novels of Jane
          Austen." Unpub. Doct. Diss. [1963], Leicester.

     (See 266.)

576 Elsbree, Langdon. "The Breaking Chain: A Study of
          the Dance in the Novels of Jane Austen, George
          Eliot, Thomas Hardy, and D. H. Lawrence." DA,
          24 (1963), 2476 (Claremont).

The dance in JA serves as an emblem of the
duties of "fidelity and complaisance," and she uses
the dance "to show how the players [in the game of
courtship] deceive themselves or play in bad faith."
Only in P does the dance give form to emotions which
transcend those of fidelity and complaisance.

577 McIlroy, Ellen LaFleur. "Realism and Anti-Realism
          in the Novels of Jane Austen." DA, 24 (1963),
          1617-18 (Syracuse).

To see JA "only as an eighteenth-century
artist, rational, behavior-oriented, bound by conventions both literary and social," is to ignore her
experimentation in realism. That experimentation
sought to make both the novelist and her heroines
compatible with society.

578 Mews, Hazel. "The Conception of the Role of Women
     in English Women Writers from 1790 to 1870."
     Unpub. Doct. Diss., 1963 (Pretoria), pp. 163-
     92 and passim.

Her heroines embody in varying degrees the
qualities JA deemed valuable, including self-
control, fortitude, intelligence, taste, and
tenderness. Eighteenth-century guides to female
conduct, by Mrs. Chapone and others, are popular
"expressions of basic principles similar to those
to which [JA] herself held fast."

579 Ten Harmsel, Henrietta. "Jane Austen's Use of
     Literary Conventions." DA, 23 (1963), 3902-03
     (Mich.).

     (See 259.)

                        1964

580 Bradbrook, Frank W. "Jane Austen: Novelist of Tra-
     dition." Unpub. Doct. Diss., 1964 (Univ. Col-
     lege of North Wales, Bangor).

     (See 301.)

581 Demarest, David Porter, Jr. "Legal Language and
     Situation in the Eighteenth Century Novel:
     Readings in Defoe, Richardson, Fielding and
     Austen." DA, 24 (1964), 2907 (Wis.).

Legal language and situation in JA identify
her with "the Johnsonian, neo-classic tradition
of the eighteenth century. Central to her vision
is the term 'judgment,' and she sets in motion a
game of detection: 'judgment' must subdue fancy and
imagination if it is to collect the unbiased evidence necessary to accurate reading of social
reality."

582 Moler, Kenneth Lloyd. "Jane Austen's Novels and
         Their Literary Milieu." Unpub. Doct. Diss.,
         1964 (Harvard).

     (See 401.)

583 Oesterreich, Helga. "Das Gespräch im Roman:
         Untersucht im Werk von Defoe, Fielding und Jane
         Austen." Unpub. Doct. Diss., 1964 (Münster),
         passim.

     JA employs four types of dialogue: direct
     discourse, experienced discourse, indirect dis-
     course, and report. Her dialogue most often falls
     into the first category. In contrast to Defoe and
     Fielding she allows the characters' dialogue to
     establish setting and thereby gives the impression
     that the novel tells itself. In her later novels
     the trend is toward interiorization (Verinner-
     lichung): the characters' unexpressed thoughts are
     used to supplement dialogue.

584 Pati, Prafulla Kumar. "Jane Austen: Her Relation-
         ship to the Romantic and Realistic Traditions
         of English Fiction." DA, 24 (1964), 4681
         (Minn.).

     "Jane Austen's close relationship to and
     synthesis of both the romantic and the realistic
     traditions enable her to express in her art her
     complex and composite personality; she also secures,
     thereby, a harmonious development for the English
     novel."

585 Westbrook, James Seymour, Jr. "Sensibility and
         Society: A Study in Themes." DA, 25 (1964),
         3560 (Columbia).

     In MP, JA "weighs the virtues of two important
     aspects of sensibility--inwardness and outward-
     ness."

                           1965

586 Harris, Stephen LeRoy. "The Mask of Morality: A
         Study of the Unconscious Hypocrite in Repre-
         sentative Novels of Jane Austen, Charles

Dickens, and George Eliot." <u>DA</u>, 25 (1965), 4699 (Cornell).

The quality of self-blindness and moral stupidity is at the heart of JA's conception of Mary Crawford and Emma Woodhouse. However, because Emma's moral quality differs significantly from Mary's, Emma proves capable of reform.

587 Heagarty, Mary Alice. "Aesthetic Distance in the Techniques of the Novel." <u>DA</u>, 25 (1965), 4687-88 (Ill.).

JA's "prose style is analyzed to show how her use of psychological detail alternating with aphorism serves to keep the reader at the distance demanded by the comic mode."

588 Woods, Sister Mary St. Francis. "Jane Austen and the Omniscient Narrative Voice." <u>DA</u>, 26 (1965), 2734 (Catholic U.).

Omniscience as JA uses it is not an inartistic narrative technique. "In her hands, omniscience is a disciplined method, complex enough to control all the elements involved in story-telling, flexible enough to be adapted to varied story situations."

1966

589 Bramer, George Robert. "The Quality of Love in Jane Austen's Novels." <u>DA</u>, 27 (1966), 1779A (Notre Dame).

In both <u>NA</u> and <u>S and S</u> a balance of the masculine principle (reason and activeness) and the feminine principle (feeling and passivity) forms the ideal love. <u>NA</u> gives a more compelling portrayal of masculine, <u>S and S</u> of feminine, strength. Critical conclusions based on the acceptance or love, rather than the hatred, in JA's novels are ultimately correct.

590 Koppel, Gene Stuart. "The Moral Basis of Jane Austen's Novels." <u>DA</u>, 26 (1966), 4663-64 (Wash. U.).

In JA's novels reason and duty supply the only
satisfactory guides for the fulfillment of responsibility to family and society. The most important
duty of parents is to educate their children morally, that is, to develop their ability to distin-
guish inner and outer reality, and to direct and
discipline themselves.

1967

591 Burrows, John Frederick. "Jane Austen's Emma: A
         Study of Narrative Art." Unpub. Doct. Diss.,
         1967 (London).

     (See 384.)

592 Duckworth, Alistair McKay. "The Improvement of
         the Estate: Self and Inheritance in Jane
         Austen's Major Fiction." DA, 28 (1967),
         1783A (Johns Hopkins).

     (See 495.)

593 Greene, Mildred Sarah Epstein. "Love and Duty:
         The Character of the Princesse de Clèves as
         Reflected in Certain Later English and
         American Novels (Studies in . . . Jane
         Austen's Sense and Sensibility and Persuasion
         . . .)." DA, 28 (1967), 230A-31A (N. M.).

     In JA's novels the Princesse-like heroine is
able to outgrow her early education and her attachment to an unstable lover and combine love and duty
in a happy marriage. Marianne Dashwood learns that
passion without esteem is no basis for marriage.
Anne Elliot is more than a "Princesse de Clèves" in
her ability to reconcile her love of Wentworth with
loyalty to Lady Russell.

594 Muellerleile, Sister St. Alfred. "The Unconven-
         tional Miss Austen; or, A Study of Jane
         Austen's Use of the Conventions of Popular
         English Fiction, 1770-1800." Unpub. Doct.
         Diss., 1967 (Chicago).

     JA transformed conventional features of late
eighteenth-century fiction "into her own significant

artistic creations." Though she used the same
materials--the theme of romantic sensibility in S
and S and the Cinderella theme in P and P are
examples--she rejected her immediate predecessors'
sentimentalism and lack of realism; she based her
novels on her own acute sense of probability and
clear moral vision.

595 Rubinstein, Elliot L. "Jane Austen's Novels: The
        Microcosm and the World Beyond." DA, 28
        (1967), 2220A-21A (Columbia).

An analysis of the relation between JA's commentary on social and cultural issues and the conflict of the individual and his restrictive social
milieu reveals that JA was not an outdated Augustan.
"One comes to understand her work instead as an
attempt to review and redefine traditional beliefs
in an age when many of the old certainties had
already been seriously challenged."

596 Slattery, Sister Margaret Patrice. "The Technique
        of Balance in the Construction of Character in
        the Novels of Jane Austen." DA, 27 (1967),
        3063A-64A (Catholic U.).

An event in JA's novels "exists primarily as the
occasion for character reaction. This concept commits the author to a use of the technique of balance,
i. e., the measuring of one character with or against
another by parallelism, or antithesis, or a combination of both." Balance is a controlling principle in
all the novels, producing characters that are convincing and structures that are aesthetically
pleasing.

597 Zimmerman, Everett. "Jane Austen and Sensibility:
        A Study of Tradition and Technique." DA, 27
        (1967), 3476A (Temple).

"The novels of sensibility are related to a
philosophical tradition usually traced to Shaftesbury and a literary tradition usually traced to
Richardson; certain aspects of both the philosophical and literary traditions are continued in Jane
Austen's works." Her problem was to resolve the
subjective demands of the self and the needs of
society.

1968

598 Brown, Lloyd Wellesley. "The Novels of Jane Austen:
     A Study of the Language of Comedy." <u>DA</u>, 28
     (1968), 4166A-67A (Toronto).

        JA enjoys a rich heritage of eighteenth-century
     traditions of comic form and expression. Her work
     also includes more original patterns. Her style
     evolves to meet the changing requirements of her
     developing insight, first using established comic
     modes, then extending itself to less traditional
     means of expression.

599 Crisp, Jane D. "Jane Austen, the Unashamed Novel
        Reader." Unpub. Doct. Diss., 1968 (Australian
        National).

        (Not seen.)

600 Kiley, Anne Watt. "The Art of Living: Jane Austen's
        Social Aesthetic." <u>DA</u>, 29 (1968), 873A (Wis.).

        "Form, style, and morality are all secondary to
     her interest in the way characters function" in re-
     lation to each other. "This social orientation is
     reflected in her attitudes toward all the arts,"
     particularly the novel. It is its truth to human
     nature in a social context that gives a novel value.

601 Kissane, Joseph Michael. "Richardson and Jane
        Austen." <u>DA</u>, 29 (1968), 1899A (Columbia).

        JA is indebted to Richardson for the characters
     of "the rake, the young lady, and the gentleman-
     hero." She draws on his "views of men and women and
     on his considerations of such matters as the effect
     of literature on the imagination, the importance of
     female education, the uses of benevolence, the
     nature of sensibility."

602 Mellen, Joan. "Morality in the Novel: A Study of
        Five English Novelists, Henry Fielding, Jane
        Austen, George Eliot, Joseph Conrad and D. H.
        Lawrence." <u>DA</u>, 29 (1968), 1543A (C.U.N.Y.).

        JA and Fielding define their moral schemes
     within a recognizable social context, generally

approved by their times. JA "is perhaps one of the
last great English novelists whose norms face no
challenge from history." But for novelists after
George Eliot, history calls all beliefs into question.

603 Sherif, Abla. Jane Austen's Persuasion. Doct.
       Diss. Zürich, 1968. Zürich: Juris, 1968.

P treats, in a more personal, less detached,
and less amused manner, themes and values characteristic of JA's other novels. Showing "a maximum
of economy, crystallization and lucidity," P combines "the Augustan virtue of control" and romanticism's stress on feelings. The book's most outstanding quality is the heroine's emotional depth.

604 Solomon, Stanley J. "Irony and the Eighteenth-
       Century Novel: Value and Vision from Richard-
       son to Jane Austen." DA, 29 (1968), 1236A
       (Temple).

"In order to employ ironic vision, classical novelists needed to write from a detached
perspective which assumed that readers would
correctly interpret the proper standards of conduct governing a moral and polite society." After
Richardson, it was not until JA that the novel
again manifested a "powerful ironic vision governed
by an author's moral concerns."

1969

605 Anderson, Walter Eldon. "Jane Austen's Novels as
       Represented Actions." DA, 29 (1969), 4448A
       (Calif., Berkeley).

The novels are defined by their kinds of
represented actions. NA, S and S, and E are organized by internal changes in the heroines; P and
P, MP, and P are organized by changes in situation
or fortune. The novels are also differentiated by
their artistic, moral, and intellectual qualities,
with P and P and E ranking highest, NA lowest, and
P "in a class by itself."

606 Beattie, Thomas Charles. "From Pride and

Prejudice to Emma: A Study of Jane Austen as
Moralist." DAI, 30 (1969), 311A-12A (Mich.).

JA's emphasis on the secular or on the religious varies from novel to novel. P and P is secular, classical, and Aristotelian. The sober religious emphasis of MP enlarges the moral perspective
she had employed in P and P, but seems uncongenial
to her creative imagination. "Emma combines a classical ethic with a Christian and presents a satisfying synthesis of the two."

607 Holly, Marcia Vivian. "Jane Austen and the Unique-
         ness of Emma." DAI, 30 (1969), 1137A (Wash.
         State).

Although JA's novels resemble each other, E
holds a "unique place . . . in being a thematically
pivotal book." Its heroine "represents the quest
of the 19th-century English woman to reconcile
traditional and modern roles, to find and define
herself, and to discover the new answers which will
enable her to live . . . as a full human being."

608 Rosenberg, Sondra. "The Wholly Greater Sum: A
         Study of Unity in the Novel." DAI, 30 (1969),
         1149A-50A (Ill.).

When a novel's theme and plot properly cohere,
as they do in E, a strong central character acts as
an important unifying element.

609 Sabiston, Elizabeth Jean. "The Provincial Heroine
         in Prose Fiction: A Study in Isolation and
         Creativity." DAI, 30 (1969), 1150A (Cornell).

Emma is part of a tradition of imaginative
provincial heroines in prose fiction. Frustrated
by her provincial setting and by her own limitations of character, she tries "to impart form and
beauty to the mediocre life" around her.

1970

610 Bryant, Ruth Carmen Woodfin. "Jane Austen's Emma:
         Art and Image." DAI, 31 (1970), 1790A
         (Texas, Austin).

In <u>E</u>, JA "accepts the fact that everyone cannot
be made good, whole, wise, or feeling without,
therefore, finding life any heavy affair. . . .
Seen from the perspective of the center of life,
fragmentation and finitude are attributes and
reminders of the whole of life which is neither
illusory nor evil nor insignificant, but always more
and always beyond the individual's ability to know
and feel."

611   Cantrell, Dorothy Dean.   "The Twentieth-Century
        Criticisms of Jane Austen's <u>Mansfield Park</u>
        and <u>Emma</u>." <u>DAI</u>, 31 (1970), 2335A-36A (Tenn.).

        "The study which devotes one chapter to a
general review of Jane Austen's reputation in the
twentieth century, two chapters to evaluations of
criticisms of the two novels, and one to a discussion of the varied approaches to Austen criticism
1900-1968 surveys and analyses all accessible books,
monographs, articles, unpublished dissertations,
introductions to editions of the novels, and reviews of the two novels published in this century."

612   Martien, Norman Gerald.   ". . . II.   <u>Mansfield Park</u>
        and Jane Austen's Heroine. . . ." <u>DAI</u>, 30
        (1970), 3468A (Rutgers).

        The progress of Fanny from a child to a
respectable young woman "operates less by development than by exclusions." She is given the traditional sentiments of a heroine, "but the novel
reveals their shortcomings just as it does the
failure of wit in the Crawfords. . . . In so
allowing the failure of both wit and sentiment,
Jane Austen undercuts her own traditions."

613   Reddick, Bryan DeWitt.   "Tone in Dramatic Nar-
        rative." <u>DAI</u>, 31 (1970), 2397A (Calif.,
        Davis).

        In <u>E</u> "the narrator's tone is authoritative.
The comparison between the narrator's simple,
succinct style and the characters' manner of
speaking flatters Mr. Knightley and Emma and
satirizes Mr. and Mrs. Elton. Emma is portrayed
by dramatic irony, not by the narrator's explicit
irony like the less central characters."

614   Sharp, Ruth Marian McKenzie. "Rational Vision and
         the Comic Resolution: A Study in the Novels of
         Richardson, Fielding and Jane Austen." DAI, 31
         (1970), 369A (Wis.).

      JA's novels illustrate the process of "rectifi-
      cation," whereby "a novelist consistently alters his
      imitation of reality in the direction of an ideal
      order."

                              1971

615   Auerbach, Nina Joan. "Reality as Vision in the
         Novels of Jane Austen and George Eliot." DAI,
         31 (1971), 4701A-02A (Columbia).

      "The subtlety with which she transmits a sense
      of spiritual magnitude to commonplace details sug-
      gests affinities with" the Romantic poets. In JA's
      early novels "the protagonist is forced to accom-
      modate herself to the demands of an unfeeling world,
      but in the later novels, the world opens out to
      accommodate the desires of the protagonist." In P
      the sea is a symbol of visionary escape from so-
      ciety.

616   Birky, Wilbur Joseph. "Marriage as Pattern and
         Metaphor in the Victorian Novel." DAI, 31
         (1971), 4704A-05A (Iowa).

      A realistic novel, P and P puts emphasis "not
      on the triumph of love over external obstacles as
      in the romantic novel, but on the selection of a
      partner in a kind of marriage market. The shape of
      the novel is determined by the climate of choice,
      and the romantic pattern is thus modified by the
      change in emphasis from goal to process."

617   Breasted, Barbara. ". . . II: Public Standards in
         Fiction: A Discussion of Three Nineteenth-
         Century Novels--George Eliot's Middlemarch and
         Jane Austen's Pride and Prejudice and Emma.
         . . ." DAI, 31 (1971), 4112A (Rutgers).

      JA "accepts traditional social roles and pub-
      lic standards and finds them essential to assess a
      character." Her heroines gain a "sharper sense of
      their own and their lover's identities through
      engaging in social life."

618   Corwin, Laura Jane. "The Concept of the Self in the
         Novels of Jane Austen." DAI, 31 (1971), 5356A-
         57A (Pa.).

         JA's characters divide into two types: the
    "protean," who define themselves by theatrical tech-
    niques, and the "stable," who see the social world
    as a reflection of the moral world and locate the
    self in this context. "The simultaneous use of so-
    cial emblems to express both emotional and moral
    commitments points to the organic relationship
    between self and society which makes the approach of
    the stable characters the basis for social harmony."

619   Delaney, Janice Fogarty. "Chapter Design in Jane
         Austen's Novels." DAI, 31 (1971), 5394A-95A
         (Temple).

         JA uses the traditions of the epistolary novel
    and the novel organized around chapters to form the
    components of fiction into chapters. She stresses
    either the chapter as scene or the chapter as one
    part of a continuing series of events.

620   Erickson, E. Joyce Quiring. "The Significance of
         Persuasion." DAI, 31 (1971), 3501A (U. of
         Wash.).

         P's significance lies "in its heroine and in
    the novel's vision of that heroine's relation to
    her society." The motivation for Anne's actions
    is not social but purely personal, and her "values,
    attitudes and mode of conduct are presented as a
    model for an obviously fragmented society."

621   Fowler, Marian Elizabeth. "Patterns of Prudence:
         Courtship Conventions in Jane Austen's Nov-
         els." DAI, 32 (1971), 917A-18A (Toronto).

         JA's heroines "make their way to the altar
    along six different paths of prudence." They
    follow those courtship conventions (involving
    money, rank, behavior, and sentiment) which aid
    them in their moral and psychological develop-
    ment.

622   Hartzler, Sara Kathryn Kreider. "Marriage as Theme
         and Structure in Jane Austen's Novels." DAI,
         32 (1971), 389A (Ind.).

JA reflects contemporary conditions and attitudes toward marriage with great accuracy. Instead of gothic and sentimental escapism, she presents a realistic assessment of the problems and moral issues facing her heroines. Her novels thus "become important social as well as artistic documents which show the human significance of the major social institution for gentlewomen of her day."

623 Helms, Alan Earl. ". . . 2. Sensibility and Sense in Jane Austen's Persuasion. . . ." DAI, 32 (1971), 3305A (Rutgers).

P reveals a new attitude on JA's part toward the nature of feeling. Anne Elliot often withdraws from society "to compose herself and ponder the meaning of her feelings. She accomplishes this by means of recollection, her principle [sic] mental occupation and the activity by which Austen distinguishes between 'good' and 'bad' characters in Persuasion."

624 Hill, Patricia Ann Newman. "The Function of Setting in Jane Austen's Novels." DAI, 32 (1971), 3252A (Auburn).

In JA's novels setting interacts with character, theme, and structure: setting acts as a stimulus to mislead or educate the heroine and is used to symbolize ideas and to organize novelistic movement.

625 Jackel, David Amrose. "Jane Austen and the Concept of the Novelist's Art, 1775-1820." DAI, 32 (1971), 3308A (Toronto).

JA knew the novelistic conventions of her time and transformed "accepted methods and commonplace materials." Unlike her contemporaries, she combined "successfully the roles of entertainer and moralist."

626 May, Leland Chandler. "Parodies of the Gothic Novel." DAI, 31 (1971), 4128A (Okla. State).

Parodies of the Gothic novel published between 1800 and 1820, including NA, did not contribute as much to the Gothic novel's demise as is usually

supposed. Still, the parodies did encourage "literature to present the actual experiences of living."

627   Metcalfe, Alvin C. "Sense and Sensibility: A Study
          of Its Similarity to the History of Sir Charles
          Grandison." DAI, 31 (1971), 4129A (Kent State).

      Sir Charles Grandison appears to be a source
for S and S because the two novels are similar in
sentiment, plot, motivation, and character development.

628   Morahan, Richard Edward. ". . . III. Jane Austen's
          Endings." DAI, 32 (1971), 3318A-19A (Rutgers).

      "Austen's endings always present a final shift
in the narrator's voice and perspective that usually
involves a withdrawal from the witty and subtle
examination of consciousness to a flatly satirical
or ironically simple-minded point-of-view."

629   North, Douglas McKay. "Inheritance in the Novels
          of Jane Austen, Charles Dickens, and George
          Eliot." DAI, 31 (1971), 5419A (Va.).

      JA's changing attitudes toward social trans-
formation can be extrapolated from her handling of
the relationship between individual and inherited
property. Anne Elliot "breaks with her public
inheritance, but then asserts in place of that
lapsed continuity a 'time-consciousness.'"

630   Raz, Robert Walter. "Syntactic Variation in Jane
          Austen's Dialogue." DAI, 31 (1971), 6584A-
          85A (Mich.).

      From JA's statements about style and from the
syntactic patterning in her novels we find that
syntax reveals the roles behind which her characters conceal themselves, that these roles are
largely defined by society, and that her heroes
and heroines conform to the roles society pre-
scribes for them.

1972

631   Beach, Luann. "A Rhetorical Analysis of Jane

Austen's Novels." DAI, 32 (1972), 5730A
(Stanford).

JA's manipulation of the narrator promotes
sympathy for, and provides judgment upon, the
characters. Technical devices and the general
tone define her narrators as distinct identities,
and the relationship between these "personalities"
and the heroines contributes to both the comic and
moral ends of the novels.

632 Brewster, Jack. "The Virtuous Heroes of the Eng-
        lish Novel." DAI, 32 (1972), 4601A-02A
        (Ind.).

George Knightley is both virtuous and heroic.
From the beginning he is in full agreement with JA's
value system and inculcates it in the fictional community. A static and peripheral hero, he represents
values that are felt to be convincing.

633 Kestner, Joseph Aloysius, III.   "Jane Austen:
        Seven Themes in Variation." DAI, 32 (1972),
        6379A-80A (Columbia).

"Seven themes emerge from an analysis of Jane
Austen's writing: improvement, intimacy, persuasion,
concealment, imagination, silence, and shyness."
"These seven themes, and the variations possible
with them, provided Jane Austen with a method she
consciously used to produce an organic whole--the
novel--from the diverse material of life."

634 Rudolf, Jo-Ellen Schwartz.   "The Novels That Taught
        the Ladies: A Study of Popular Fiction Written
        by Women, 1702-1834." DAI, 33 (1972), 1695A
        (Calif., San Diego).

MP derives from the aims and formulas of the
"tea-table novel," a genre of popular literature
"characterized by its didactic purpose of teaching
young unmarried women how to maneuver through the
intricacies of eighteenth-century moral and social
rules."

635 Whitten, Benjamin Goodman, Jr.   "Jane Austen's
        'Comedy of Feeling': A Critical Analysis of
        Persuasion." DAI, 32 (1972), 4031A (Calif.,
        Davis).

"The general narrative point of view, together
with the rhetorical guidance of narrative tone,
allows the reader to observe objectively the psychological handicaps, inconsistencies of behavior,
and misconceptions Anne displays and must overcome,
while at the same time the narrative vantage at
Anne's position allows him to respond sympathetically
to her genuine strong feelings and appreciate her
real strength of character."

636 Wilhelm, Albert Earl. "Word Clusters in Jane
        Austen's Major Novels." DAI, 32 (1972), 5206A-
        07A (N.C., Chapel Hill).

        JA's themes are clarified by analyzing sig-
nificant word clusters within the individual novels.
In terms of development JA "moves from a heavy
dependence upon abstractions in her early novels
to a greater use of word clusters whose root words
are concrete."

                         1973

637 Nelson, Carolyn Christensen. "Patterns in the
        Bildungsroman as Illustrated by Six English
        Novels from 1814 to 1860." DAI, 33 (1973),
        3597A-98A (Wis.).

        Unlike later nineteenth-century English novels
in the Bildungsroman tradition, MP, which shows
"the education of the individual as a social initia-
tion," concludes with the protagonist assuming her
place in the established society.

III.   Mentions

638 Palmer, Arnold. Movable Feasts: A Reconnaissance
        of the Origins and Consequences of Fluctuations
        in Meal-Times with Special Attention to the
        Introduction of Luncheon and Afternoon Tea.
        New York: Oxford Univ. Press, 1952, p. 27 and
        passim.

        JA, like "other people of leisure and fashion,"
     breakfasted at ten o'clock.

1953

639 Furbank, P. N., and F. J. H. Haskell. "[An Inter-
        view with] E. M. Forster." ParisR, No. 1
        (1953), p. 39. Forster's remarks on JA appear
        also in Writers at Work: The Paris Review
        Interviews, ed. Malcolm Cowley (New York:
        Viking Press, 1958), p. 34.

        "'What did you learn from Jane Austen tech-
     nically?'"

        "'I learned the possibilities of domestic
     humor. I was more ambitious than she was, of
     course; I tried to hitch it on to other things.'"

640 Lawrence, D. H. "A Propos of Lady Chatterley's
        Lover," in Sex, Literature and Censorship.
        Ed. Harry T. Moore. New York: Twayne, 1953,
        p. 119. This essay appeared originally in
        1930.

        "This old maid typifies 'personality' instead
     of character, the sharp knowing in apartness instead
     of knowing in togetherness, and she is, to my feel-
     ing, thoroughly unpleasant, English in the bad,
     mean, snobbish sense of the word, just as Fielding
     is English in the good, generous sense."

641 Liddell, Robert. Some Principles of Fiction.

London: Cape, 1953, pp. 23-24 and _passim_.

Unlike the modern novelist, JA could rely on the existence of an "organic community," which forms a "permanent background" to her novels.

642 Trilling, Lionel. "A Portrait of Western Man."
     Listener, 11 June 1953, pp. 969-71.

What JA contemplates in her novels is "the drama of spirit at war with itself." Her irony is the "divine irony" that dramatizes the irreconcilable antinomies of human nature. She is first among the novelists to recognize the dependence of spirit on matter and circumstance, and she first clarified the categories of sincerity and vulgarity, of personality and character.

643 Wright, Andrew H. "Irony and Fiction." _JAAC_, 12
     (1953), 114.

Comedy sees human incongruities as corrigible; irony sees them as irremediable. Thus _E_, which contains elements of both modes of apprehension, "can be read on more than one level."

1954

644 Clark, E. V. "The Private Governess in Fiction."
     ContemporaryR, 186 (1954), 166-67.

Typical of those in most fiction, the governesses in JA's novels are treated with kindness, but (perhaps excepting Miss Taylor of _E_) never as equals.

645 Forster, E. M. _Aspects of the Novel_. New York:
     Harcourt, Brace & World, 1954 [1927], pp. 65-66 and 73-77.

JA "is a miniaturist, but never two-dimensional. All her characters are round, or capable of rotundity." They "give us a slightly new pleasure each time they come in."

646 Muir, Edwin. "The Dramatic Novel," in _The Structure_

of the Novel. London: Hogarth Press, 1954
[London: L. and V. Woolf, 1928], pp. 42-47 and
passim.

JA is the first consummately successful English
practitioner of the dramatic novel. This form involves "an intensification of action," "strict interior causation," "no external framework," and the
view that character has consequences. "The dramatic
novel shows that both appearance and reality are the
same, and that character is action, and action
character."

1955

647   Nicolson, Harold. Good Behaviour: Being a Study of
          Certain Types of Civility. London: Constable,
          1955, pp. 233-35.

"The society which she depicts is mean and
competitive, almost wholly uninterested in intellectual, spiritual or aesthetic values, and wastes
time, energy and even passion upon the meaningless
subtleties of social status." It is "an incompa-
rable analysis of the stratification of English
upper-middle and lower-middle society at the time of
the Industrial Revolution."

648   Ward, A. C. Illustrated History of English Litera-
          ture. New York: McKay, 1955. III ["Blake to
          Bernard Shaw"], 135-38 and passim.

Preserving "an utter serenity in her novels,"
JA distills "the essences of human nature in what
is no more than a tiny crucible of experience.
. . . By bringing the domestic novel to perfection Jane Austen also brought it to its terminus."

1956

649   James, Henry. "The Lesson of Balzac," in The
          Future of the Novel: Essays on the Art of
          Fiction. Ed. Leon Edel. New York: Vintage,
          1956, pp. 99-101. This essay appeared orig-
          inally in 1905.

"The key to Jane Austen's fortune with

posterity has been in part the extraordinary grace
of her facility, in fact of her unconsciousness."

650 McKillop, Alan Dugald. The Early Masters of English
       Fiction. Lawrence: Univ. of Kansas Press, 1956,
       pp. 95-96.

       "Richardson handed on to Jane Austen the tradi-
tion of a judgment of society by the intelligent
feminine mind, secured by an accepted social and
moral system."

651 O'Connor, Frank. The Mirror in the Roadway: A Study
       of the Modern Novel. New York: Knopf, 1956,
       p. 98 and passim.

       "So aware is [JA] of people that she can almost
transfer entirely the narrative responsibility from
events to character. She can make the character
produce the events that she needs to sustain
interest."

652 Praz, Mario. The Hero in Eclipse in Victorian Fic-
       tion. Trans. Angus Davidson. New York: Oxford
       Univ. Press, 1956, p. 317 and passim.

       JA's novels may be likened to a piece of
Hepplewhite furniture, "the kind of English furniture that has polished surfaces, strong, delicate
joints and unemphatic mouldings." This furniture
is characterized by "honesty of workmanship,
absence of emphasis, and fitness to" its purpose.

653 Reeves, James. The Critical Sense: Practical
       Criticism of Prose and Poetry. London:
       Heinemann, 1956, pp. 41-43.

       "Under cover of her ever-polite but ever-
vigilant irony," JA was able to maintain her "own
private standards while appearing to conform to
those of society."

654 Scrutton, Mary. "Addiction to Fiction." TC, 159
       (1956), 363.

       In NA, "Jane Austen was perfectly right to
snipe at the hypocrisy that subordinated [the
novel] to the essay."

655   Thomson, Patricia. The Victorian Heroine: A Chang-
         ing Ideal, 1837-1873. New York: Oxford Univ.
      Press, 1956, pp. 58-59.

      Throughout her novels JA implies "that the
      resemblance between the sexes was greater than their
      disparity, that to a large extent their vices and
      virtues were interchangeable. But still, many years
      later, feminists were making little headway in
      persuading the public of the truth of this point,
      made so effortlessly by Miss Austen."

                              1957

656   Brace, Gerald Warner. The Age of the Novel.
      Boston Univ. Press, 1957, p. 13.

      For JA "the only life worth living is upper
      class life."

657   Bradbrook, Frank. "Samuel Richardson," in From
         Dryden to Johnson. (Vol. 4 of The Pelican
         Guide to English Literature.) Ed. Boris Ford.
      Harmondsworth, Middlesex: Penguin, 1957, pp.
      301-02 and 309-11.

      (See 301.)

658   Cecil, Lord David. "The Forms of English Fic-
         tion," in The Fine Art of Reading and Other
         Literary Studies. Indianapolis: Bobbs-Mer-
      rill, 1957, pp. 137-38 and 144-46.

      With JA, the reader "feels he is watching
      something happening in real life. Yet he is left
      with a sense of completeness and symmetry which,
      alas, real life seldom gives." As she reconciles
      "the claims of reality and pattern," so does she
      also reconcile "those of reality with the claims
      of her comic vision."

659   Coveney, Peter. Poor Monkey: The Child in Litera-
         ture. London: Rockliff, 1957, p. 66.

      MP "is as much a novel about education as any
      in the language, and for this reason it was neces-
      sary for the story to begin with Fanny's child-
      hood."

>5660 Earnest, Ernest. "The Catty School of Writing."
SatR, 29 June 1957, p. 8.

Mrs. Elton, an example of JA's catty women, is
presented in the "context of essentially likeable
human beings."

661 Frye, Northrop. Anatomy of Criticism: Four Essays.
Princeton: Princeton Univ. Press, 1957, p. 308
and passim.

The interest "in ideas and theoretical statements is alien to the genius of the novel proper,
where the technical problem is to dissolve all
theory into personal relationships. In Jane
Austen . . . church, state and culture are never
examined except as social data."

662 Goodheart, Eugene. "Thomas Hardy and the Lyrical
Novel." NCF, 12 (1957), 215.

Unlike that of Hardy, "the greatness of Jane
Austen and Henry James consists precisely in the
extent of their awareness of the intimate connection that exists between spirit and manners."

663 Stamm, Rudolf. Englische Literatur. (Wissen-
schaftliche Forschungsberichte. Geisteswis-
senschaftliche Reihe, 11.) Bern: Francke
Verlag, 1957, pp. 327-28.

To understand JA, we must learn if the limited
range of her novels was externally or internally
imposed, and if it was consciously or unconsciously
sought.

664 Varma, Devendra P. The Gothic Flame: Being a
History of the Gothic Novel in England: Its
Origins, Efflorescence, Disintegration, and
Residuary Influences. London: Barker, 1957,
pp. 4-5.

"The list of seven horrid novels provided by
Jane Austen in her Northanger Abbey, far from
being haphazard, is by itself a chronicle of the
origin, efflorescence, and disintegration of Gothic
Romance, revealing not only the various types of
Gothic fiction but also the consequential phases of

its development from one shade to another."

665   Watt, Ian. The Rise of the Novel: Studies in Defoe,
        Richardson and Fielding. Berkeley and Los
        Angeles: Univ. of California Press, 1957, pp.
        296-99.

        JA solves the two narrative problems presented
        by Richardson and Fielding by combining the advan-
        tages of both "realism of presentation and realism
        of assessment." She faces the problems of economic
        individualism raised by Defoe and reflects the
        increasing importance of women in the literary
        scene.

666   West, Rebecca. The Court and the Castle: Some
        Treatments of a Recurrent Theme. New Haven:
        Yale Univ. Press, 1957, pp. 110-15 and passim.

        JA "was unable to feel any interest in woman
        as a redemptory figure leading man up to heaven.
        . . . What preoccupied her was the lot of Sophia
        Western's grand-daughters here on earth." "The
        terrible feature of Jane Austen's world is her best
        characters' complete realization that they must
        never live candidly and seek salvation by faithful-
        ness to a moral code which set principle above
        opportunism."

1958

667   Borden, Mary. "Personal Experience and the Art of
        Fiction." EDH, 29 (1958), 95.

        For JA, as for other women writers, the ideal
        life experience "is not rich and varied, but spartan,
        meagre, and restricted."

668   Cary, Joyce. Art and Reality: Ways of the Creative
        Process. New York: Harper, 1958, p. 53 and
        passim.

        "Jane Austen took the Anglican world as given
        to her, loved it, and enlarged upon it. Its ideals,
        so firmly grasped and strongly accepted, set her
        free. Her beautiful clarity, her mastery, is that
        of one who has no moral doubts, whose judgment is

always confident. Her command of form is due to her
command of a moral idea--her greatness to the fact
that her moral idea was true within its context."

669 Sittler, Joseph. The Structure of Christian Ethics.
     Baton Rouge: Louisiana State Univ. Press, 1958,
     pp. 20-21.

     JA exposes "the absurd incongruities between
form and fact, the dear delusions so sweetly anes-
thetic to a conventional society." Demonstrating
"the fundamentally ethical nature of the craft of
the artist," she speaks "the truth about the life
of man" and lets "real cats out of phoney bags."

670 Steinmann, Martin, Jr. "The Old Novel and the New,"
     in From Jane Austen to Joseph Conrad: Essays
     Collected in Memory of James T. Hillhouse. Ed.
     Robert C. Rathburn and Martin Steinmann, Jr.
     Minneapolis: Univ. of Minnesota Press, 1958,
     p. 296.

     As exemplified by the first chapter of P and P,
"the old novel is . . . not indifferent to the
dramatic"; rather, "the dramatic is not enough." JA
"must, like an essayist, introduce her scene with
generalizations and, when it is over, summarize its
particulars."

671 Sutherland, James. English Satire. Cambridge,
     Engl.: Univ. Press, 1958, pp. 116-22.

     "There is no question of disillusionment with
such a writer as Jane Austen. She has not lost her
illusions, because she never had any, and what may
seem satirical is often no more than her habitually
precise discrimination." Her vision is "singularly
clear and undisturbed."

672 Woolf, Virginia. "Phases of Fiction," in Granite
     and Rainbow: Essays. New York: Harcourt,
     Brace, 1958, pp. 114-20. This essay appeared
     originally in The Bookman, 1929.

     "To suggest that there is anything that lies
outside men and women would be to cast the shadow
of doubt upon the comedy of their relationships
and its sufficiency." "Pride and Prejudice, because

it has such integrity of its own, never for an
instant encroaches on other provinces, and, thus,
leaves them more clearly defined."

1959

673 Allott, Miriam. Novelists on the Novel. New York:
     Columbia Univ. Press, 1959, passim.

     JA "transposes the pleasurably 'romantic' into
the key of ordinary everyday experience." Hers is
a rational art, "obedient to eighteenth-century
notions of formal discipline" and shaped by a
"temperament which dislikes waste and feels com-
pelled to tidy up life's customary messiness."

674 Barrett, Mary Ellin. "20 Women Every Woman Should
     Know." Glamour, 41 (May 1959), 90-91.

     P and P "is the greatest how-to-get-a-man novel
of all time. Here is a young lady who is unflinch-
ingly honest, intelligent, direct, humorous, willing
to admit her prejudices unjustified . . . and eventually triumphant."

675 Bewley, Marius. The Eccentric Design: Form in the
     Classic American Novel. New York: Columbia
     Univ. Press, 1959, p. 15 and passim.

     "Her values pre-existed in the materials and
conditions of her art, even if it took her genius
to reveal them. Her art is essentially an art of
ironic illumination, of revealing in a new light
what had been there all along. Her judgements and
insights have the sureness and strength that come
from the corroboration of traditional sanctions."

676 Harkness, Bruce. "Bibliography and the Novelistic
     Fallacy." SB, 12 (1959), 61.

     The Rinehart edition of P and P, though based
on Chapman, ignores the three-volume construction of
the novel and numbers the chapters serially throughout. This format cannot but confuse the reader and
is suggestive of a general editorial irresponsibility toward novels.

1960

677   Bayley, John. The Characters of Love: A Study in
        the Literature of Personality. London: Con-
        stable, 1960, pp. 214-17 and passim.

        "For Jane Austen a loving absorption in indi-
        vidual personalities always precedes the working out
        of patterns of discernment. . . . It was people
        whom she found complex and intriguing--morality was
        simple enough."

678   Clive, Geoffrey. The Romantic Enlightenment. New
        York: Meridian, 1960, p. 154.

        "Kierkegaard took issue with the sense of
        propriety and security permeating the novels of
        Jane Austen. The celebrated opening sentence of
        Pride and Prejudice . . . bespeaks a trust in
        impersonal providence Kierkegaard hated with all
        his heart and all his mind."

679   Daiches, David. The Novel and the Modern World.
        Rev. ed. Chicago: Univ. of Chicago Press,
        1960 [1st ed., 1939], pp. 2-3 and passim.

        JA "took a stable and hierarchic society
        absolutely for granted in the complete assurance
        that her readers shared the view of what is sig-
        nificant in human experience that is implied in
        the structure of her novels."

680   Jefferson, D. W. "A Note on Ivy Compton-Burnett."
        Rev. Eng. Lit., 1 (Apr. 1960), 19-20.

        "What Miss Compton-Burnett inherits from Jane
        Austen is partly a tradition of literary and social
        manners," and also a vocabulary that "afforded
        opportunities for understatement, for the discreet
        or witty disclaimer."

681   Legouis, Émile, and Louis Cazamian. A History of
        English Literature. Trans. Helen Douglas
        Irvine. Rev. ed. London: Dent, 1960 [1st ed.,
        1926-1927], pp. 963-66 and passim.

        JA's realism "is more truly psychological
        than that of Richardson, for it is free from the

tragic obsessions of moral conscience. . . . There
is nothing more objective than these stories with
their spirit of gentle tolerance, one might even
say their naïveté, if a subtle suggestion of irony
did not hover over every page, revealing a sharpness of vision that could be unmercifully severe."

682 Mudrick, Marvin. "Character and Event in Fiction."
     YR, 50 (1960), 210 and 215.

     "Jane Austen is quite as fastidious a writer
as James, and the fastidiousness of her language is
always in the service of her mastery of event." A
fiction of novel length is required to draw a
character such as Elizabeth Bennet.

683 Poirier, Richard. The Comic Sense of Henry James:
     A Study of the Early Novels. New York: Oxford
     Univ. Press, 1960, p. 19 and passim.

     "In Jane Austen, the ironic variety of possible
interpretations [of any act] is made possible by her
adherence to a stable set of social conventions."

684 Priestley, J. B. Literature and Western Man. New
     York: Harper, 1960, p. 143.

     Excepting JA, "who had no more to do with the
Romantics than if they had been on the moon," the
Romantic age "failed in the novel proper."

685 Tave, Stuart M. The Amiable Humorist: A Study in
     the Comic Theory and Criticism of the Eigh-
     teenth and Early Nineteenth Centuries.
     Chicago: Univ. of Chicago Press, 1960, p. 147.

     "The humorist's true line of descent came not
through Jane Austen--she was unique, a cheerful wit,
equally free of innocence and indecency--but rather
through Scott."

686 Watson, Winifred. "Two Chelsea Doctors: J. M.
     Whistler's London Background." The Lady,
     27 Oct. 1960, pp. 533-35.

     (A short illustrated biography of Charles
Thomas Haden, the doctor who in 1815 attended Henry

Austen and is frequently mentioned in JA's letters, and of his son, Sir Francis Seymour Haden.)

1961

687   Bayley, John.   "The Novel and the Life Standard."
        LondonMag, 8 (Feb. 1961), 63-64.

        JA does not categorize her characters as being more or less "on the side of life." This Lawrentian standard of value is inapplicable to JA.

688   Bland, D. S.   "Endangering the Reader's Neck: Back-
        ground Description in the Novel." Criticism, 3
        (1961), 128-31.

        JA does not use landscape description "to en-hance situation, as in Mrs. Radcliffe," but rather to reveal "character, mood, and situation."

689   Blunden, Edmund.   "On Regency Fiction: A Fragment."
        E&S, 14 (1961), 58-60.

        Although JA was not widely read in the early nineteenth century, Archbishop Whateley's "idola-trous" article in the Quarterly Review (1821) made her better known.

690   Booth, Wayne C.   The Rhetoric of Fiction. Chicago:
        Univ. of Chicago Press, 1961, p. 163 and passim.

        "Jane Austen goes relatively deep morally, but scarcely skims the surface psychologically."

691   Garsh, Gabriel.   "The Problem of Class in the En-
        glish Novel." Venture, 2 (1961), 77-78.

        Like other nineteenth-century English novelists, JA deals "with the direct and intense relations be-tween individuals, but everything is carefully set in the treasured framework of class."

692   Hardy, Barbara.   "The Change of Heart in Dickens'
        Novels." VS, 5 (1961), 49.

Unlike <u>Robinson Crusoe</u> or <u>Martin Chuzzlewit</u>, E
is a novel of gradual moral progress rather than
sudden conversion.

693 Heath, William. <u>Elizabeth Bowen: An Introduction</u>
      <u>to Her Novels</u>. Madison: Univ. of Wisconsin
      Press, 1961, <u>passim</u>.

      Elizabeth Bowen admired JA and learned from
      her the ability to see through manners to morals.

694 Johnson, Pamela Hansford. "If She Writes, Must She
      Be a Lady?" <u>New York Times Book Review</u>, 31
      Dec. 1961, p. 1.

      JA might be called a "Lady Novelist" on the
      highest level.

695 McCarthy, Mary. "Characters in Fiction," in <u>On the</u>
      <u>Contrary</u>. New York: Farrar, Straus and Cudahy,
      1961, pp. 287-88.

      "If you examine the works of Jane Austen . . .
      you will find that the 'real people' in her books
      are not so often the heroes and heroines as the
      minor characters."

696 Wilson, Angus. "The Novelist and the Narrator," in
      <u>English Studies Today: Second Series</u>. Ed. G.
      A. Bonnard. Bern: Francke Verlag, 1961, pp.
      49-50.

      "If I have to choose any novel that seems to
      me to have been narrated as nearly perfectly as
      possible I shall select Jane Austen's <u>Emma</u>. . . .
      The irony implied in [Emma's] vision of life is
      the central theme of the book, so that the theme
      grows with the action and both grow with her moral
      enlightenment; and in all this the reader is sat-
      isfactorily yet never grossly ahead."

1962

697 Bowen, Elizabeth. "Truth and Fiction," in <u>After-</u>
      <u>thought: Pieces about Writing</u>. London: Long-
      mans, 1962, pp. 129-30.

JA used dialogue properly, both to move the story forward and to reveal character.

698   Karl, Frederick R. The Contemporary English Novel.
      New York: Farrar, Straus and Cudahy, 1962, p.
      83 and passim.

      JA uses "irony as a comic freeing force and as
      a means of returning her characters to a social
      norm."

699   Mullik, B. R. English Literature: Its Background
      and Development. Delhi, India: Chand, 1962,
      pp. 115-17.

      "Jane Austen brought good sense and balance to
      the English novel which during the Romantic age had
      become too emotional and undisciplined. . . . She
      did for the English novel precisely what the Lake
      poets did for English poetry--she refined and sim-
      plified it, making it a true reflection of English
      life."

700   Phelps, Gilbert. A Short History of English Litera-
      ture. London: Folio Society, 1962, pp. 123-24
      and passim. Phelps's comments on JA appear
      also in his A Survey of English Literature:
      Some of the Main Themes and Developments from
      Beowulf to 1939 (London: Pan, 1965), pp. 187-
      89 and passim.

      Though a classicist, JA is still wholly of her
      times: she insists upon restraint, but the restraint
      is exercised upon genuine feelings; she "gave ex-
      pression to the reaction against ready-made codes
      and to the assertion of the sanctity of individual
      responsibility and judgment which were such impor-
      tant aspects of the Romantic Revival."

1963

701   Baker, Sheridan. "The Idea of Romance in the
      Eighteenth-Century Novel." SELit, English No.
      (1963), pp. 59-60. Baker's comments on JA
      appear also in PMASAL, 49 (1964), 519-20.

      "This is the center of Jane Austen's comedy:

this self-containing, self-deceiving mind, her leg-
acy from Locke by Sterne." "Emma, like a true comic
character, never learns her lesson: her ultimate illusion is that she has learned it."

702   Blanke, Gustav H. "Aristokratie und Gentleman im
      englischen und amerikanischen Roman des 19. und
      20. Jahrhunderts." GRM, 13 (1963), 287.

JA's novels chart the decay of the aristocracy
and the rise of the bourgeoisie. A change in the
meaning of "gentleman" reflects this historical
development. No longer does gentlemanliness derive
from an inherited title; rather, the character of a
gentleman must be earned by civility, virtue, and
nobility of spirit.

703   Cox, C. B. The Free Spirit: A Study of Liberal
      Humanism in the Novels of George Eliot, Henry
      James, E. M. Forster, Virginia Woolf, Angus
      Wilson. New York: Oxford Univ. Press, 1963,
      p. 96 and passim.

There are times when JA's "ironic treatment of
human folly is so bitter that it undermines all
faith in the possibility of a reasonable society,
but these are comparatively rare."

704   Hough, Graham. "Morality and the Novel," in The
      Dream and the Task: Literature and Morals in
      the Culture of Today. London: Duckworth,
      1963, pp. 44-50. Parts of this essay appear
      also in Listener, 2 May 1963, pp. 747-48 [and
      see corr., W. R. Martin, 30 May, p. 915]. See
      also 713.

Bradbury's contention (see 184) that morality
is the essence of JA's art ignores our actual
experience of reading. The characters, the episodes, the social texture, "the mere contingent
facts interest, amuse, delight--not only the moral
pattern that is seen behind them."

705   Jack, Ian. English Literature, 1815-1832. (The
      Oxford History of English Literature, 10.)
      Oxford: Clarendon Press, 1963, pp. 248-50
      and passim.

JA demonstrably influenced the novels of Thomas

Henry Lister, particularly his Arlington (1832),
which uses amateur theatricals in a way that re-
calls MP.

706   Kennedy, Margaret. "The Novelist and His Public."
      EDH, 32 (1963), 76.

      "There are . . . a number of scholarly men who
profess an almost fanatical admiration for Jane
Austen. Upon investigation it turns out that they
think they would have married Elizabeth Bennet, in
Pride and Prejudice, could they but have met her."

707   Parry, John. A Guide through English Literature.
      London: Univ. of London Press, 1963, pp. 166-
      68.

      "It is remarkable that Jane Austen succeeds in
making interesting all this gossip about characters
who are empty-headed and devoid of idiosyncrasies.
. . .   She approaches the novel as a conscious
artist, polishing and shaping where other writers
[of the period] are content to let the narrative
flow on of its own accord."

                              1964

708   Bloom, Edward A. The Order of Fiction: An Intro-
      duction. New York: Odyssey Press, 1964, pp.
      106-07.

      In P and P, JA "uses setting as a necessary
background, depending upon it to support somewhat
larger effects incident to the genteel and pros-
perous society of which she writes."

709   Elliott, George P. "The Novelist as Meddler."
      VQR, 40 (1964), 108-09.

      Though there is substantial agreement in JA
between the novelist's value system and that of the
fictional society, yet she recognizes "a disparity
between official reason and private motive, between
society's requirements and the heart's need."

710   Friedson, Anthony M. Literature through the Ages.
      New York: Sterling, 1964, pp. 74-76.

To JA, the most noted novelist of manners,
"both social class and income group" are important.
She creates drama out of "conflicting codes of manners in the rigid social structure."

711 Greene, Donald. "The Sin of Pride: A Sketch for a
        Literary Exploration." NMQ, 34 (1964), 20-21.

In P and P "pride (emotional weakness) and
prejudice (intellectual weakness) are inevitably
bound together." These two deficiencies are exactly
the subject of the novel.

712 Jensen, Franklin L. "Mark Twain's Comments on Books
        and Authors." ESRS, 12 (June 1964), 17-18.

Mark Twain on JA: "I could read [Poe's] prose
on salary, but not Jane's. Jane is entirely impossible. It seems a great pity that they allowed her
to die a natural death." "Every time I read Pride
and Prejudice I want to dig her up and beat her over
the skull with her own shinbone."

713 Lodge, David. "The Critical Moment 1964." CritQ, 6
        (1964), 268-69.

Contrary to Hough's assertion (see 704), "there
is no doubt that the kind of interests aroused by
Emma are fundamentally moral."

714 Loofbourow, John. Thackeray and the Form of Fic-
        tion. Princeton: Princeton Univ. Press, 1964,
        pp. 74-75 and passim.

The plot of E "is exquisitely correlated with
dramatic structure, distinct and iridescent as a
Platonic idea. . . . Nowhere does the novel's
imaginative content supersede its objective structure or transcend its clear, communicative medium;
and this is both an advantage and a limitation."

715 Macauley, Robie, and George Lanning. Technique in
        Fiction. New York: Harper & Row, 1964, pp.
        175-76 and passim.

"Jane Austen's kind of fiction was intensive.
She was more interested in varieties of the same

experience than in varieties of experience that bear
wide contrast and make broad comparisons."

716 Ray, Gordon N. Bibliographical Resources for the
        Study of Nineteenth Century English Fiction.
        Los Angeles: School of Library Service, Univ.
        of California, 1964, passim.

        According to a survey of holdings in nine-
        teenth-century English fiction in twenty-nine col-
        lections, there are sixteen copies of first edi-
        tions of P and P and eighteen of S and S.

717 Sacks, Sheldon. Fiction and the Shape of Belief: A
        Study of Henry Fielding, with Glances at Swift,
        Johnson and Richardson. Berkeley and Los
        Angeles: Univ. of California Press, 1964, pp.
        12-13, 16-19, and passim.

        "Miss Bates' volubility is represented in such
        a manner that Emma's single act of gross discourtesy
        to her chattering acquaintance is seen as at once
        understandable and culpable." E's resolution guar-
        antees each individual a fate equal to his moral
        worth.

718 Ward, J. A. "Dining with the Novelists." Person-
        alist, 45 (1964), 405.

        Instead of "meal scenes" (with the exception
        of E), JA "prefers other social occasions for group-
        ing her characters--like balls, musicals, and
        strolls, in addition to the teas."

                              1965

719 Hoyt, Charles Alva. "Muriel Spark: The Surrealist
        Jane Austen," in Contemporary British Novel-
        ists. Ed. Charles Shapiro. Carbondale:
        Southern Illinois Univ. Press, 1965, pp. 125-
        43.

        (Mentions the contrast of the two novelists.)

720 Hutchens, Eleanor Newman. Irony in Tom Jones. Uni-
        versity, Ala.: Univ. of Alabama Press, 1965,
        pp. 149-55 and passim.

Shifting momentarily into the voices of her
characters, as she does in E, JA underlines "the
absurdity or eccentricity of their views by means of
incongruous connotations. The effect is one of
mature amusement, and of urbanity, that is basic to
Jane Austen's style."

721   Levin, Harry. "Janes and Emilies, or the Novelist
      as Heroine." SoR, NS 1 (1965), 744-47.

In contrast to the "brooding intensities" of
Emily Brontë, JA is the archetypically "analytic"
novelist: she is satirical, detached, and dispassionate.

722   Mayhead, Robin. Understanding Literature. Cam-
      bridge, Engl.: Univ. Press, 1965, pp. 64-68 and
      passim.

JA's art is subtle and concentrated: she can
simultaneously inform us factually about an event
or person, criticize people and values, and foreshadow her story's later developments.

723   Price, Martin. "The Picturesque Moment," in From
      Sensibility to Romanticism: Essays Presented
      to Frederick A. Pottle. Ed. Frederick W.
      Hilles and Harold Bloom. New York: Oxford
      Univ. Press, 1965, pp. 265-68.

In her use of the picturesque, JA stresses
"the moral qualities revealed in the control of
taste."

724   Souvage, Jacques. An Introduction to the Study of
      the Novel, with Special Reference to the En-
      glish Novel. Gent: E. Story-Scientia, 1965,
      p. 41 and passim.

MP is characteristic of "the old novel": instead of the dramatization modern fiction relies on,
it uses "such narrative methods as summary, description, exposition, commentary and character analysis."

1966

725   Ashraf, A. "Perspectives of Charlotte Brontë from

Her Letters." <u>CalR</u>, 180 (1966), 60-61.

"Jane Austen's restraint is poles apart from Charlotte Brontë's extravagance. Their temperaments were utterly different and G. H. Lewes's advice of disciplining her taste and imagination to the degree of Jane Austen was futile."

726 Beker, Miroslav. "The Theme of Plain Honesty in English Literature (From the Renaissance to Jane Austen)." <u>SRAZ</u>, Nos. 21-22 (1966), p. 286.

"By and large [JA's] world is too urbane for clear outlines of plain and stern honesty."

727 Bradbury, Malcolm. "The Short Stories of Angus Wilson." <u>SSF</u>, 3 (1966), 117-19.

Like JA, Wilson "is a writer of intense moral concern, a moral realist devoted to the analysis of man in his social context."

728 Cohn, Dorrit. "Narrated Monologue: Definition of a Fictional Style." <u>CL</u>, 18 (1966), 107.

JA was the first writer to make extended use of the narrated monologue (<u>erlebte Rede</u>), especially to depict her heroine's "moments of inner crisis."

729 Colby, Vineta and Robert A. <u>The Equivocal Virtue: Mrs. Oliphant and the Victorian Literary Market Place</u>. N.p.: Archon, 1966, p. 65.

Mrs. Oliphant's "Lucilla Marjoribanks is the spiritual grand-daughter of Jane Austen's Emma Woodhouse."

730 Hough, Graham. "From: An Essay on Criticism." <u>CritQ</u>, 8 (1966), 140.

"We do not ask in reading Jane Austen 'But where are the lower classes?' Or if we do we are foolish."

731 Lodge, David. <u>Language of Fiction: Essays in</u>

Criticism and Verbal Analysis of the English
Novel. New York: Columbia Univ. Press, 1966,
pp. 13-15.

JA's vision is characterized by "an ironic
detachment combined with a carefully discriminating sympathy and understanding." She imposes order
"with assurance and tact upon the flux of human
emotion and irrationality."

732 Malins, Edward. English Landscaping and Literature,
         1660-1840. New York: Oxford Univ. Press, 1966,
         pp. 129-39 and 155-58.

Four of JA's heroines--Fanny Price, Marianne
Dashwood, Catherine Morland, and Elizabeth Bennet--
"have in common a genuine love of the Picturesque,
with a consequent dislike of more formal landscaping."

733 Praz, Mario. "Ritratto di signora," in Cronache
         letterarie anglosassoni. Rome: Edizioni di
         storia e letteratura, 1966. IV, 319-23. This
         essay appeared originally in Il Tempo, 30 June
         1965. See also 379.

E and James's The Portrait of a Lady are
similar in plot and characterization.

734 Spearman, Diana. The Novel and Society. New York:
         Barnes & Noble, 1966, pp. 150-52.

"Death as well as poverty, serious illness as
well as sunken ships, are absent from her books
because she was writing comedy, which is a kind of
abstract art. This does not mean that they lack
[seriousness] . . . but merely that they show it in
a different dimension from tragedy."

735 Stevick, Philip. "The Theory of Fictional Chap-
         ters." WHR, 20 (1966), 234.

"If part of the pleasure [of the first two
sentences of Chapter Sixteen of E] . . . is in the
ironic juxtaposition of the curling of hair and
the onset of misery, part of one's pleasure may
also derive from the perception that the ancient
art of beginning a new episode has been carried
off with consummate skill."

1967

736 Chandler, Alice. "The Name Symbolism of Captain
        Vere." <u>NCF</u>, 22 (1967), 88.

    JA may have considered the pejorative con-
notations of "Fairfax" when she used the name in <u>E</u>.

737 Crane, R. S. "Every Man His Own Critic," in <u>The
        Idea of the Humanities and Other Essays Crit-
        ical and Historical</u>. Chicago: Univ. of
        Chicago Press, 1967. II, 211-14.

    Mudrick (see 5) is wrong to suppose that in <u>P</u>
the treatment of Mrs. Musgrove and her son has no
pretext. JA presents this episode to show "Wentworth's gratuitous kindness to both [mother and
son] and gives it the emphasis it has, just at the
moment, after the awful first meeting with Anne,
when we need especially to think well of him."

738 Golden, Morris. "The Novel as Education." <u>HussR</u>,
        1 (1967), 12.

    "For Jane Austen, social approval--not, as
for her predecessors, yielding to the appetites--
is the great temptation, and while succumbing is
never condoned, in all the novels but <u>Mansfield
Park</u> it elicits our sympathy."

1968

739 Daiches, David. <u>More Literary Essays</u>. Chicago:
        Univ. of Chicago Press, 1968, pp. 34-35.

    As can be seen in <u>P and P</u> and <u>E</u>, JA "con-
stantly uses misunderstanding as a means of
revealing, chastening, and educating her characters, though it is only the good characters who are
chastened and educated--the bad are only exposed
and mocked."

740 Ellmann, Mary. <u>Thinking about Women</u>. New York:
        Harcourt, Brace & World, 1968, pp. 115-18 and
        <u>passim</u>.

    JA uses sexual stereotypes in her fiction,

including "the giddy girl" and "the practical man."
"The last novels become 'male' in the stereotyped
sense that they argue suspicion of whatever seems
more attractive than dutiful."

741   Foltinek, Herbert. Vorstufen zum viktorianischen
        Realismus: Der englische Roman von Jane Austen
        bis Charles Dickens. (Wiener Beiträge zur
        englischen Philologie, 71.) Vienna: Braumül-
        ler, 1968, pp. 6-17 and passim.

        JA marks the beginning of a discrete period of
        literary history that ends with the young Charles
        Dickens. Her works determine the direction of the
        novel between 1817 and 1837 and contain the roots
        of the most important realistic novels of the
        nineteenth century.

742   Hickman, Peggy. Silhouettes. (Collectors' Pieces,
        12.) New York: Walker, 1968, pp. 9, 11, and
        18-19.

        (Reproductions and descriptions of JA and her
        family in silhouette.)

743   Lévy, Maurice. Le Roman Gothique anglais, 1764-
        1824. (Publications de la Faculté des
        Lettres et Sciences Humaines de Toulouse, A9.)
        Toulouse: Association des Publications de la
        Faculté des Lettres et Sciences Humaines de
        Toulouse, 1968, pp. 506-10.

        NA, which relies completely on Mrs. Radcliffe
        for the Gothic elements it parodies, is more than
        just a Gothic pastiche. It contains a theme dear
        to the author of S and S: literature, JA humorously
        warns the reader, can lead him away from the path
        of reason and common sense.

744   Miyazaki, Koichi. Igirisu Shosetsu Ronko. Tokyo:
        Kaitaku-sha, 1968.

        (Not seen.)

745   Owen, J. C. "Utopia in Little: Mary Russell Mitford
        and Our Village." SSF, 5 (1968), 245-46.

Like JA, Mary Russell Mitford lets "other pens dwell on guilt and misery," but she describes the scenery JA takes for granted.

746 Price, Martin. "The Other Self: Thoughts about Character in the Novel," in Imagined Worlds: Essays on Some English Novels and Novelists in Honour of John Butt. Ed. Maynard Mack and Ian Gregor. London: Methuen, 1968, pp. 289 and 296-97.

"The shallow stage of Jane Austen is a scene where discrimination--tact, intelligence, self-awareness--can play out its part, unconfused by darker or deeper impulses." She "moves below the surface of manners to the moral urgencies which underlie it."

747 Quigly, Isabel. Pamela Hansford Johnson. London: Longmans, Green, 1968, p. 6.

Like most women novelists, JA describes only a woman's world and sees people and events from a domestic and feminine viewpoint.

748 Rosen, Marvin S. "Authors and Publishers: 1750-1830." Science and Society, 32 (1968), 227-28.

JA's quarrel with Crosbie and Company over Susan is typical of the difficulties then current between publishers and authors.

749 Saagpakk, Paul F. "A Survey of Psychopathology in British Literature from Shakespeare to Hardy." L&P, 18 (1968), 150.

As evidenced by Mr. Woodhouse and Lady Susan, JA, "although following the tradition of classicism, created psychopathological characters, too."

750 Turner, Paul. "Novels, Ancient and Modern." Novel, 2 (1968), 23.

Both MP and P illustrate modifications of a separation theme that can be traced back to the Greek "novel." "The adventures of the separated

lovers become less sensational; the separation tends
to become psychological rather than physical; and
the long series of seducers . . . dwindles to one
apiece."

751 Watt, Ian. "Introduction' to The Augustan Age: Ap-
     proaches to Its Literature, Life, and Thought.
     Ed. Ian Watt. New York: Fawcett Premier, 1968,
     p. 19.

     "What the French call le phlègme anglais" be-
     came "by the end of the eighteenth century . . . the
     established social ideal, as we can see in the stiff
     upper lips of Jane Austen's heroes."

752 Watt, Ian. "Serious Reflections on The Rise of the
     Novel." Novel, 1 (1968), 218.

     "The contradiction between Augustan values on
     the one hand, and feminine and youthful attitudes
     on the other," is revealed in JA's novels, which
     "dramatize the process whereby feminine and adoles-
     cent values are painfully educated in the norms of
     the mature, rational and educated male world."

753 Watt, Ian. "Two Historical Aspects of the Augustan
     Tradition," in Studies in the Eighteenth Cen-
     tury: Papers Presented at the David Nichol
     Smith Memorial Seminar, Canberra, 1966. Ed.
     R. F. Brissenden. Toronto: Univ. of Toronto
     Press, 1968, p. 86.

     Despite chronology, we think of JA as Augustan,
     because of her sharp "discrimination between true
     and false norms; and for this no detail of speech,
     dress, or manners is too small to be morally diag-
     nostic."

754 Wilson, Angus. "Sexual Revolution." Listener, 10
     Oct. 1968, p. 458.

     JA "disliked Clarissa" for "she disliked the
     vicious rape by Lovelace."

1969

755 Brace, Gerald Warner. The Stuff of Fiction. New
     York: Norton, 1969, pp. 44-45 and passim.

"One of the best-planned novels in existence,"
P and P shows that JA "was able to develop a logical
neoclassical structure at the same time she was
animating it with an effect of dramatic spontaneity."

756   Gross, John. The Rise and Fall of the Man of Let-
         ters: A Study of the Idiosyncratic and the
         Humane in Modern Literature. New York: Macmil-
         lan, 1969, pp. 278-79.

         F. R. Leavis' contention (see 48) that JA was a
formative influence on George Eliot and Henry James
is "a complete exaggeration."

757   McNamee, Lawrence. Ninety-Nine Years of English
         Dissertations. Commerce, Texas: East Texas
         State Univ., 1969, pp. 56-60.

         Though there was only one dissertation on JA
before 1935, her popularity "spiraled in the
fifties. This surge lasted until 1963," by which
time twenty-eight in all had been produced.

758   Priestley, J. B. The Prince of Pleasure and His
         Regency, 1811-20. New York: Harper & Row,
         1969, pp. 197-98. and passim.

         "Her novels are subtle works of art, highly
selective in their detail, but her letters bring us
close to quiet upper-middle-class life in the
Regency, to people who were neither fashionable
and raffish nor evangelical puritans."

759   Sacks, Sheldon. "Golden Birds and Dying Genera-
         tions." CLS, 6 (1969), 285-88.

         In P and P, JA "for the first time in the his-
tory of English fiction" created a kind of comedy in
which the barriers to comic resolution are internal
and require subtle psychological changes for their
removal. "Indeed, the plots of Austen's major
novels are crucial experiments in expanding the
bounds of morally serious comedies."

760   Sherbo, Arthur. "Character Description in the Nov-
         el," in Studies in the Eighteenth Century En-
         glish Novel. N. p.: Michigan State Univ. Press,
         1969, pp. 197-98. and 204.

Some novelists, of whom "Jane Austen is one,
seem instinctively to regard their characters as
embodiments of one or more particular attitudes
and hence do nothing, if indeed they are capable of
doing anything, about making them come physically
alive."

1970

761 Baetzhold, Howard G. Mark Twain and John Bull: The
     British Connection. Bloomington: Indiana Univ.
     Press, 1970, pp. 296-97.

Although Twain could see, as did his friend
Howells, the sharpness with which JA drew character
and the sureness of her touch, Twain said that "he
could not fully appreciate them since they became
apparent only when Austen dealt with 'odious characters.'"

762 Breuninger, Margarete. Function und Wertung des
     Romans im frühviktorianischen Romans. (Studien
     zur englischen Philologie, 14.) Tübingen:
     Niemeyer Verlag, 1970, pp. 23-25, 97-103, and
     passim.

"Jane Austen's famous protest against the
depreciating statement 'Oh! it is only a novel!' led
to the conjecture that the difficulties the novel
met with on its way to recognition as a literary
genre . . . are mirrored in fiction itself."
References to novelists and novel-reading in her
work show that JA often defines characters "by
their literary likes or dislikes" and condemns the
romantic novel as sentimental and unrealistic.

763 Caudwell, Christopher. Romance and Realism: A
     Study in English Bourgeois Literature. Ed.
     Samuel Hynes. Princeton: Princeton Univ.
     Press, 1970, pp. 67-68.

In JA, the last eighteenth-century novelist,
"norms have become so established that freedom to
move within them is as limited as is possible for
a novelist to endure." Her novels are "like an
exquisitely bright, sharply focussed, minute magic
lantern show."

764 Greene, Donald. The Age of Exuberance: Backgrounds

to Eighteenth-Century English Literature. New
York: Random House, 1970, pp. 27-28.

That JA can portray intelligent and personable
clergymen as heroes of her novels illustrates the
advance in the status of that profession.

765 Hildick, Wallace. Thirteen Types of Narrative. New
York: Potter, 1970, pp. 11-12 and passim.

One of JA's achievements in P and P is that, as
detached narrator, she not only manages repeatedly
to compress into a short space a great deal of information, but she does so with grace and smoothness.

766 Howell, Elmo. "Eudora Welty's Comedy of Manners."
SAQ, 69 (1970), 469.

"The work of Eudora Welty . . . is at best
comparable to that of Jane Austen as appraised by
Scott": it is capable of rendering "'ordinary com-
mon-place things and characters interesting.'"

767 O'Dowd, M. C. "Writing and Injustice." Contrast,
6 (June 1970), 53-54.

To the extent that "Jane Austen, a member of
the land owning class, sister of two admirals, an
unrepentant snob . . . thought about politics at
all [she] could have been nothing but a reaction-
ary."

768 Preston, John. The Created Self: The Reader's Role
in Eighteenth-Century Fiction. New York:
Barnes & Noble, 1970, pp. 11-12.

JA's art "calls on irony to render the narrative intelligence as a kind of third dimension
to the action, or as a colour filter, not visible
itself but affecting all the tones in the scene."

769 Stevick, Philip. The Chapter in Fiction: Theories
of Narrative Division. Syracuse: Syracuse Univ.
Press, 1970, passim.

JA subtly varies "the beginnings and endings,
the technical shifts, the relations between chapters." As units, her chapters are means to the

achievement of ironic effects and help her attain
clarity, adjust "form to idea," and "order the parts
as precisely as possible within the whole." Her
chapter endings frequently reveal "rhythmic, epi-
grammatic, summary qualities."

770   Stoll, John E. "Psychological Dissociation in the
         Victorian Novel." L&P, 20 (1970), 64-66.

      E is the first nineteenth-century English nov-
el where "the psychological implications of the
moral code by which the characters are grouped and
disposed of are disastrous and suggest an irreconcilable conflict between the psychologically verifiable and the morally ideal." Since its characters are ranked by the relative predominance of
judgment over fancy, E employs a "moral code per-
petuating psychological dissociation."

771   Williams, Raymond. The English Novel from Dickens
         to Lawrence. New York: Oxford Univ. Press,
         1970, pp. 18-24.

      JA paradoxically achieves "a settled and
remarkably confident way of seeing and judging" a
phase of English social history notable for its
confusion and change. In her later novels she
develops "an everyday uncompromising morality which
is in effect separable from its social basis and
which, in other hands, can be turned against it."

772   Withim, Philip. "The Psychodynamics of Litera-
         ture." PsyR, 56 (1970), 576-81.

      "Emma's strong ego flies toward a necessary
match with Knightley's strong superego," but "of
course Emma has a strong superego as well. . . .
Actually though, with Emma it is not so much a
negative superego as a positive ego ideal."

                              1971

773   Barish, Jonas A. "Antitheatrical Prejudice in the
         Nineteenth Century." UTQ, 40 (1971), 277-81.

      Contrary to Trilling's assertion (see 59),
"the point at Mansfield Park is not so much that

Henry or Maria Crawford [sic] will mar their integrity by taking roles in the play as that their flair for impersonation" indicates "the erosion or even the absence of such integrity." To JA "the road that leads from the play-acting at Mansfield to the adultery in town is neither circuitous nor mysterious."

774 Gindin, James. Harvest of a Quiet Eye: The Novel of Compassion. Bloomington: Indiana Univ. Press, 1971, pp. 17-19.

"Jane Austen's fiction shows a struggle between form and content, an interest divided between working out the formal patterns of the novel and the pressure of sympathies and attitudes that burst from confined form."

775 Hyams, Edward. Capability Brown and Humphry Repton. London: Dent, 1971, p. 127 and passim.

Rushworth's intended improvements "would have required two or three days' work, during which time he would have stayed in the house as a guest."

776 Lodge, David. The Novelist at the Crossroads and Other Essays on Fiction and Criticism. Ithaca: Cornell Univ. Press, 1971, passim.

"The more closely we look, the more apparent it becomes that there is no aspect of Jane Austen's language that is innocent of persuasive purpose, that her choices of diction and syntax are at every point creating, ordering and judging the experience she offers to us."

777 Speirs, John. Poetry towards Novel. London: Faber and Faber, 1971, pp. 202-04 and passim.

"It is possible to see Crabbe and Jane Austen as still in the line from the Augustans, though developing in their art new psychological insights into the individual in relation to the family and to society."

778 Trow, George W. S., and Michael O'Donoghue. "Jane Austen. Isn't That the Kind of Cupcake They

Used to Sell at the A&P?" National Lampoon, 1 (Oct. 1971), p. 31.

(A humorous advertisement for English literature.)

779 Weinstein, Mark A. "Imagination and Reality in Romantic Fiction." WC, 2 (1971), 126-27.

Suspicious of Romanticism, JA dramatized "the dangers of the projection onto external reality of idiosyncratic vision and personal feeling" as well as "the value of accumulated experience and the need to observe closely and reflect carefully on that experience. The basic assumption is that, although truth is deceptive and the road to it difficult, there is an objective reality--about persons, things, oneself--that can finally be discovered by the qualified observer."

1972

780 Anon. Review of The Journals and Letters of Fanny Burney (Madame D'Arblay), Vols. I and II, ed. Joyce Hemlow et al. TLS, 15 Dec. 1972, pp. 1531-32.

Like Fanny Burney, Jane Austen has as her subject "the impossibility of escaping from intolerable people. . . . Jane Austen's novels seem to have been created as an oyster creates a pearl, by irritation and abrasion."

781 Bateson, F. W. Essays in Critical Dissent. Totowa, N. J.: Rowman and Littlefield, 1972, pp. 250-51.

P is an example of the satiric novel, where values are used to deflate things. Realistic detail serves as a comment on human society.

782 Bedient, Calvin. Architects of the Self: George Eliot, D. H. Lawrence, and E. M. Forster. Berkeley and Los Angeles: Univ. of California Press, 1972, p. 115 and passim.

Like other nineteenth-century English novelists,

JA "relinquished the eternal in an attempt to take hold of the temporal." She was an empiricist of human life.

783 Elsbree, Langdon. "The Purest and Most Perfect Form of Play: Some Novelists and the Dance." Criticism, 14 (1972), 364-65.

"In Jane Austen, the dance is explicitly conceived of as the purest kind of play. . . . The relationship of the individual to his society in her novels is his relationship to a play community, and his success depends upon how faithfully he follows the rules . . . whether in dancing or marriage."

784 Gill, Richard. Happy Rural Seat: The English Country House and the Literary Imagination. New Haven: Yale Univ. Press, 1972, pp. 243-46 and passim.

The houses JA describes in her fiction usually function symbolically. She began, in NA, by burlesquing the Gothic novel's use of medieval abbeys, and, in her later novels, "turned this manipulation of the house to more straightforward purposes of revealing character and extending theme."

785 Goldknopf, David. The Life of the Novel. Chicago: Univ. of Chicago Press, 1972, p. 204.

"In a Jane Austen novel, the very constriction in scope of interest makes a moral statement: cultivate your own garden. Such an attitude has [now] become morally reprehensible and for the novelist pragmatically impossible. To be realistic, a novel must take the whole world into account."

786 Gose, Elliott B., Jr. Imagination Indulged: The Irrational in the Nineteenth-Century Novel. Montreal: McGill-Queen's Univ. Press, 1972, pp. 16-17.

JA, who does not trust exaggerated emotion or reveal much concern for dreams, belongs "to a tradition that can be traced to Aristotle. His key conception was that art is mimetic, that it imitates an action in the real world."

787 Lascelles, Mary. <u>Notions</u> <u>and</u> <u>Facts</u>: <u>Collected</u>
     <u>Criticism</u> <u>and</u> <u>Research</u>. Oxford: Clarendon
     Press, 1972, p. 252 and <u>passim</u>.

     (Among other mentions of JA, there is a memori-
     al tribute to R. W. Chapman and his edition of the
     novels.)

788 Moynahan, Julian. "Pastoralism as Culture and
     Counter-Culture in English Fiction, 1800-
     1928: From a View to a Death." <u>Novel</u>, 6
     (1972), 23-27.

     "The movement from Jane Austen's Emma Woodhouse
     to George Eliot's Gwendolen Harleth or Hardy's Tess
     is one from a type of high pastoral comedy to a type
     of tragedy, from the incorporation of a value to its
     alienation."

789 Norton, Rictor. "Aesthetic Gothic Horror." <u>YCGL</u>,
     No. 21 (1972), p. 37.

     "The grotesque and the macabre, which readers
     of Jane Austen's <u>Northanger</u> <u>Abbey</u> mistakenly believe
     were used to parody the Gothic novel, are the artis-
     tic devices by which a Gothic novelist reestablishes
     a healthy balance for a mind too engrossed with the
     sublime and with terror."

790 Tennyson, G. B. "Commentary." <u>NCF</u>, 27 (1972),
     248-49.

     Between 1967 and 1971 JA ranked seventh in the
     number of submissions to <u>NCF</u>. In 1971 taken alone
     she ranked fifth and doubled the 1970 submissions.

791 Trilling, Lionel. <u>Sincerity</u> <u>and</u> <u>Authenticity</u>.
     Cambridge, Mass.: Harvard Univ. Press, 1972,
     pp. 72-80 and <u>passim</u>.

     Like Rousseau, JA uses as a standard of judg-
     ment "the sentiment of being, with all that this
     implies of self-sufficiency, self-definition, and
     sincerity." Yet except in the case of <u>MP</u>, "she
     judges not as Rousseau does, categorically, but as
     Hegel does, dialectically."

792 Ward, William S., comp. <u>Literary</u> <u>Reviews</u> <u>in</u>

British Periodicals, 1798-1820: A Bibliography, with a Supplementary List of General (Non-Review) Articles on Literary Subjects. New York: Garland, 1972. I, 136.

(A bibliographical listing of fifteen reviews, 1812-1818, of JA's novels.)

1973

793 Allen, Walter. "The Virtues of the Epistolary Novel." TLS, 26 Jan. 1973, p. 98.

"The fact that [JA] was so thoroughly steeped in Richardson may have prevented her from competing with him" in the epistolary mode.

794 Moers, Ellen. "Money, the Job, and Little Women." Commentary (New York), 55 (Jan. 1973), 57-61.

Money "may be the first obviously feminine thing about [JA's] novels, for money and its making were characteristically female rather than male subjects in English fiction." JA's concern with the connection of money and marriage and with the professions of her heroes reflects her realistic attention to the economic problems of young women.

Indexes

Index of Authors

Reference is to item numbers.
"R" prefix indicates a book review.

Jordan, John E., R258,
R259, R266, R281, R301,
R347, R375, R405, R406,
R445, R463.

Karl, Frederick R., 249,
698.

Kaul, A. N., 470.

Kauvar, Elaine M., 471.

Kawamoto, Shizuko, 353,
400.

Kearful, Frank J., 277.

Kennedy, Margaret, 4, 706.

Ker, W. P., 67.

Kermode, Frank, R281.

Kestner, Joseph A., III,
502, 503, 531, 633.

Kettle, Arnold, 164, 237,
354, 397, 541.

Keynes, Geoffrey, 395.

Kiely, Robert, 532.

Kiley, Anne Watt, 600.

King, Noel J., 21.

Kinsley, James, 458, 474,
477, 493, 508.

Kirkham, Margaret, 382,
R482.

Kirschbaum, Leo, 142.

Kissane, James, 472, 601.

Kliger, Samuel, 312, 447.

Knight, Charles A., 473.

Knight, Richard, 355.

Knoepflmacher, U. C., 356,
R493, R495, R508.

Koljević, Svetozar, 143.

Kondo, Ineko, 77.

Koppel, Gene, R406, 590.

Krieger, Murray, 504.

Kroeber, Karl, 430, 505.

Kronenberger, Louis, 191,
278, 431.

Krutch, Joseph Wood, R107.

Kumar, Anita S., 192.

Kunkel, Francis L., 193.

Lamont, Claire, 474, 530.

Lane, Margaret, 314, 343.

Lanning, George, 715.

Lansdale, Nelson, 97.

Lascelles, Mary, 194, 195,
223, 224, 225, 250, 264,
265, 279, 303, 304, 312,
382, 415, 447, 481, 533,
541, 787.

Laski, Marghanita, 144, 432.

Latham, Jacqueline E. M.,
280.

Lauber, John, 475, 506, 534.

Lawrence, D. H., 640.

Lawry, J. S., 433.

Leavis, F. R., 48.

Leavis, Q. D., 98, 112, 312, 396, 450.

Legouis, Émile, 681.

Lerner, Laurence, 226, 357, 481.

Levin, Harry, 721.

Levine, George, R505.

Levine, Jay Arnold, 168.

Lévy, Maurice, 743.

Lewis, C. S., 49, 164, 237, 481.

Liddell, Robert, 227, 641.

Linder, C. A., 507.

Link, Frederick M., 99, 567.

Litz, A. Walton, 169, 170, 281, 312, R347, 358, R406, 447, 541.

Lloyd, J. D. K., 55, 196.

Lobb, K. M., 78.

Lochhead, Marion, 79, 359.

Lock, F. P., 476, 535, 536.

Lodge, David, 197, 315, 397, R505, 508, 713, 731, 776.

Logan, Campbell, 171.

Logan, James V., R33.

Loofbourow, John W., R281, R375, 434, 714.

Loomis, Emerson Robert, 563.

Lucas, John, 477.

Lynch, P. R., 360.

Macaulay, Robie, 715.

MacCarthy, B. G., R301.

MacInnes, Helen, 22.

Macintyre, Angus, 84.

Magee, William H., 316.

Malins, Edward, 732.

Mallinson, Anne, 361.

Maniar, U. M., 282.

Manning, Olivia, 398.

Mansell, Darrel, Jr., 362, 435.

Marcus, Mordecai, 172, 447.

Marshall, Percy, 198.

Marshall, Sarah Latimer, 399.

Marshall, William H., 363.

Martien, Norman Gerald, 612.

Martin, W. R., 145, 146, 317, 364, 704.

Matache, Liliana, 436, 437.

Mathew, Ray, R33, R227.

Mathison, John K., 100, R182.

Maxwell, J. C., R234, 362.

Maxwell-Mahon, W. D., R406.

May, Leland Chandler, 626.

Price, Martin, 723, 746.

Priestley, J. B., 147, 230, 684, 758.

Pritchett, V. S., 10, R33, 324.

Quigly, Isabel, 747.

Ragg, Laura M., R106.

Rawson, C. J., 115, R182, 243, 256.

Ray, Gordon N., 716.

Raybould, Edith, 102.

Raymond, John, 116.

Raz, Robert Walter, 630.

Reddick, Bryan DeWitt, 613.

Rees, David, R227.

Reeves, James, 653.

Renwick, W. L., 231.

Rivers, Isabel, R405.

Robson, M. A., 52.

Rogers, Timothy, R347, R375.

Rohmann, Gerd, 483.

Rosen, Marvin S., 748.

Rosenberg, Sondra, 608.

Rosenfeld, Sybil, 202.

Rosser, G. C., 369.

Rubinstein, Annette T., 25.

Rubinstein, E., 445, 446, 447, 595.

Rudolph, Jo-Ellen Schwartz, 634.

Rugg, Winnifred King, 11.

Ryals, Clyde de L., 484.

Ryle, Gilbert, R266, 325, 405.

Saagpakk, Paul F., 749.

Sabiston, Elizabeth Jean, 609.

Sacks, Sheldon, 717, 759.

Salter, Emma Gurney, R33.

Sanders, Helen Morse, 555.

Sandstrom, Glenn Arthur, 564.

Sano, Masahiko, R258.

Schaefer, William D., R375, R384, R401, R406.

Schemm, Mildred Walker, 288.

Schirmer, Duke, 175.

Schneider, Sister M. Lucy, 326.

Schoeck, R. J., 70.

Schorer, Mark, 12, 80, 126, 127, 237, 397.

Scrutton, Mary, 53, 654.

Selwyn, E. G., 128, 343.

Seronsy, Cecil C., 81.

Servotte, Herman, 289, 573.

Watson, J. R., 487.

Watson, Winifred, 150, 686.

Watt, Ian, 180, 216, 237, R259, R266, 665, 751, 752, 753.

Watts, Mary, 547.

Webb, William, 295.

Wedgwood, C. V., 352.

Weinsheimer, Joel, 548.

Weinstein, Mark A., 779.

Wellington, Gerald Welles-ley, Duke of, 373.

Welsh, Alexander, 238.

Welty, Eudora, 453.

West, Rebecca, 666.

Westbrook, James Seymour, Jr., 585.

White, Edward M., 239, R262, 374, 570.

Whitten, Benjamin Good-man, Jr., 635.

Widmer, Eleanor Joan Rackow, 568.

Wiesenfarth, Joseph, 332, 375, 517.

Wildi, Max, 333, 408.

Wilhelm, Albert Earl, 636.

Williams, Raymond, 771.

Wilson, Angus, 213, 405, 409, 696, 754.

Wilson, Edmund, 237.

Wiltshire, John, R266, R281, 296, R301, 518.

Withim, Philip, 772.

Wölcken. F., R40.

Wolfe, Thomas P., 519.

Wood, Frederick T., R33, R259, R281.

Woodring, Carl, R347, R375, R406.

Woods, Sister Mary St. Francis, 588.

Woolf, Leonard, 481.

Woolf, Virginia, 164, 237, 672.

Worth, George J., R357.

Wright, Andrew H., R16, 33, 83, 215, 237, 240, R281, 297, R301, 312, R327, 343, R357, R375, 447, R528, 560, 643.

Wycherley, H. Alan, 410.

Zietlow, Paul N., 298.

Zimmerman, Everett, 411, 454, 455, 597.

Index of Jane Austen Titles

Index of Subjects

227, 281, 301, 401, 451,
780; <u>Cecilia</u>, 227, 243,
264, 271, 284; <u>Diary</u>,
115; <u>Evelina</u>, 53, 368,
401.

Byron, George Gordon Noel,
Lord, 96.

Calvin, John, 325.

Camus, Albert, 51.

Carroll, Lewis, 51.

<u>Champion</u>, 546.

Chance, 298, 381, 548.

Chapman, R. W., 787.

Chapone, Hester, 578.

Chapters, 8, 505, 619,
735, 769.

Characterization, 4, 5, 7,
8, 10, 28, 31, 54, 69,
70, 82, 84, 90, 102,
106, 109, 113, 120, 122,
138, 152, 162, 164, 173,
178, 179, 182, 225, 227,
230, 245, 249, 250, 251,
259, 260, 266, 282, 296,
310, 314, 327, 330, 340,
345, 347, 389, 405, 408,
412, 416, 463, 466, 472,
474, 482, 483, 505, 506,
521, 525, 549, 553, 596,
601, 618, 623, 630, 631,
632, 645, 646, 651, 677,
682, 687, 695, 707, 760,
761, 784.

Charm, 33, 125, 405, 469,
475.

Chawton, 38, 97, 343, 355,
361.

Chesterfield, Philip

Dormer Stanhope, Earl of,
<u>Letters</u> <u>to</u> <u>His</u> <u>Son</u>, 105.

Children, <u>see</u> Family.

Chronology of Composition,
209, 225, 258, 281, 367,
396, 551.

Cinderella, <u>see</u> Fairy Tale.

Civility, 112, 423.

Clemens, Samuel, <u>see</u> Twain,
Mark.

Clergy, The, 14, 52, 62, 79,
128, 156, 163, 263, 357,
764.

Coleridge, Samuel Taylor,
"Kubla Khan," 467.

Comedy, 11, 27, 49, 51, 54,
89, 101, 126, 128, 133,
164, 179, 185, 191, 194,
195, 224, 225, 247, 249,
258, 262, 269, 273, 278,
301, 307, 311, 323, 327,
328, 343, 344, 352, 357,
389, 405, 412, 418, 420,
431, 447, 457, 463, 466,
470, 487, 492, 501, 508,
547, 587, 598, 643, 658,
672, 701, 734, 759, 788.

Commitment, 5, 59, 239,
339, 463, 524, 545.

Community, 103, 281, 505,
641.

Compton-Burnett, Ivy, 680.

Conclusions, 18, 74, 164,
205, 227, 258, 259, 296,
298, 334, 412, 505, 518,
549, 628.

Congreve, William, 334.

Cooper, Anthony Ashley, Earl

308, 310, 311, 312, 313,
315, 316, 323, 325, 327,
333, 334, 337, 339, 340,
341, 344, 347, 356, 357,
358, 363, 364, 370, 374,
378, 380, 388, 394, 398,
401, 405, 408, 411, 414,
416, 450, 451, 463, 468,
477, 484, 489, 494, 495,
503, 521, 525, 531, 540,
548, 549, 552, 569, 586,
590, 602, 604, 606, 618,
666, 668, 669, 675, 677,
690, 692, 693, 704, 713,
717, 723, 727, 746, 753,
759, 770, 771, 785.

More, Sir Thomas, Utopia,
442.

Mozart, Wolfgang Amadeus,
185.

Myth, 73, 94, 347, 517.

Names, 20, 45, 119, 377,
549, 736.

Narrative Point of View,
7, 32, 33, 60, 85, 117,
140, 151, 174, 182, 194,
203, 225, 258, 266, 281,
289, 310, 332, 345, 351,
384, 398, 414, 436, 437,
440, 450, 468, 483, 505,
519, 522, 531, 540, 549,
555, 559, 565, 573, 583,
588, 613, 628, 631, 635,
665, 696, 720, 724, 765.

Narrator, see Narrative
Point of View.

Nature, 65, 153, 154, 164,
260, 281, 312, 489, 558.

Neoclassicism, 9, 267,
281, 388, 434, 459, 489,
581, 700, 755.

Newton, Sir Isaac, 87.

Novel as Art, 237, 341, 490,
600.

Novel as Genre, 100, 277,
281, 368, 654, 762.

Novel Conventions, 5, 101,
173, 225, 227, 250, 259,
301, 541, 594, 625.

Novel, Domestic, 5, 648.

Novel, Epistolary, 167, 258,
522, 540, 619, 793.

Novel of Manners, 137, 337,
522, 710.

Novel, Popular, 173, 258,
259, 281, 493, 525, 594,
634.

Novel Readers, 429, 505,
549, 706.

Novel, Romantic, 101, 532,
584, 616, 762.

Novel, Sentimental, 258,
259, 454, 470, 574.

Novel Tradition, 9, 48, 98,
106, 113, 168, 259, 271,
281, 289, 290, 301, 341,
371, 401, 495, 500, 505,
549, 584, 609, 637, 644,
650, 691, 724, 741, 747,
750, 770, 782.

Oliphant, Margaret, 406;
Miss Marjoribanks, 729.

Ordination, 62, 159, 260,
263, 269, 317, 382.

Parents, see Family.

Parody, see Burlesque.

Parsons, Eliza, Castle of